Reconstructing Theology

*A Critical Assessment of the Theology of
Clark Pinnock*

D0996091

Reconstructing Theology

A Critical Assessment of the Theology of
Clark Pinnock

Edited by
Tony Gray
and
Christopher Sinkinson

paternoster
press

First published in 2000 by Paternoster Press

06 05 04 03 02 01 00   7 6 5 4 3 2 1

Paternoster Press is an imprint of Paternoster Publishing,
P.O. Box 300, Carlisle, Cumbria, CA3 0QS, UK
and
P.O. Box 1047, Waynesboro, GA 30830–2047, USA
Website: www.paternoster-publishing.com

British Library Cataloguing in Publication Data
A catalogue record for this book is available from the British Library

ISBN 1-84227-037-0

Cover Design by Aquablade, Lancaster
Typeset by WestKey Ltd, Falmouth, Cornwall
Printed in Great Britain by Bell & Bain, Glasgow

Contents

Part 3

Foreword

My first and only personal meeting with Clark Pinnock took place in Louisville Kentucky in the spring of 1987. At that time, I was a professor at the Baptist theological seminary in that city, an institution embroiled in the then-raging controversy within the Southern Baptist Convention. Pinnock had been brought to campus by school administrators as a positive example of conservative evangelical scholarship. They wanted to show the moderate/liberal-dominated faculty that not all evangelicals were obscurantists, fundamentalists or polemicists. Pinnock was a celebrated biblical inerrantist (as he still claims to be, to my knowledge), but he could speak movingly and thoughtfully in complete English sentences. He could quote Barth, Pannenberg and Rahner with ease. He was cosmopolitan in his contacts and transdenominational in his sympathies. He was also eminently likeable. Still, it was a hard sell for most members of the faculty. They remembered an even earlier version of Clark Pinnock: an angry, vociferous Calvinist demagogue, as one of them called him, who had used his platform as a professor at New Orleans Baptist Theological Seminary to criticize colleagues for their lack of evangelical fidelity and to call for a root and branch reformation within the SBC. The newer, nicer Pinnock was a hard pill for some of the old veterans to swallow. But Pinnock was winsome and persuasive and gained the respect of even some of his former foes. I, among others, welcomed his urbane evangelical theology as a corrective to the narrow-minded openness which prevailed on the faculty at that time.

A decade and a half can be a long time in the history of theology: just think of how Karl Barth changed his mind between 1915 and

1930. Clark Pinnock is a theologian in motion and his thought has continued to change, not so much by evolving as by leaping from one strategic centre of gravity to another. In some ways, Pinnock is not unlike John Smyth, the notorious progenitor of the English Arminian Baptists who, within the space of a dozen years, moved from being an Anglican to a Puritan to a Separatist to a Baptist to a Waterlander Mennonite. When one of his opponents called him 'a wavering reed and a variable chameleon', Smyth readily admitted the charge of inconstancy but felt no need to apologize for it. His latter thoughts, he said, were often better than his former. He vowed to renounce his errors every day as soon as he could discover them!

Like Smyth, what Pinnock lacks in constancy, he makes up for in honesty. He understands himself to be on a theological pilgrimage with many twists and turns and unexpected vistas along the way. While some may criticize Pinnock for his theological instability and shifting loyalties, the willingness to question and re-examine one's theology is not a fault but a virtue. Had Luther, Zwingli and Cranmer been unwilling to do this, we would never have had the Reformation. Had Barth remained stuck in theological liberalism, twentieth-century theology would have been much the poorer. But change, in ideas as well as living organisms, can be destructive as well as formative. Doctrine can deviate as well as develop. Jesus promised that the Holy Spirit would lead the church into all truth, but he also endowed the church with the gift of discernment for he knew it would need to distinguish genuine Spirit-led developments from distortions shaped by the spirit of the age.

Prior to his conversion and introduction to evangelicalism as a teenager, Pinnock was brought up in a liberal church. One could perhaps read the trajectory of his theological journey as a slow and sometimes painful return to his pre-conversion liberal moorings, although he himself would doubtless want to see it as a deeper enrichment of the evangelical impulse. As Brian Gerrish has shown, this was precisely how Friedrich Schleiermacher saw his own theological work as well. However, there is no rule which says that one's theological pilgrimage must be unidirectional. So long as Pinnock continues to change and grow, and to engage in the kind of dialogue set forth in this volume, there is the possibility (some may say the hope) that he may realize, contra John Smyth, that some of his former thoughts are better than his latter.

In his response to these essays, Pinnock refers to himself as a 'theological maverick'. In their various chapters, the contributors to this volume test the extent to which this is an apt description of Pinnock and his theological work thus far. One chapter is essentially supportive of the Pinnock project, although it too offers important course corrections. The others, however, while recognizing the many strengths in Pinnock's perspective, rightly see him as a revisionist theologian whose work is seriously flawed with respect to both its biblical basis and its accountability to the apostolic tradition embodied in historic Christian orthodoxy. It is a measure of Pinnock's stature as a theologian and his influence within the academy that the contributors take his work so seriously and engage his ideas in such a tough-minded way. The contributors themselves are rising evangelical scholars, each well trained in his own discipline and well aware of the wider theological terrain. In his response, Pinnock commends them for their excellence as well as their civility in treating him with fairness and respect. In fact, this volume is a good model of the kind of substantive theological engagement evangelicals need to pursue in the construction of a vibrant Christian orthodoxy, one that is both faithful to the Holy Scriptures and alert to emerging trends and challenges in the contemporary world.

The essays in this volume do not offer a complete critique of Pinnock's theology, but they pose significant questions about three areas of his thought. Is the so-called openness theism espoused by Pinnock and others really as biblical as it claims to be? How is Pinnock's theology, especially his denial of comprehensive divine foreknowledge, related to the Christian tradition of the past two millennia? Where does Pinnock's model of soteriological inclusivism fit in the context of contemporary religious pluralism? None of these issues is new. Indeed, they have formed a large part of the staple diet of mainline Protestant and progressive Roman Catholic theology for the past one hundred years. What is new is the claim that the solutions offered by openness theologians should find a happy home among evangelicals as an expression of tolerable diversity within this Christian tradition.

It is a good (and very evangelical) thing that Pinnock wants to hold himself accountable to the Holy Scriptures. Certain forms of

classical theism have indeed played down the personal character of
God and his interactivity with the world and history. The Nicene
doctrine of the Holy Trinity was developed in part to counter the
pagan notion of God as a transcendent monad devoid of communi-
cability and love. No one can read Athanasius, Augustine, Luther,
Calvin or Wesley without realizing how committed they were to
the compassionate, covenantal, dynamic God of the Bible. But they
did not deem it necessary to deny *creatio ex nihilo* (as consistent process theologians must), or divine foreknowledge of future contingents (as openness theologians do), in order to affirm the
relationality and responsiveness of the one true God. Only by a hermeneutic of selective literalism can openness theologians claim biblical support for their dogma of a limited God. For example, they
interpret quite literally biblical statements about God's repentance,
citing this as evidence that God really does not know the future with
precision. But they gloss over other biblical texts which say that
God also 'forgets' aspects of the past, that he does not remember the
sins of his people (cf. Is. 43:25). Are we to suppose then that God
suffers from amnesia as well as ignorance of the future? Openness
theism teaches that God cannot know the future (although he can
know what he intends to do in the future), for the future is not
'there' to be known. Yet Jesus predicted not only the death of Peter,
but the precise mode of his martyrdom (Jn. 21:18–19). Was this just
an educated guess, a holy hunch? The consensual tradition of orthodox biblical interpretation has been able to account for such texts
without breaching the sovereignty of the biblical God who is the
Lord of the future as well as the creator of heaven and earth.

Pinnock has likened himself to Martin Luther defending the
principle of *sola scriptura* against the tradition-bound theology of
John Eck at the Leipzig Debate in 1519. This echoes Hegel's portrayal of Luther as 'the all-illuminating sun which follows that
day-break at the end of the Middle Ages'. But this is a complete misunderstanding of Luther's legacy. He was no modern rugged indi-
vidualist, no lonely seeker after truth. At both Leipzig and Worms
Luther was arguing *against* tradition *from* tradition, or better put, he
was arguing from a shallower tradition to a profounder one. To the
end of his life, he saw himself as a faithful and obedient member of
the one, holy, catholic, and apostolic church, the church he sought
to reform on the basis of the word of God. Among Reformation

characters, Pinnock is perhaps better compared to Faustus Socinus, a brilliant and admirable man with strong evangelical leanings. (Like Pinnock he too was once a Calvinist.) As leader of the Polish Brethren, Socinus developed an evangelical rationalist theology which led him to break with the historic Christian doctrine of God's omniscience as well as the Trinitarian and Christological consensus of the early church. Pinnock is no Socinian, nor is he a consistent process theologian. But some of the same impulses which moved Socinus along his theological trajectory are evident in Pinnock's world of thought as well.

As Christians committed to the biblical God who became incarnate in Jesus Christ, we can applaud Pinnock's rejection of the static, loveless, uninvolved God of Aristotelian philosophy, the God Thomas Hardy once referred to as 'the dreaming, dark, dumb Thing that turns the handle of this idle Show'. Pinnock is right to scream in protest against such a God. The biblical God is a God of relationships: he is compared to a loving father, a caring mother, a tender shepherd, a faithful husband, a generous friend. But the God of grace is also the God of glory, as that maverick preacher Harry Emerson Fosdick put it so well in his great hymn. Divine sovereignty and significant human freedom are not competitive exclusives. It is not as though God and human beings were locked together in a finite room with a limited supply of oxygen – the more God breathes with his big lungs the less air there is for his human creatures. God is not in the suffocating business. We need not bring him down to size in order to lift up the true humanity of men and women made in his image. God's goodness is not threatened by his greatness. God's grace and glory coalesce.

In the course of his long and sometimes bitter dispute with his former fellow-traveller Rudolf Bultmann, Karl Barth once said that the best answer to a bad theology is a better one. A better theology is required for a healthy church. This book, both the essays and Pinnock's response to them, is a good example of faith seeking understanding and is thus a worthy contribution toward that goal.

Timothy George

Contributors

Simon Gathercole read classics and theology at King's College, Cambridge, and is now a lecturer at Aberdeen University. He has written articles on Augustine and Albert Schweitzer and is currently co-authoring a monograph on the book of Tobit.

Timothy George is Dean of Beeson Divinity School, Stamford University, and Senior Editor of *Christianity Today*.

Tony Gray is theological books editor for Paternoster Press. He has published articles on the doctrine of hell, openness theology, and systematic theology. He is co-editor of *Solid Ground* (Leicester: Apollos, 2000), and author of *The Potted Guide to Theology* (Carlisle: Paternoster Press, 2000).

Nathan MacDonald is a graduate of Emmanuel College, Cambridge, and is presently engaged in doctoral studies at Durham University on monotheism and Deuteronomy.

Christopher Partridge is Senior Lecturer in Theology and Contemporary Religion, University College Chester, Chester. He has written articles on both theology and contemporary religion, *H.H. Farmer's Theological Interpretation of Religion: Towards a Personalist Theology of Religions* (Toronto Studies in Theology, 76; Lewiston: Edwin Mellen Press, 1998), and edited and introduced *H.H. Farmer, Reconciliation and Religion: Aspects of the Uniqueness of Christianity as a Reconciling Faith*, Gifford Lectures 1951 (Lewiston: Edwin Mellen Press, 1999).

Clark Pinnock is Professor of Theology at McMaster Divinity College, Hamilton, Ontario.

Patrick Richmond is Curate at the Church of the Martyrs, Leicester. He read medicine at Balliol College, Oxford, and, after doing a doctorate in physiology there, spent six months in Pakistan working with drug addicts. He returned to Oxford to read theology and train for ordination in the Church of England. Besides publications in physiology, he is a contributor to *Euthanasia and the Churches*, ed. Robin Gill (London: Cassell, 1998).

Christopher Sinkinson completed his PhD at Bristol University on the theology of John Hick. He has published articles on religious pluralism, authored a booklet on John Hick, and is currently Assistant Pastor at a church in Bournemouth.

Daniel Strange has just completed his PhD at Bristol University on Clark Pinnock's inclusivism regarding the unevangelized. His first degree was also at Bristol University. He has published articles in *World Faith Encounters* and the *Evangelical Quarterly*. He is currently working for UCCF with theology and religious studies students.

Introduction
Tony Gray

How do we understand God? What assumptions do we have when we use the word 'god'? If we presume that our contemporary world knows what we as Christian theologians mean, then we are probably wrong. In fact, a number of prominent Christian thinkers have started to use the word without a capital letter, for that very reason.[1] People presume a certain picture of god, which may well be very far off from a biblical picture of God.

For Christian communication in a postmodern world this is of course a vital issue. However, the issue is an important one, even within the Christian community. Among evangelical Christians there is diversity even on how one would define a 'biblical picture of God'. Does God have knowledge of the future (did God know for certain that I was going to write this introduction)? Is God 'static', or does God change (can he weep and rejoice and forget and change his mind)? Does God work through non-Christian religions (does God save those who turn their hearts towards him in repentance, even if they have never heard the name of Christ)? These and other issues are now up for discussion.

The Canadian theologian Clark Pinnock has, for a while now, been at the centre of such debates. While the debates and issues are not in themselves new, the context is. For here is Pinnock, a well-respected and self-confessed evangelical, giving theological reflection which is by and large out of synch with a traditional evangelical theology. The consensus of evangelicalism has, for most of

---

[1] See N.T. Wright in the 'Introduction' to *The New Testament and the People of God.*

this century at least, disagreed with the conclusions Pinnock has come to. He has challenged the tradition; he has started to reconstruct evangelical theology. According to Pinnock, the God the Bible portrays does not have certain and exhaustive knowledge of the future. He may well change. And he will work through non-Christian religions.

It is because Pinnock has sought to challenge accepted understandings of these doctrines in such a consistent way that the editors of this volume thought it worth interacting with his theology. For this reason, we brought together a team of evangelical scholars, all of them relatively young, to tackle some of the central issues Pinnock deals with. The choice of those relatively new to academic theology was deliberate, for apart from being familiar with new and recent material, the authors demonstrate that a dissatisfaction with traditional doctrine is not a characteristic universally widespread among younger generations. Some have labelled 'Openness Theology' the theology for a new generation. Indeed, when Pinnock spoke at a conference in the UK in 1997 it was entitled 'A Theology for Revival', something which would accompany the new things God was doing. So we hope that this volume will not come across as died-in-the-wool traditionalists reacting to some new fad! All of the contributors to this volume want to achieve two things – to interact with Pinnock at a clear and detailed level, and to remain thoroughly biblical and evangelical.

These two commitments demand some explanation. This collection consists of fairly detailed papers that deal with detailed issues. An attempt has been made to prevent them becoming too technical, while at the same time ensuring that we follow the very best academic standards. There is no need for name-calling or caricaturing, of establishing straw men and women to win arguments, or of defending labels just for the sake of it. If we hold our positions with good conscience, then we must demonstrate this to be the case using the gifts God has given us to the best of our abilities. That the papers make sense and may (or may not) win arguments is down to God's grace, not our wisdom!

Secondly, the essays are concerned with what is biblical, and what is evangelical. All involved in this project, including Pinnock, wish to hold that all doctrine and practice emerge out of our final authority – the Christian Scriptures. In particular Part 1 deals with some of the detailed exegetical issues involved in constructing a doctrine of God, and the response by Pinnock will highlight the need for hermeneutical questions to be addressed. As for the question 'Who is an evangelical?', this of course must also emerge from our understanding of Scripture. It is a pressing question, for many are claiming that evangelicalism is fragmenting, and more personally, that Clark Pinnock, although claiming the name for himself, has now moved beyond the boundaries of evangelicalism. Of course this is a complex question, and one which is probed at various points in Parts 2 and 3. There are a number of ways to define 'evangelical' – sociologically, in terms of piety, historically and doctrinally. The contributors to this volume are perhaps concerned most of all with these last two areas. At times Pinnock is accused of, for one reason or another, moving beyond a 'traditional' evangelical position, and to this Pinnock replies. No one in fact has a monopoly on the term 'evangelical' (a term used by Barth, Brunner, Stott and Carson, to name but a few!), and for this reason Scripture must always be the final authority, not for how we use a term, but for how we understand faith.

However, it must be born in mind that we have no desire to ostracize or condemn, to label or caricature, merely to understand, refine, and to further the debate. In this collection of essays it is a position we question, not a character. Our desire is to see clearly what Scripture understands as true and right doctrine, and to see whether Pinnock's work coincides with this. I remember very vividly John Wenham, shortly before his death, urging me not to get too hung up on the word 'evangelical'. Although it is important, what Scripture wants to know is whether someone is right with God (a follower of God, a Christian), and whether their life and belief measure up to Scripture. This is surely a challenge for all theologians, whichever labels they attract or claim or deny.

And of course, that challenge is central to the three Parts that follow. Part 1 deals with the biblical understanding of God and how Pinnock sees in Scripture a doctrine of God that challenges the tradition. Part 2 examines some historical and doctrinal matters that illustrate how these questions have been addressed in the tradition, and how Pinnock's theology fits into that history. And Part 3 very clearly addresses the question of who is a Christian, or rather, who is saved.

We hope that this book will make a small but significant contribution to the many debates that it covers. We are extremely grateful that Clark Pinnock has been willing to give the time to read our efforts and respond so graciously. And as we commend this book, we pray that we all will come to know and serve our God better, understand his ways more clearly, that we can glorify him in everything we do – including our theology!

1

Biographical Essay: Clark H. Pinnock: The Evolution of an Evangelical
Daniel Strange

Some theologians are idealogues, so cocksure about the truth that they are willing to force reality to fit into their own system; others are not so sure and permit reality to change them and their systems instead. I am a theologian of the latter type.[1]

In this essay I wish to give a biographical study of the Canadian Baptist theologian Clark H. Pinnock, giving a flavour of his pilgrimage in theology which has spanned five decades. In understanding the current work of a particular scholar, it is always helpful to understand the context within which he or she works, the theological background from which they have come, and the influences that have shaped their thought. From this it may even be possible to predict where they will go next in their theological journey.

Within the evangelical community, especially in North America, Clark Pinnock is one of the most stimulating, controversial and influential theologians, and a study of his work raises important questions about the nature and identity of contemporary evangelicalism. His work also provides an interesting 'case study' as to the nature of systematic theology: how change and development in one area of doctrine impacts and influences every area; how the criteria of internal consistency and coherence shape our theological frameworks; how emotion, intuition and rationalism influence our

---

[1] C.H. Pinnock, 'Foreword' in R.C. Roennfeldt's published doctoral thesis, *Clark H. Pinnock On Biblical Theology: An Evolving Position*, xv.

theologizing; and how and why theologians feel forced at times to make paradigmatic shifts in their thinking.

The essay will be divided into three parts. Firstly, I will chart, chronologically, Pinnock's life and work in three distinct phases; describing the main elements of his thinking and the influences that have shaped this thinking. Secondly, I will draw attention to some characteristic features of Pinnock's theology. Finally, I will briefly assess Pinnock's continuing impact and significance on evangelical Christianity.

An outline of Pinnock's life and work

Phase 1: Up to 1970: In the Calvinist paradigm

Pinnock was born in Toronto in 1937 and grew up in the environment of a liberal Baptist church. It was through the influence of his grandmother that he became a Christian in 1949, and he received nurturing from Youth for Christ: 'I was introduced to God in the context of the fundamentalist portraiture of the Gospel. It alerted me to the fact that there are a lot of modernists out there who had vacated the house of authority and sold our birthright for a mess of irrelevant pottage.'[2] Pinnock says that the writers he was introduced to as 'sound' in the 1950s, were all theologically Reformed: John Murray, Cornelius Van Til, Carl Henry and J.I. Packer. Looking back he says that he did not realize a Calvinistic hegemony in post-war evangelicalism: 'it is no surprise that I began my theological life as a Calvinist who regarded alternate evangelical interpretations as suspect and at least mildly heretical. I accepted the view I was given that Calvinism was just scriptural evangelicalism in its purest expression, and I did not question it for a long time.'[3]

After completing his first degree in Ancient Near East Studies at the University of Toronto, he went to Manchester University and did his doctoral research on Pauline pneumatology under F.F. Bruce. Around this time he developed a close association with

---

[2] C.H. Pinnock, 'I Was a Teenage Fundamentalist', 18.
[3] C.H. Pinnock, 'From Augustine to Arminius: A Pilgrimage in Theology' in idem (ed.), *The Grace of God and the Will of Man*, 17.

Francis Schaeffer and even worked at L'Abri for a time. Although Schaeffer was the main influence on Pinnock's early work on 'cultural apologetics', Pinnock believed that more traditional 'evidentialist' apologetics were needed if faith was not to become another irrational 'upper-story leap'[4] (to use a famous Schaefferism). In his evidentialist field, Pinnock was influenced by the work of John Warwick Montgomery.[5]

For Pinnock, successful evangelism depended on the declaration of a specific message and foundational to this message was the Calvinist view of salvation since any other resulted in Christian synergism and a repudiation of salvation by grace alone.[6]

In the mid-sixties he began teaching New Testament studies at New Orleans Baptist Theological Seminary but soon moved into the department of systematic theology. A charismatic experience in 1967 would be very influential in Pinnock's life and work. While at a Bible study he received an 'infilling of the Spirit' and caught a glimpse of the dimension of the Spirit which the New Testament describes. Ever since that moment Pinnock has been a fervent advocate of charismatic renewal and Pentecostalism (although he has remained within the Baptist denomination), and this conviction has received more detailed theological treatment in recent work.

Apart from apologetics, Pinnock's main interest in this period was biblical authority and revelation. In 1971 he wrote his first important work, *Biblical Revelation: The Foundation of Christian Theology*,[7] which at the time was called, 'the most vigorous scholarly statement of verbal, plenary inspiration since Warfield'.[8] This work advocated a strong yet nuanced version of biblical inerrancy and infallibility. Again looking back, Pinnock notes three factors which determined the nature of this work. At this time he thought it epistemologically fundamental to prove a perfect Bible in which

---

[4] See Pinnock's 1971 'Appendix: On Method in Christian Apologetics' in his *Set Forth Your Case: Studies in Christian Apologetics*, 131f.
[5] Pinnock refers especially to Montgomery's *The Shape of the Past: An Introduction to Philosophical Historiography*.
[6] See C.H. Pinnock, *Evangelism and Truth*, 29–39.
[7] With the 'Foreword' by J.I Packer.
[8] Lewis, G.R., review of *Biblical Revelation*, in *Eternity* (January 1972), 50. Quoted from R.V. Rakestraw, 'Clark H. Pinnock: A Theological Odyssey', 253.

there were no errors or contradictions. He writes in the conclusion of *Biblical Revelation*, 'to cast doubt on the complete veracity and authority of Scripture is a criminal act creating a crisis of immense proportions for theology and faith'.[9] Secondly, Pinnock notes that this view of the Bible is only possible within the predestinarian framework of Calvinism:

> Since God is thought to decree and control everything, he can also be thought of as controlling and determining the text of the Bible through the supernatural inspiration of it . . . one might [also] deduce that it would partake of the attribute of divine truth itself and be perfectly inerrant in every respect.[10]

Finally, Pinnock realizes that his earlier view was a militant one, intolerant of any other view of Scripture even though it claimed to be 'evangelical'. Only three years before in his *A New Reformation: A Challenge to Southern Baptists*, he had called for the Southern Baptist Convention to expel any non-inerrantist professors. Writing in 1993 about this time he says, 'This does not make one an easy going fellow ecumenically as others may testify from knowing me during those years.'[11] This whole period sees Pinnock fighting against the spectre of liberalism and relativism which had infiltrated many churches and taken away the only, 'valid knowledge of redemption'[12] – that is the authoritative revelation of the Bible.

Phase 2: 1970–86; The slow realization of a paradigm shift and the conversion to Arminianism

From 1969–74, Pinnock taught at Trinity Evangelical Divinity School. It was during his tenure there that he underwent a second 'conversion', the impact of which would eventually filter down to every area of his thought. Pinnock was teaching the doctrine of the perseverance of the saints in the book of Hebrews.[13] He found that

---

[9] Pinnock, *Biblical*, 228.
[10] 'Foreword', Roennfeldt, *Clark H. Pinnock*, xviii.
[11] Ibid. xix.
[12] *Biblical*, 104.
[13] This is the belief that those who are saved, the elect, will be kept by the grace of God and will persevere until they are glorified.

he could not square this doctrine with the passages in Hebrews that urge us to persevere or the stern warnings about falling away from Christ (Heb. 3:12; 10:26). He was also strongly influenced by I. Howard Marshall's study in the entire New Testament of the same problem, *Kept by the Power of God: A Study in Perseverance and Falling Away*. Pinnock writes:

> The exhortations and the warnings could only signify that continuing in the grace of God was something that depended at least on the human partner. And once I saw that, the logic of Calvinism was broken in principle, and it was only a matter of time before the larger implications of its breaking would dawn on me. The thread was pulled, and the garment must begin to unravel, as indeed it did.[14]

What had happened here? One perspective from which one could analyse this change, is Pinnock's new construal of the relationship between divine sovereignty and human freedom and responsibility. He writes, 'I began to doubt the existence of an all-determining fatalistic blueprint for history and to think of God's having made us significantly free creatures able to accept or reject his purposes for us.'[15] Moral responsibility required him to believe that human actions are not determined either internally or externally. This is described by philosophers as categorical freedom, so while reasons and causes can always affect our decisions, they cannot determine them, and the agent can always categorically do otherwise than he or she did.

Pinnock believed that in creating humans in his image, God gave them this relative autonomy of self-determination, and it is only this definition of freedom that can firstly, account for the mutuality and relationality we see between God and his creatures, and secondly, is the only account of freedom which does not make us responsible for our sin. Significant freedom shows itself in the fact that we are sinners who have God's plans: 'our rebellion is proof that our actions are not determined but free – God's plan can be frustrated and ruined'.[16] Pinnock believed this to be existentially true on an

---

[14] 'Augustine', 17.

[15] Ibid. 18.

[16] C.H. Pinnock, 'God Limits His Knowledge' in R. Basinger and D. Basinger (eds.), *Four Views on Predestination and Freewill*, 147.

intuitional level: 'Universal man almost without exception talks and feels as if he were free . . . this fundamental self perception, I believe, is an important clue to the nature of reality.'[17]

So far this debate will be a familiar one with those acquainted with the theological and philosophical positions known as Calvinism and Arminianism. In light of this revelation concerning the nature of freedom, Pinnock realized that he had to reformulate certain areas of his soteriology: 'Just as one cannot change the pitch of a single string on a violin without adjusting the others, so one cannot introduce a major new insight into a coherent system like Calvinian theology without having to consider many other issues.'[18] Thus humanity was never so depraved (either in its natural state or because of a restoring grace) that it could not freely respond to grace; predestination, rather than being an all-determining plan for the world and our lives, was a set of all-inclusive goals that could be accepted or rejected: 'it became possible for me to accept the scriptural teaching of the universal salvific will of God and not feel duty-bound to deny it as before';[19] election was conditional and based on the human response to faith; the atonement was unlimited in its scope and included everyone in its provision (Pinnock admits that this meant that he had to reduce the precision in which he understood Christ's substitution to take place); saving grace was resistible and could be spurned, and believers could fall away and lose their salvation. At this stage of Pinnock's thinking he had yet to formulate the theological theories that would explain many of these truths he wanted to affirm.

Pinnock believes that these changes were not made only out of logical necessity and the need to be internally consistent, or because they felt 'right' on an intuitional level. Rather he believed that the biblical text demanded such a change, the 'dark shadow of Calvinism'[20] was lifting for him to see the Bible in a new light:

---

[17] C.H. Pinnock, 'Responsible Freedom and the Flow of Biblical History' in idem (ed.), *Grace Unlimited*, 95.
[18] 'Augustine', 18.
[19] Ibid. 19.
[20] Ibid. 21.

Obviously what is happening here is a paradigm shift in my biblical hermeneutics. I am in the process of learning to read the Bible from a new point of view, one that I believe is more truly Evangelical and less rationalistic. Looking at it from the vantage point of God's universal salvific will and of significant human freedom, I find that many new verses leap up from the page, while many familiar ones take on new meanings. In the past I would slip into my reading of the Bible dark assumptions about the nature of God's decrees and intentions. What a relief to be done with them![21]

From an initial question concerning the perseverance of the saints, Pinnock had started a chain reaction in his thinking which resulted in a complete paradigmatic shift in his theology. This could conveniently be called a move to Arminianism although as we shall see, the recent implications for the doctrine of God which Pinnock has seen, possibly push him beyond this category. This said, Pinnock in the 1970s and 1980s became one of the leading spokesmen and figureheads of the Arminian wing of the evangelical community, editing two books of collected essays by a variety of contemporary Arminian scholars, *Grace Unlimited* (1975), and *The Grace of God and the Will of Man: A Case For Arminianism* (1989).[22] The overriding concern of these books is to assert the love of God, his universal salvific will and the unlimited nature of atonement: 'we reject all forms of theology which deny this truth and posit some secret abyss in God's mind where he is not gracious'.[23]

Outside soteriological issues, Pinnock was continuing to make changes in other areas of doctrine, purging the Calvinistic framework that had influenced his earlier thought. One area where there was a major change was Pinnock's doctrine of Scripture itself.[24] Admitting that it took him ten years to realize the significance of his paradigm shift for issues of revelation, Pinnock's 1985 book, *The Scripture Principle* sees him moving away from Warfield's view

---

[21] Ibid.

[22] It is interesting that I. Howard Marshall, the theologian who started Pinnock's thinking on these issues, contributes two essays to these books.

[23] 'Introduction' in Pinnock, *Grace Unlimited*, 11.

[24] For a very detailed study on Pinnock's doctrine of Scripture comparing *Biblical Revelation* and *The Scripture Principle* see Roennfeldt, *Clark H. Pinnock*.

which he claims is too rationalistic and docetic in its treatment of the biblical text. Rather he was now free to understand the human character of the text, and the result is more of a concomitant view of inspiration where God supervises the writers in varying degrees, and is a partner in the creation of the text rather than a coercive determining influence. Pinnock comments on this view, 'Respecting the Bible means accepting it humbly in the form in which it comes. The effect of this realisation was to make the category of biblical inerrancy less intelligible unless quite broadly defined and then it sounded a little meaningless.'[25] Perhaps a fair description would be to say that the Bible is inerrant in its 'macropurpose',[26] that is its 'salvific/paraenetic intention',[27] as set down in 2 Timothy 3:16. Pinnock believes that this shift on inspiration and inerrancy is another necessary move if he is to be logically consistent. On those non-Calvinist evangelicals who hold to plenary verbal inspiration, Pinnock says that they 'do not think systematically and limit their Calvinism to this one subject'.[28]

Finally Pinnock's 'political theology' at this time reflects his paradigm shift. Before 1970, Pinnock describes his position as part of the mainstream which supported democratic capitalism although he admits he had not reflected much on this area of theology. However, while at Trinity, Pinnock became involved with the 'Sojourners' group which adopted an Anabaptist understanding of discipleship, ethics and the state. Price comments that this was a rejection of 'the historic Calvinist belief in the state as the Christian common-wealth with its "Christ the Transformer of Culture" model'.[29] He even voted for a communist candidate in the 1974 Vancouver civic election.[30] As regards his teaching career, Pinnock, in 1977, had become Associate Professor of Systematic Theology at McMaster Divinity College, Hamilton, Ontario.[31]

---

[25] 'Foreword', Roennfeldt, *Clark H. Pinnock*, xx.

[26] R.M. Price, 'Clark H. Pinnock: Conservative and Contemporary', 157–83, 178.

[27] Ibid.

[28] *Scripture*, 101, 102.

[29] Price, 'Clark H. Pinnock', 168.

[30] This was during Pinnock's brief tenure at Regent College, Vancouver, 1974–77.

[31] He is presently still teaching there, now as Professor.

Phase 3: 1986 until the present:[32] *The transition to free-will theism and the category of Openness*

As I have already said, Pinnock's 'conversion' to a more Arminian view of soteriology, impacted on every area of his theology. However, to describe this change from the perspective of freedom is only to understand part of a much more fundamental and comprehensive change in Pinnock's thinking. Pinnock's crisis over the perseverance of the saints had made him rethink what he calls his 'root metaphors' for God. He defines these metaphors as 'basic portrayals of God which affect how we view and relate to him'.[33] Rather than having a root metaphor which stressed absolute sovereignty and power, Pinnock's metaphors of God now revolved around the ideas of a loving parent and a personal, relational God who was involved in reciprocal 'give and take' relationships with his creatures. A presupposition integral to this view was a certain way of construing freedom.

In the last ten years, Pinnock has realized that there are further implications of adopting a root metaphor of a personal God and a categorical view of freedom if one is to be biblically faithful, internally consistent and emotionally satisfied. This has led him, in more detail, into the territory of the doctrine of God, a journey in which he has been accompanied by like-minded evangelicals, namely Richard Rice, David Basinger, William Hasker and John Sanders.[34] The outcome has been the proposal of a new theistic paradigm variously called 'free-will theism', 'creative love theism' or 'the Openness of God'. This proposal places itself between the model of classical theism (which is accused of being heavily influenced by Neo-Platonism and which exaggerates God's transcendence), and process theology (which stresses a radical immanence). Pinnock summarizes his model as such:

---

[32] I have chosen the year 1986 to mark Pinnock's third phase because it was in this year that he began to publish material explicitly on the doctrine of God, the first being the essay 'God Limits His Knowledge'.

[33] C.H. Pinnock and D. Brown, *Theological Crossfire: An Evangelical/Liberal Dialogue*, 66.

[34] All these writers have edited a book which could be called the manifesto for 'free-will theism'. See C.H. Pinnock et al. (eds.), *The Openness of God: A Biblical Challenge to the Traditional Understanding of God*.

> Our understanding of Scripture leads us to depict God, the sovereign Creator, as voluntarily bringing into existence a world with significantly free personal agents in it . . . In line with his decision to make this kind of world, God rules in such a way as to uphold the created structures and, because he gives liberty to his creatures, is happy to accept the future as open, not closed and a relationship with the world that is dynamic not static . . . Our lives make a difference to God – they are truly significant.[35]

There are three particular doctrines which form the basis of this model of God: the 'social analogy' of the Trinity, God's transcendence and immanence in creation, and a reformulation of the divine attributes. The third of these has proved the most controversial and deserves a brief summary.

Pinnock and the other free-will theists have had to rethink the nature of divine sovereignty. God is sovereign in that he created the world *ex nihilo* and does not rely on anything for his existence (contra process theism). Indeed God could have created a world in which he determined everything, but he has not done this. In fact he has created creatures with genuine autonomy and so has accepted limitation on his divine power. Therefore God's sovereignty is not in the form of dominion but in God's ability to anticipate obstructions to his will and deal with them. Omnipotence is not the power to determine everything but the power to deal with every circumstance that can arise: it is an omnicompetance. Similarly there have been questions raised and revisions made to the doctrines of impassibility, immutability and God's timeless eternity.

The most contentious aspect of this proposal is a redefinition of divine omniscience. Pinnock not only rejects the Calvinist belief in fore-ordination but also the traditional Arminian doctrine of foreknowledge, because it is seen to contradict significant freedom: 'I could not shake off the intuition that such a total omniscience would necessarily mean that everything we will ever choose in the future will have already been spelled out in the divine knowledge register, and consequently the belief that we have significant choices would be mistaken.'[36] So God knows everything that is

---

[35] 'Systematic Theology' in idem et al., *Openness*, 104.
[36] 'Augustine', 25.

logically knowable but does not and cannot know future human actions although he can accurately predict many human decisions based on his exhaustive knowledge of past and present.

Pinnock sees many benefits in adopting this model of theism. God is said to be pictured in more dynamic terms: he takes risks and opens himself to genuine rejection and failure. This is the stuff of personal relationships where one partner not only acts but reacts to the other. Such a view also can deal with the many biblical passages which speak of God rejoicing, repenting, grieving, changing his mind, being frustrated, etc. These are not anthropomorphisms but literal statements about God. Finally, such a view provides a powerful theodicy, for although God knows that evil will occur, he does not know what specific instances will arise from free human decisions.

In adopting this view of God, Pinnock has finally come to understand the full implications of his 1970 'conversion'. From the perspective of free-will theism, not only Calvinism is to be rejected but traditional Arminianism which is to be seen as merely an epicycle of the Reformed paradigm. Pinnock calls all evangelicals to make a paradigm shift to this new proposal which he believes is a truly biblical position.

Although the 'Openness of God' has been Pinnock's main concern in recent years, other important areas of theology have received detailed treatment and can be seen to be inextricably linked to the 'Openness' worldview and vision. All these areas come to fruition in Pinnock's latest work, *Flame of Love: A Theology of the Holy Spirit* (1996) which is the most comprehensive overview and summation of his theological vision to date. I will briefly mention a few of these areas.

Firstly, Pinnock is very open to truth found in other Christian traditions; indeed he believes the Holy Spirit to be at work throughout the Christian world uniting Christian traditions. So in *Flame of Love* we see a catholic Pinnock drawing from a variety of traditions (traditions which in the past have been seen to be the antithesis of evangelical theology and methodology), to explain those areas of theology which he feels evangelicalism has been ill-equipped to tackle. So, for example, he goes to the Cappadocian Fathers and Greek Orthodoxy for the 'social analogy' of the Trinity; Irenaeus, Greek Orthodoxy and Barth for a revised doctrine of kenotic 'Spirit Christology' and a 'recapitulation' theory of the atonement; Greek Orthodoxy again for the holistic view of salvation called theosis. However, in spite of all these influences, Pinnock still calls this work evangelical.

Linked to this has been Pinnock's work in the 'theology of religions' which is further evidence of an openness in his thinking.[37] Taking the foundational axioms of the universal salvific will of God, and the particularity of Christ, Pinnock has formulated a position which he calls 'modal inclusivism'.[38] Again the inspiration for this is not primarily evangelicalism (although he refers to the influences in his formative years of C.S. Lewis and Norman Anderson) but the statements of Vatican II. He writes, 'I make no apology as an evangelical in admitting an enormous debt of gratitude to the Council for its guidance on this topic.'[39] In Pinnock's model, the possibility of salvation must be universally accessible if God loves the whole world and Christ died for the whole world. God may use elements of other religions to offer the Holy Spirit's prevenient grace to someone who has not come into contact with the gospel proclamation. An unevangelized person can be saved through explicit faith in God as revealed in general revelation or by implicit faith through acts of love which are equally a response to grace. Therefore Pinnock believes that an atheist can be saved by 'accepting the mystery of their being, which is the goal of his or her life'.[40] This proposal has some similarities and affinities to John Wesley's doctrine of prevenient grace and Karl Rahner's 'supernatural existential'. Behind all this theological formulation is a firm belief of a wideness in the mercy of God and an optimism in the number of people who will eventually be saved (*Heilsoptimismus*): 'Christian theology must speak of universality and inclusion.'[41] In explicitly adopting inclusivism, Pinnock is definitely on virgin territory for an evangelical theologian.

---

[37] Pinnock's main work on this is his book *A Wideness in God's Mercy: The Finality of Jesus Christ in a World of Religions*. Since this book, though, Pinnock has developed and nuanced his argument considerably. See his essay 'An Inclusivist View' in D. Okholm and T.R. Phillips (eds.), *More Than One Way? Four Views of Salvation in a Pluralistic World*, 93–124; and ch. 6 of *Flame*, 'Spirit and Universality', 185–215.

[38] See Pinnock, 'Inclusivist', 100.

[39] Ibid. 97, n. 4.

[40] Ibid. 119.

[41] Ibid. 93.

Finally, Pinnock has continued to be open to the work of the Spirit in the life of the church, and *Flame of Love* is a firm endorsement of charismatic renewal. He says of Pentecostalism that it is 'a mighty twentieth-century outpouring of the Spirit. I think of this as the most important event in modern Christianity.'[42] Indeed on a personal note he mentions his indebtedness to the Toronto Blessing for the influence it had over the writing of *Flame of Love*: 'the flow of grace and love in this remarkable wakening can only be marveled at'.[43]

Some paradoxical features of Pinnock's theology

Clark Pinnock's *modus operandi*, is that of seeing theology as an adventure, and a matter of curiosity. He admits that sometimes he doesn't know where he is going in his thinking or how he will get back, and he admits that in this respect he is serendipitous, not having a 'big plan' or 'system' that he is working with. Price perceptively comments on this fact:

> Pinnock wants to avoid deductively imposing some neat and simple *a priori* scheme on the stubborn 'phenomena' of reality. He must be honest and take each case as it comes, responding to each as seems appropriate. This hermeneutic of reality keeps him open to change as reality itself is changing.[44]

This means that while some areas of his theology have moved in one direction, other areas have moved in the opposite direction. The main area where this is evident is in his latest thoughts on political theology. Although Pinnock has repudiated Calvinistic soteriology and the Calvinist portrayal of God, he has moved away from his 'radical' Anabaptist phase of the 1970s towards a 'neo-Puritan' vision and Reformed hermeneutic with respect to the Old and New Testaments. As Rakestraw notes, 'He is excited about the resurgence of this theonomy teaching in the later writing of Francis

---

[42] *Flame*, 18.
[43] Ibid. 250, n. 10.
[44] Price, 'Clark H. Pinnock', 183.

Schaeffer, in the efforts of the New Right . . . and even urges Christians in his land to work hard to move the country, "in the direction of a Christian commonwealth".[45]

As a conservative risk-taker, Pinnock is not afraid to experiment with new ideas and there is somewhat of a playfulness to his theology. He says that he has the ability to make changes without losing his evangelical moorings and that he has been able to manage this intellectually because he can retrieve the best conservative thought from the past as well as realizing that there are contemporary questions (e.g. religious pluralism) that have to be dealt with. In this Pinnock places himself with a number of theological allies, Barth, Bloesch, Fackre, Ward, Oden and Grenz, who are both conservative and contemporary. Pinnock says, 'By mixing all this together, I found it possible to construct a reformed (not Reformed) evangelical theology and I suspect that whatever appeal it has is due to the fact that there is a large group in the churches who want a theology like this.'[46] Perhaps the *raison d'être* behind *Flame of Love* demonstrates the above point most clearly. Pinnock believes that this is a work which does not deny or repudiate the evangelical heritage from which he has come. Rather his resolve in this work was to pick up anything that evangelicalism had neglected, and put it back. His aim was to enrich the feast and to re-emphasize certain areas. So Spirit Christology is emphasized but this is not to negate Logos Christology. Recapitulation and salvation by resurrection is stressed, but this is not to deny substitution or the element of judgement in the cross. Theosis is emphasized as a large model of salvation, but this is not to deny justification by faith, rather justification is only a small part of soteriology, the wider perspective being union with God. Of course the question Pinnock's theology raises is, when does re-emphasis become over re-emphasis and therefore mark a definitive change? For example, in *Flame of Love*, he rejects the purpose of the atonement as being 'primarily penal'.[47] On this he says, 'This is a delicate point for me to discuss. First, it was the view of John Calvin and has been the distinguishing mark

---

[44] Price, 'Clark H. Pinnock', 183.

[45] Rakestraw, 'Clark H. Pinnock', 263.

[46] 'Foreword', Roennfeldt, *Clark H. Pinnock*, xviii.

[47] *Flame*, 106.

of Evangelicalism . . . It is risky to seem to be calling it into question.'[48]

All these points demonstrate a major paradox in Pinnock's theological project. Pinnock has been criticized for his theological instability and his changes of mind over a variety of issues. However this 'change' is rarely a going back over old positions (the noticeable exception being his political views). Rather than being a sign of instability, it could be argued that this changing is a sign of thoroughness and a striving to work through the full implications of earlier presuppositions. It is more like an evolution of thought moving in one direction than a regression which is unstable and whimsical. From 1970 and Pinnock's 'conversion' to the relational model of God and categorical freedom, there has been a systematic (albeit subconscious) attempt by Pinnock to be internally consistent and coherent in his theology. This can be seen in many areas of his work. On the atonement, where he realized early on that strict penal substitution led inexorably to limited atonement, the seventies and eighties saw him looking for an appropriate model before finally adopting the model of recapitulation. He rejected total depravity because it implied monergism in the work of salvation rather than synergism. Again he has thought about many theories before adopting the Orthodox distinction between image and likeness and a version of prevenient grace which still enables him to say we are saved by grace through faith. Then there is the denial of exhaustive divine omniscience which is seen to contradict real freedom. Ironically Pinnock is perhaps more critical of traditional Arminianism than Calvinism because it is confused and inconsistent, lying midway between the Calvinist position and free-will theism. Pinnock admits that the Calvinist paradigm is a consistent one but is fatally flawed both biblically and experientially.

A final point worth remembering about Pinnock is that he does not concentrate his work in one area of systematics, but roams the theological world writing on a variety of issues. He realizes that a disadvantage to working in this manner is that no one area is given comprehensive treatment, but is left without detailed explanation, with the result sometimes that there can be ambiguity over what he means. While this may give rise to the accusation of superficiality

---

[48] Ibid.

and crudeness in expounding certain ideas, a benefit of this approach is that it is easier to see how one area of systematics fits into Pinnock's wider theological concerns, as he has written on so many areas.

Pinnock's impact upon Evangelicalism

Robert Rakestraw comments in somewhat diplomatic manner that Pinnock's influence on the content of evangelical theology will be 'more in forging new patterns of thought than in honing or defending established Evangelical doctrines'.[49] It is fair to say that within the context of the evangelical community Pinnock is influential and yet highly controversial. Perhaps it would be unfair to call him the *enfant terrible* of evangelicalism. He still is a member of the Evangelical Theological Society (although he notes that some have been expelled from this organization for less radical views than his), and he believes that he is tolerated because he has been part of the evangelical community for over forty years. Away from the Establishment his work has been grasped enthusiastically by Wesleyans and Pentecostals, the latter group seeming to 'adopt' him as their theologian.[50]

Perhaps Pinnock's lasting legacy to the evangelical community will be that his work raises perennial questions concerning the nature and identity of evangelicalism itself. Alister McGrath comments that Pinnock 'has been the catalyst for much rethinking within the Evangelical movement'.[51] Pinnock still believes there to be a Reformed hegemony in the evangelical establishment and that it is this wing that has ostracized him and his theology: 'The Reformed group has occupied this position among us and to a degree still does and so is in a strong position to equate evangelical theology with their own viewpoint and declare who is in and who is out of

---

[49] Rakestraw, 'Clark H. Pinnock', 269.

[50] Pinnock's influence is not restricted to North America. In November 1997 Pinnock was the keynote speaker at a major conference organized by Ichthus, Pioneer, Holy Trinity Brompton and YWAM, endorsing *Openness*.

[51] A.E. McGrath, 'Response to Clark Pinnock' in Okholm and Phillips, *Four Views*, 129.

the movement.'[52] So Pinnock is highly critical of, for example, the 'Alliance of Confessing Evangelicals' (ACE) because it excludes not only his views but the views of more orthodox Wesleyans and Pentecostals: 'Evangelicalism in its recent form [e.g. ACE] began with a birth defect in method that has to be overcome if there is to be excellent work. Fortunately the corrections are being made.'[53] Enter free-will theism with which Pinnock believes evangelicalism can grow out of propositionalism and omnicausalism and face the future with integrity and promise. In 1997 he stated:

> I love the Evangelical heritage but have been burdened by difficulties such as these [propositionalism and omnicausalism] my whole life. They have impeded me from producing the quality of work that I would have wished. Fortunately a new generation is coming along which recognises the problems and (I hope) will be able to transcend them more effectively in future.[54]

So we see a situation emerging with definite battle lines drawn out. Both Pinnock and his critics accuse each other of the same things, that is, a move away from the biblical testimony and a dependence upon logical rationalism and intuitive experience. This debate has a long way to go and evangelicals are just beginning to tackle it.[55]

Clearly Pinnock is an emotive theologian who is not afraid to ask difficult questions of the evangelical movement. A trait of his personality is that he is always ready to give an opinion and is not afraid to publish quickly, some say too quickly, before he has thought through all the implications of a particular position. A glance at his prolific bibliography is testimony to this. This means that he has often become the figurehead (perhaps not intentionally) of many of the controversial issues which have confronted evangelicalism in

---

[52] C.H. Pinnock, 'Evangelical Theologians Facing the Future: An Ancient and a Future Paradigm', Keynote address for the 33rd Annual Meeting of the Wesleyan Theological Society, 7–8 November 1997.

[53] Ibid. 6.

[54] Ibid. 16.

[55] See e.g. M. Erickson, *The Evangelical Left: Encountering Postconservative Evangelical Theology*; J.H. Armstrong, *The Coming Evangelical Crisis*; Norman Geisler, *Creating God in the Image of Man? The New Open View of God – Neotheism's Dangerous Drift*.

the last two decades: the authority of Scripture (as a 'limited inerrantist'), the role of other religions (as an inclusivist), the nature of hell (as an advocate of annihilationalism), the charismatic renewal and the place of spiritual gifts (a strong advocate), and the doctrine of God (as a free-will theist).

But can Pinnock still be called an evangelical theologian? As we have seen, this depends on your definition of evangelicalism. Perhaps, though, Pinnock should take solace from the adage that those you criticize the most are usually the ones closest to you. Certainly if we are to take Pinnock's own sociological definition of evangelicalism as a loose coalition based on a number of family resemblances, then it will be easy to categorize his theology as evangelical.[56]

However, categorizing Pinnock on the theological spectrum may be a more difficult task than this, and Pinnock himself realizes that as a theological maverick who is open to change, this is a difficult, painful, yet hopeful question to answer:

> Not only am I not often listened to, I am also made to feel stranded theologically: being too much of a free thinker to be accepted by the Evangelical establishment and too much a conservative to be accepted by the liberal mainline. Sometimes I do not know where I belong. But I am not discouraged by this because, being a creature of hope, I can imagine a future where Evangelicals and liberals mature and come around to more sensible middle positions. I will not object to some views of mine being accepted belatedly if not now.[57]

Whether this prophecy will come true is like much of Pinnock's theology, stimulating, provocative and open to debate.

---

[56] Pinnock lists these resemblances as 'commitment to the biblical message as the supreme norm; belief in a transcendent personal God who interacts with creation and acts of history; a focus on the transforming grace of God in human life, and the importance of mission to bring the [sic] goodness to the whole world' ('Evangelical', 3).

[57] 'Foreword', Roennfeldt, *Clark H. Pinnock*, xvi.

Part 1

2

From Augustine to Arminius, and Beyond[1]
Nathan MacDonald

'Our image of God must go' was how the *Observer* heralded the appearance of John A.T. Robinson's *Honest to God* on 17 March 1963. Such a slogan would be an appropriate description of the challenge Clark Pinnock's books and articles have placed before North American Evangelicalism. The doctrine of God has long been an interest of Pinnock's. An interest that has seen a theological journey from Calvinism[2] to what he and the other contributors to *The Openness of God* call 'the open view of God'.[3] This journey has had a number of recognizable stages. The first stage in the seventies led to Pinnock questioning the idea of God's timelessness, immutability and impassibility. In the mid to late eighties he moved on to questions of God's omniscience and sovereignty. The final stage was the early nineties in which Pinnock and others presented a theological system based around their new understanding of God. I will review each of these stages in more detail.

Pinnock's interest in the doctrine of God extends back to 1973 when he wrote 'The Problem of God' which sought to indicate the chief issues in the defence of the Christian doctrine of God against the attack by modern thinking. Pinnock noted the challenge of process theology, and argued that part of the response must be to

---

[1] I am grateful to both Dr Walter Moberly and Dr Peter Williams for reading drafts of this essay and for their helpful comments.
[2] For Pinnock's own account of his journey see 'From Augustine to Arminius: A Pilgrimage in Theology' in idem (ed.), *The Grace of God and the Will of Man: A Case For Arminianism*.
[3] Pinnock et al. (eds.), *The Openness of God: A Biblical Challenge to the Traditional Understanding of God*, 8.

'engage in careful rethinking of several traditional concepts which adhere to Christian theism, such as timelessness, immutability and impassibility, so that having understood them correctly we can deliver the doctrine from caricature and unfair criticism'.[4] This rethinking lead him in 1979 to 'neo-classical theism' which stood between the Charybdis of classical theism and the Scylla of process theism. Pinnock argued that classical theism is guilty of combining the Bible and Greek Philosophy, a dynamic ontology and a static ontology. Christian theology needed to affirm that God can suffer; God is in time, but everlasting; God is constant, but can change.[5]

The second stage of Pinnock's theological journey took place in the mid-eighties, and led to Pinnock's restatements of divine omniscience and sovereignty. Until this period Pinnock held the classical Arminian view that God had not ordained everything, but that he foreknew all. However, increasingly Pinnock questioned the philosophical plausibility of this idea. For, if God foreknew everything how could there be significant human freedom? Thus, in 1985, he wrote:

> Reason may tell me, for example, that if God knows the future exhaustively, then every detail of it is fixed and certain and the freedom most humans believe they have (and which Scripture itself seems to say that we have) is an illusion. Biblical teaching about foreknowledge appears to contradict biblical teaching about human freedom, and it is nigh unto impossible to see how the puzzle can be resolved rationally.[6]

A resolution was what Pinnock sought in his contribution to the volume *Predestination and Free Will* in which four different views on divine sovereignty and human freedom were presented.[7] The idea of foreknowledge was rejected, and God's omniscience redefined:

---

[4] C.H. Pinnock, 'The Problem of God', 15.

[5] C.H. Pinnock, 'The Need for a Scriptural, and Therefore a Neo-Classical Theism' in K.S. Kantzer and S.N. Gundry (eds.), *Perspectives in Evangelical Theology: Papers from the Thirtieth Meeting of the Evangelical Theological Society*, 37–42.

[6] C.H. Pinnock, 'How I Use the Bible in Doing Theology' in R. Johnston (ed.), *The Use of the Bible in Theology*, 31.

[7] D. Basinger and R. Basinger (eds.), *Predestination and Free Will: Four Views of Divine Sovereignty and Human Freedom*.

God knows all things that can be known. He has a complete knowledge of the past and present, but the future remains undetermined. This entailed a different understanding of predictive prophecy, 'most of it is easily accounted for by God's predicting – on the basis of what he knows – what is going to happen, or by God's announcing ahead of time what he plans to do in such and such a circumstance or by some combination of these two factors'.[8] Thus through his rejection of foreknowledge Pinnock had added a fourth area of the traditional doctrine of God that needed redefining.[9]

Pinnock had realized in 1985 that a rejection of divine foreknowledge entailed a different understanding of sovereignty.[10] In giving freedom to his creatures God had eschewed a sovereignty of domination. God's plans are often thwarted, as the present state of the world evidences, but he works things together for good Sovereignty is persuasion, not coercion or domination.

In *Predestination and Free Will* Pinnock's arguments were not primarily biblical. This gap was soon filled by his reading of Terence E. Fretheim's *The Suffering of God*.[11] In his fourth chapter Fretheim, an Old Testament scholar, argued that 'there are a variety of texts which point to a divine limitation with respect to God's knowledge of the future'.[12] There are passages where God says 'perhaps' or uses the conditional 'if', passages where God consults humans about what to do, and passages where God seems to be questioning himself.

Fretheim, though, seems to have provided Pinnock not only with biblical arguments, but also with a framework with which to synthesize his ideas of God. Fretheim begins *The Suffering of God* with a discussion of metaphorical language for God. Fretheim

---

[8] C.H. Pinnock, 'Response to B. Reichenbach' in Basinger and Basinger, *Predestination*, 139.

[9] 'God Limits His Knowledge' in Basinger and Basinger, *Predestination*, 143–62; C.H. Pinnock, 'Between Classical and Process Theism' in R. Nash (ed.), 320–25. My thanks to Professor Pinnock for making this article available to me.

[10] 'How I Use', 31.

[11] *The Suffering of God: An Old Testament Perspective*. A revealing comparison may be made between Fretheim's fourth chapter and Pinnock, 'Augustine', 25–6.

[12] Fretheim, *Suffering*, 45.

speaks of the Bible having 'controlling metaphors',[13] and it is this idea that Pinnock takes over into his theology and leads to the latest stage in Pinnock's development of the doctrine of God.[14] This final synthesis has a number of different names: 'free-will theism' in *Theological Crossfire*,[15] 'the open view of God' in *The Openness of God*,[16] and 'creative love theism' in *Unbounded Love*.[17] In all three books the concerns of Pinnock that we have already seen are re-expressed, especially in *The Openness of God*. What is new is the language of 'root metaphor' or 'model'. Pinnock argues that people have a 'root metaphor' of what God is like: 'Root metaphors for God are very influential. These are the basic portrayals of God which affect how we view and relate to him.'[18] The root metaphor many evangelicals have is one of God as monarch or judge, and Pinnock believes that a more biblical model is that of God as loving parent. Thus at the heart of Pinnock's doctrine of God is the statement in 1 John, 'God is love', and the Trinity as an interrelating and loving fellowship.

For Pinnock the root metaphor acts as a lens through which any other statements about God are seen. Thus Pinnock faces the reader with a choice of models: either God as 'aloof monarch' or 'caring parent'.[19] There can be only one root metaphor. The root metaphor controls the meaning of other metaphors, thus in the case of the metaphor of caring parent:

---

[13] Ibid. 11.

[14] The influence of Fretheim's ideas on metaphor upon J. Sanders, another exponent of openness theism, is clear in his 'God as Personal' in Pinnock, *Grace of God*, 165–80, and possibly also on R. Rice, 'Divine Foreknowledge and Free-Will Theism' in Pinnock, *Grace of God*, 121–39. Pinnock refers the reader to these articles in 'Systematic Theology' in idem et al., *Openness*, 191, n. 6.

[15] C.H. Pinnock and and D. Brown, *Theological Crossfire: An Evangelical/Liberal Dialogue*, 67.

[16] *Openness*, 8.

[17] C.H. Pinnock, and R.C. Brow, *Unbounded Love: A Good News Theology for the 21st Century*, 20.

[18] Pinnock in Pinnock and Brown, *Crossfire*, 66.

[19] 'Systematic', 103

Creative love theism celebrates a different set of theological categories from those of the forensic model. Even when the images overlap (both models see God as Judge, for example), the meaning is somewhat different. When it thinks of God as Judge, creative love theism does not think of him as a law-court judge, but as a judge of the biblical type (recall how judges in the Old Testament cared about liberating oppressed people and putting things right). Both models may speak of God as a king, but with different views of the meaning of sovereignty. When creative love theists think of monarchy, we do not picture an all-determining power but a Davidic king who protects and shepherds his flock and delegates power to others. Jesus' metaphor of the Father who loves us unconditionally is the central image in creative love theism rather than Judge or Sovereign, and it controls the meaning of these other metaphors.[20]

On the other hand, with the metaphor of God as 'aloof monarch' we have a static model of God, based on a synthesis of Greek philosophy and the Bible. In this model anything which speaks of God as a person, as changing or suffering is interpreted as an anthropomorphism. The choice is one model, or the other.

Before we begin a critical analysis of Pinnock's doctrine of God in the light of the Old Testament a few general points of appreciation should be made. Pinnock's work is characterized by a number of admirable qualities. First, Pinnock has striven to be biblical in his theology. Secondly, Pinnock's thinking always has one eye on the practical issues of Christian living, such as prayer. Thirdly, Pinnock's concern is evangelistic. A true, biblical presentation of God, he believes, will be attractive to unbelievers. Fourthly, Pinnock is disarmingly honest about what he wishes the Bible did say.[21]

Preliminary response

The challenge of Pinnock to classical theism – though it is questionable whether nearly two thousand years of diverse theological

---

[20] Pinnock and Brow, *Unbounded*, 29.
[21] See e.g. 'How I Use', 30.

reflection can be characterized in this way – is whether its God is the God of the Bible. This challenge can be reversed: is Pinnock's God the God of the Bible? This essay asks a slightly narrower question: is Pinnock's God the God of the Old Testament? Or, alternatively, when the writers of the Old Testament used *elohim* did they mean what Pinnock means by 'God'? The issue could not be more crucial, for the danger of an incorrect doctrine of God might be idolatry.[22] False images may be intellectual, not only made of wood or stone.

At the very heart of the issue for Pinnock is the notion of metaphor. Nearly all our language about God uses metaphor. Metaphors describe the incomprehensible God in comprehensible ways. Metaphors presuppose a basic *continuity* between the metaphor and the object described. They also imply elements of *discontinuity*, for the metaphor has only a resemblance to the object. Thus God as shepherd describes his care for his people ('his sheep'). God, however, is not a shepherd because we are human beings, not sheep. Such an understanding of metaphor is basic for any understanding of the God of the Bible. Most readers of the Bible have such an understanding of metaphor, although they probably have not consciously thought about it. Pinnock argues further that everyone has a root metaphor or model of God. Root metaphors 'are the basic portrayals of God which affect how we view and relate to him'.[23] He believes the root metaphor for classical theism has been the image of God as judge or sovereign – legal metaphors. Pinnock argues that this needs to be replaced with an image of God as a loving Father. Further, this metaphor controls the meaning of other metaphors of God, such as God as judge, or king.[24]

Pinnock's root metaphor is God as loving Father, which finds its fundamental basis in the statement 'God is love' (1 Jn. 4). Love is at the heart of who God is, because God is a loving Trinity. In this essay I will argue a number of things. First, that it is in no way self-evident that the statement 'God is love' should receive hegemony over other statements about God. Instead, I will try and sketch some of

---

[22] For theological error as idolatry, see M. Halbertal and A. Margalit, *Idolatry*, 108–79. See also Fretheim, *Suffering*, 2.

[23] Pinnock in Pinnock and Brown, *Crossfire*, 66.

[24] *Unbounded*, 39.

the richness and complexity of the biblical picture of God found in the book of Exodus. Secondly, that Pinnock either ignores certain aspects of the Bible's teaching on God, or redefines them in a way that is reductionistic. Thirdly, that any attempt, whether by classical theism or openness theism, to define God around one metaphor is ill conceived.

Entering into the Bible's portrayal of God

'God is love' (1 Jn. 4:8,16) is an attractive statement around which to base a description of the Bible's portrayal of God. Not only attractive to a world which desires intimacy with the divine, but also because it is one of the few instances in the Bible of a third person statement about God.[25] However, it is not clear that such a statement should dominate our understanding of God such that everything else that the Bible says about God should be redefined in its light. For one thing John's primary concern in 1 John 4 is not to define who God is, but to indicate what love is. John 'spells out precisely the nature of the love which is demanded from every believer'.[26] He does this by reference to God's actions. For John our understanding of the nature of love is so poor it can only be explained with reference to God's love. Thus to explain God's nature by love, and not love by God's nature, is to seriously misunderstand what John is doing. It is only by considering God's actions in the Old and New Testaments that we understand the nature of God's love, and how it differs from human ideas about love. Secondly, we must question whether the Bible's third person statements about God should receive prime place in trying to express what is said about God in the Bible. That such statements should prove attractive to systematicians is not surprising as systematicians aim to speak about God in the third person. However, most of the Bible's language about God is couched in I-Thou discourse, the language of engagement. All of this says that while 'God is love' is a theologically profound and important statement, it is not obvious that it

---

[25] Other instances include 'God is spirit' (Jn. 4:24) and 'God is light' (1 Jn. 1:5).

[26] S.S. Smalley, *1,2,3 John*, 235.

should be viewed as the most fundamental statement about the nature and character of God found in the Bible.

Very similar things can be said about 'God as Father' and the Trinity. Although 'God as Father' is of enormous importance to Jesus it rarely figures in the Old Testament. It is not clear why it should be more important than, say, God as husband. The Trinity too is theologically of great significance, but the early church's discussions on the Trinity took place within the framework of God's oneness. The *shema*, 'Hear O Israel, YHWH, our God, YHWH is one', has no less a place in Christianity than in Judaism (Deut. 6:4; cf. Mk. 12:29, NIV).[27]

A single essay could scarcely do justice to the rich portrayal of God found in the Bible. It will be useful, however, to sketch at least something of what the Bible says about God. In the Old Testament there is, perhaps, no better place to begin such a sketch than in the book of Exodus. The exodus is, in the Old Testament, the supreme act of revelation.[28] Not only that but in Exodus we find a concern with the name of God unlike any other book. This is significant because 'it is a common place of Hebrew thought that a name may say something about the character of its bearer (e.g. Gen. 32:28; Ruth 1:20; 1 Sam. 25:25)'.[29] The name of God is discussed in Exodus 3, 6 and 34, but is also an important theme of chapters 3 to 14. Thus in studying what Exodus has to say about the name of God we may hope to discover something about the character of God.

In Exodus 3 God reveals himself to Moses in the burning bush as 'YHWH, the God of your fathers'.[30] He has seen the oppression of his people in Egypt and will come down to rescue them and take them to the land he promised. As Pinnock correctly indicates, Exodus 3:14 cannot be used as a metaphysical statement of God's

---

[27] It is interesting to note that 'YHWH is one' is also a third person statement about God.

[28] In many ways similar to Christ being the supreme act of revelation in the New.

[29] R.W.L. Moberly, *The Old Testament of the Old Testament: Patriarchal Narratives and Mosaic Yahwism*, 5.

[30] The exact sense in which YHWH reveals his name to Moses and the relationship between Exodus 3 and 6, and between those chapters and the patriarchal narratives, have long been the subject of great debate. See B.S. Childs, *Exodus*, 47–89, 108–20.

immutability.[31] Instead, the difficult *'ehyeh 'ăšer 'ehyeh* possibly is God announcing that 'his intentions will be revealed in his future acts, which he now refuses to explain'.[32] In particular the future acts of the plagues and the Red Sea. When Moses goes to the Israelites and performs the miracles God has told him to do, the people believe (5:30–31). The response from Pharaoh, however, is quite different. He replies with a contemptuous 'Who is YHWH?' (5:2). His oppressive actions lead to the Israelites becoming discouraged and they no longer believe (5:20–21). The disbelief of the Israelites and Pharaoh leads to the second revelation of YHWH in Exodus 6. At the heart of this revelation by God is the important affirmation 'I am YHWH' which occurs six times in Exodus 5:22 to 7:7 (6:2,6,7,8,29; 7:5). To the patriarchs God did not reveal himself as YHWH (6:3), but now, through his actions in Egypt and at the Red Sea, Israel and Egypt will come 'to know that I am YHWH' (6:7; 7:5).[33] Thus the second revelation of God to Moses responds directly to Pharaoh's 'Who is YHWH?' God will show 'I am YHWH.' In the subsequent chapters God's power over the plagues shows that Israel's God is 'I am YHWH' (7:17; 8:6,22; 9:14,29; 10:2).[34] Finally, in the destruction of the Egyptian army the Egyptians will come to 'know that I am YHWH' (14:4,18) and Israel again believes in YHWH and Moses (14:31).

What then do we learn about God in these chapters? Or, in the terms that Exodus uses, what does it mean 'to know that I am YHWH'? First, he is the God who saves his people. Thus when God speaks his ten commandments to Israel at Sinai he begins, 'I am YHWH your God who brought you out of Egypt' (Ex. 20:2). Secondly, he is the God who brings judgement. It is not only Israel who comes to understand who YHWH is, but also the Egyptians. The connection between the phrase 'know that I am YHWH' and judgement is intensified in Ezekiel and, more terrifyingly, turned against

---

[31] 'Systematic', 106.

[32] Childs, *Exodus*, 76.

[33] For a form-critical analysis of the phrase 'know that I am YHWH' see the stimulating essay by W. Zimmerli, 'Knowledge of God according to the Book of Ezekiel' in W. Brueggemann (ed.), *I Am Yahweh*, 29–98.

[34] There are some differences in the use of the phrase 'know that I am YHWH' in Exodus. For a source-critical solution see Childs, *Exodus*, 130–42.

Israel as Walther Zimmerli has shown (e.g. Ezek. 6:11–14).[35]
Thirdly, God hears and feels the suffering of his people. God is capable of anger, love, compassion and other emotions. Fretheim makes the point neatly when he describes Pharaoh as the only 'Unmoved Mover' in Exodus.[36]

Fourthly, God appears as sovereign. Sovereign not only over nature (and in particular nature in Egypt, Ex. 8:22; 9:14,29), but also over Pharaoh's heart. As is well known these chapters contain the famous occasion of Pharaoh's heart being hardened by God. On the one hand there are references to Pharaoh's hardening his own heart (e.g. Ex. 8:11,28), and on the other to God hardening Pharaoh's heart (e.g. Ex. 9:12; 10:1).[37] References to God hardening Pharaoh's heart do not begin until the sixth plague (9:12), and Pharaoh does not harden his own heart from after the seventh plague (9:35) as Fretheim has noted. However, the problem of YHWH hardening Pharaoh's heart cannot be eased in this way because before Moses confronts Pharaoh on the first occasion God has told Moses that he will harden Pharaoh's heart so that he will not let the people go (4:21–3).[38] In these same verses God foretells that Pharaoh will refuse to let Israel go, and therefore God will kill the firstborn of Egypt. Whichever way one turns the issue of divine causality faces the reader.

A fifth aspect is worth noting from these chapters, though it concerns the human actors of the story, and God only indirectly. This aspect is that human beings are responsible agents. This is seen with Moses, whom God persuades to act as his agent in chapters 3 and 4. It is seen with Israel whom God brings eventually to acknowledge him and Moses (14:31), despite her doubts and unbelief. Even with Pharaoh God's encounter is genuine. God speaks to Pharaoh with the conditional 'if' (8:2,21; 9:2; 10:4).

It is clear that many of these five aspects of God's character and actions in the Exodus narrative stand in considerable tension with

---

[35] Zimmerli, 'Knowledge', 92–4.

[36] T.E. Fretheim, 'Suffering God and Sovereign God in Exodus: A Collision of Images', 31–56.

[37] There are, of course, other references where it says only, 'Pharaoh's heart was hardened.'

[38] Fretheim seems to me to be unsatisfactory here in his attempt to explain the text as having an 'openness to the future' (T.E. Fretheim, *Exodus*).

one another, tensions which are not easily, if at all, resolvable. Thus
God's act of salvation and act of judgement can appear to be two
contradictory aspects of his character, but are in fact closely related,
as is seen most clearly, within Christian theology, on the cross.
Fretheim subtitles his article on the suffering God and sovereign
God in Exodus 'A collision of images'.[39] Similarly, God's sovereignty and human freedom, or responsibility, also appear in tension.
A faithful reading of the text of Exodus must maintain these tensions, and resist the temptation to collapse any one of them into the
others.

In what Walter Brueggemann describes as a 'credo of
adjectives'[40] the name of God is the focus of attention in Exodus
34:6–7:

> YHWH, YHWH, a God merciful and compassionate, slow to anger, and
> abounding in steadfast love and faithfulness, keeping steadfast love to
> the thousandth generation, forgiving iniquity, transgression and sin,
> yet by no means clearing the guilty, visiting the sins of the fathers upon
> the children and their children's children until the third and fourth
> generation.

This credo is significant for a number of reasons, besides being one
of the few conscious reflections on Yahweh's name. First, it occurs
at the climax of one of the most important events in Israel's history,
the making of the golden calf, when Israel's relationship with
Yahweh, even her very existence, is under threat. Secondly, this is
one of the few statements in the Old Testament that is quoted on
more than one occasion.

What is immediately noticeable is that the same tensions that we
have already seen are expressed here. In the first half of the verse we
have statements about YHWH's faithfulness and mercy, and most
relevant to Israel, his forgiving of sin. Yet, it is 'sin' (in both cases the
Hebrew *ʿāwōn* is used) that God will not clear and will visit to the
third and fourth generation. The tension is so strong that
Brueggemann goes as far as to say, 'while some interpretative

---

[39] Fretheim, 'Suffering God and Sovereign God'.
[40] W. Brueggemann, *Theology of the Old Testament: Testimony, Dispute and Advocacy*, 215.

manoeuvrability is possible in relating the two statements to each other, in the end I suggest that these two characterizations of Yahweh are in profound tension with each other, and finally they contradict each other'.[41]

The tension at the heart of this credo is found in the story of the golden calf (Ex. 32–34) of which it is such an intimate part.[42] For, though through Moses' intercession God relents from the judgement he had planned, three thousand Israelites are still killed, and the sin of the golden calf remains unpunished (32:34). We should observe, however, that there is an asymmetrical relationship between these two aspects of God's character. God's *steadfast love* is kept for a thousand generations, but his wrath against sin is visited only to the third or fourth generation. God's mercy will ultimately prevail because God has chosen Israel.[43]

Though the relationship between God's love and wrath is asymmetrical we must avoid collapsing God's wrath into his love. The biblical writers use the credo in both directions. For example, Jonah uses it when bemoaning God's forgiving of Nineveh (Jon. 4:2), and Nahum uses it in the context of the destruction of Nineveh (Nah. 1:3). The credo provides a challenge to much modern theology as Brueggemann draws out:

> Our contemporary adjudication of this issue concerning Yahweh is bound to be as problematic as it was in ancient Israel. We have a strong propensity to insist that Yahweh's gracious fidelity has surely, decisively overridden Yahweh's harsh propensity to sovereignty, so that we hope for a God of love. Such an argument is often presented as a certain Christian discernment of God; but such Christian discernment depends, in large part, on a very selective reading of the New Testament.[44]

Pinnock's view of God is exactly the sort that Brueggemann is protesting against, and the sort that Exodus 34:6–7 will not allow. It is

---

[41] Brueggemann, *Theology*, 227.
[42] These chapters present a number of difficult literary problems. See R.W.L. Moberly, *At the Mountain of God: Story and Theology in Exodus 32–34*.
[43] Israel's election lies at the very heart of these three chapters.
[44] Brueggemann, *Theology*, 271–2.

significant then that both Richard Rice in his essay on the biblical support for openness theism, and Pinnock and Robert Brow in *Unbounded Love* quote only the first part of this credo, avoiding those parts that are problematic for their view of God.[45]

Before we leave Exodus 34:6–7 we must note its link to Exodus 32:7–14 and the 'repentance of God'. Exodus 32:7–14 tells how God told Moses about Israel's apostasy in worshipping the golden calf. God tells Moses to leave him alone in order that he may destroy the Israelites. Moses intercedes for the people reminding God of three things: that God himself rescued the people from Israel, that God's actions would seem shameful to the Egyptians, and that God had made certain promises to the Patriarchs. On hearing this God repents of the disaster he was going to bring on Israel (32:14).

What should be made of the Old Testament when it talks about God 'repenting'. For many, such language seems extremely problematic. The Old Testament text itself gives us clear indications that we should proceed with care in talking of God's 'repentance'. Walter Moberly writes:

> The Hebrew writers show a certain awareness of possible problems of language in their use of terminology. Hebrew has two different words for 'repent', *šûb* and *niham*, and usually (though not invariably) uses *šûb* of people and *niham* of God . . . It is unfortunate that contemporary English has no obvious rendering for this Hebrew conceptuality – alternatives to 'repent,' such as 'relent,' 'regret,' or 'change mind,' may solve some problems, but they easily create others.[46]

For this reason we should not be too hasty to dismiss those who explain the use of language about 'repentance' for God as an anthropomorphism. However, too often such a judgement is premature without a consideration of what the Old Testament says about God's 'repenting', or what the implications might be that nearly all our language about God is metaphorical. Therefore, a careful

---

[45] R. Rice, 'Biblical Support for a New Perspective' in Pinnock et al., *Openness*, 30–31 and 178, n. 25. Pinnock and Brow, *Unbounded*, 68.

[46] R.W.L. Moberly, ' "God is Not a Human That He Should Repent" (Numbers 23:19 and 1 Samuel 15:29)' in T. Linafelt and T.K. Beal (eds.), *God in the Fray: A Tribute to Walter Brueggemann*, 115.

consideration of what God's 'repentance' means is necessary. We should observe a number of things.

First, God's repentance is an integral part of the Old Testament's presentation of God. The actions of God in this chapter, his anger and repentance are summarized in the credo of Exodus 34:6–7. Thus Childs writes on the repentance of God in Exodus 32:14, 'if it is read in its full context, it epitomizes the essential paradox of the Hebrew faith: God is "merciful and gracious . . . but will not clear the guilty"'.[47] Thus when Jonah cites the credo he says, 'I knew that you are a God, compassionate and merciful, slow to anger, and abounding in steadfast love, *and repenting from evil*' (Jon. 4:2; cf. Joel 2:13, NIV).[48] We cannot, then, marginalize the Old Testament's references to God's repentance, or redefine them in the light of Numbers 23:19, 'God is not a human, that he should lie, nor a mortal, that he should repent' (cf. 1 Sam. 15:29).

Secondly, God is said to repent either because of the intercession of a prophet, as here, or because people repent of sin (e.g. Joel 2:13–14). Thus God's repentance expresses his responsiveness to his people or the prophet. Therefore what the Old Testament describes as God's repentance is central not only to the Old Testament's presentation of God but also to the Christian presentation of God. For the Christian gospel affirms that if we repent of our sins God will forgive us (1 Jn. 1:9).

Thirdly, God's repentance takes place within the context of God's complete freedom. In the context of Exodus 34:6–7 God announces the proclamation of his name, YHWH, with the statement 'I will be gracious to whom I will be gracious, and will show mercy on whom I will show mercy' (33:19, NRSV). God repents in response to human intercession or repentance only when he has invited intercession or repentance. Thus on Exodus 32:7–14 Childs writes, 'God vows the severest punishment imaginable, but then suddenly he conditions it, as it were, on Moses' agreement. "Let me alone that I may consume them." The effect is that God himself leaves the door open for intercession.'[49] Similarly, in Jonah, the possibility is left open for repentance by the announcement of

---

[47] Childs, *Exodus*, 568.
[48] See Rice, 'Biblical Support', 31.
[49] Childs, *Exodus*, 567.

judgement in *forty* days. God is not leaving them to stew in their juices before annihilating them, but opening the door for repentance.[50] In 1 Samuel 15 God is completely sovereign with regard to Saul. He has made him king and he can also revoke that (1 Sam. 15:11,35).

Fourthly, and on the other hand, God's repentance usually occurs in a context when God is most bound in acting. This is reflected in Exodus 32 where Moses reminds God that he brought Israel out of Egypt, and made his covenant with their forefathers. Israel is God's elect, and he has bound himself to them. God is completely free in his actions towards them, but because of his faithful promise he cannot do anything less than preserve the people and bring them into the land (32:13). In Jonah God repents because of his nature as a God who is merciful and compassionate (Jon. 4:2). Taken together both points indicate that 'when God is most free to act, God is most bound in that acting'.[51]

Fifthly, there are passages which affirm that 'God does not repent'. The exact sense in which God cannot repent is made clear in Numbers 23:19 and 1 Samuel 15:29 where it is placed in parallelism with 'God is not a human being that he should lie'. When God makes promises he will stand by them. In these too God is both free and bound. He freely binds himself to his elect with promises that cannot be broken (Num. 23:19; 1 Sam. 15:29; Ps. 110:4). In the case of David (1 Sam. 15:29; Ps. 110:4), though he commits terrible sin God has still chosen him and his election cannot be undone (2 Sam. 7).

In the light of these observations we should make a distinction between unconditional promises from God, such as the election of David, and those passages where the people have sinned and face God's judgement unless someone intercedes for them, or they repent of their sins.[52] Thus when God announces judgement and

---

[50] In light of this Pinnock can hardly be right when he claims, 'Their repenting was not something God knew in advance would happen. He was planning to destroy them but changed his mind when they converted' (Pinnock, 'Systematic', 122).

[51] Moberly, 'God is Not a Human', 114.

[52] Robert Chisholm speaks of decrees and announcements. The first are unconditional declarations, and the second are conditional statements of divine declaration (R.B. Chisholm, 'Does God "Change His Mind"?', 378–99).

then turns from that judgement there is either an explicit or implicit conditionality to his announcement. This is quite different from Pinnock's presentation of God who makes one decision, and then, surprised by human repentance, changes his decision.[53] As we have already seen it is God who opens the door for intercession, or repentance, in his divine freedom. God is free, acting how he wishes (Ex. 33:19; cf. Jer. 18:1–10), but also the relationship with human beings is real 'in which everything is to be gained or lost according to how human beings live within that relationship with God. It depends on God, and it depends on human response.'[54]

Thus those passages which speak of God's repentance and non-repentance do not sit comfortably with openness theism which does not wish to speak of God's sovereign freedom in his actions with human beings or his election of certain individuals or people. Nor do they sit comfortably with the more rigid expressions of classical theism which threaten human responsibility.[55] Human responses matter.

Aspects of God's character and actions

I have so far tried to sketch something of the character of God found in the book of Exodus. I have shown that basic to the Old Testament's portrayal of God are many tensions. I will now try to indicate a number of features of God's character and actions seen in the Old Testament which are difficult for the open view of God. The aim of this should not be misunderstood. What is being presented is not a rounded biblical view of God, but only several features of the biblical view of God which fit uncomfortably in open theism, or do not fit at all.

First, God may cause humans to do evil. We have already seen that in the case of Pharaoh the 'problem' of divine causality cannot

---

[53] Pinnock, 'Systematic', 122.

[54] Moberly, 'God is Not a Human', 121.

[55] For a careful consideration of the questions of divine mutability and immutability from a theologian who understands and appreciates the classical expositions of Christian theology, but is prepared to criticize them if necessary, see K. Barth, *Church Dogmatics* II.1, 495–9, and III.4, 108–9. I am grateful to Walter Moberly for these references.

be circumvented. However, this is not the only place where God is seen, in some sense, to be in control of human evil. God is said to have turned the hearts of the Egyptians to hate the Israelites (Ps. 105:25). God also hardens the heart of King Sihon so that the Israelites fought him and took his land (Deut. 2:30). Similarly, God hardened the Canaanites *in order that* they might be destroyed (Josh. 11:20). God may even cause his own people's heart to be hardened (Is. 6:10), and to stray from his ways (Is. 63:17).[56] God sends evil spirits on individuals and groups: on Abimelech and the Shechemite leaders (Judg. 9:23) and on Saul (1 Sam. 16:14; 18:10). It is God who deludes the false prophets (Ezek. 14:9; cf. Deut. 13:4). In 1 Kings 22:23 God sends a 'lying spirit' into the prophets in order that Ahab may be deceived and be killed at Ramoth Gilead.

On the other hand, there are texts that speak of God working for good in human hearts. Both David and Solomon ask that God might direct the people's hearts to himself (1 Chr. 29:18; 1 Kgs. 8:57–60). After exiling the people God promises to circumcise the people's hearts (Deut. 30:6; cf. Deut. 10:16). In Jeremiah God will write the law on their hearts (Jer. 31:31–4), and in Ezekiel God promises to give the people a new heart and spirit (Ezek. 11:19–20; 36:26–7). God is said to have stirred the hearts of Zerubbabel and Joshua to do the work of rebuilding the temple (Hag. 1:12–14). In Proverbs the king's heart is said to be in the hand of God 'he turns it wherever he will' (21:1, NRSV). Similarly, in Proverbs 19:21 'the human mind may devise many plans, but it is the purpose of YHWH that will be established'.

Clearly, the Old Testament often presents God working in humans in a way that Pinnock's redefinition of sovereignty will not allow. Such verses do not fit into a portrayal of God giving freedom to humans such that he never determines or coerces, but only woos.[57] It is also impossible to square these verses with Pinnock's rejection of the idea of salvation as a change of state, or even his mocking of the idea of salvation as a 'heart-transplant'.[58] In the light of God's promises to give his people a new heart and spirit in Ezekiel, the

---

[56] In both cases the *hiphil* (causative) is used.

[57] 'Systematic', 113–17.

[58] C.H. Pinnock, *Theology for Revival, Lecture 11: Relationality, Prayer and Other Topics*.

language of 'heart-transplant' might be an appropriate modern restatement of what God does.

Pinnock, however, challenges us as to whether 'significant human freedom' can be preserved in view of these texts. A closer examination of these and other texts reveal that human freedom and responsibility are maintained. In 1 Kings 8:57 Solomon desires that God may incline the people's hearts to him to keep his commands, yet in verse 61 he exhorts the people to devote themselves to God and keep his commands. Any exposition of Proverbs 19:21 and 21:1 must understand these verses within the overall thrust of Proverb's message that our behaviour has consequences. The prophet who is deceived in Ezekiel 14:9 is held responsible for his sin, and receives punishment for it. This, and other passages, which speak of God's deceiving the false prophets must also be read against Jeremiah's assertion that false prophets speak 'visions of their own minds' (Jer. 23:16, NRSV).

The juxtaposition of divine action and human action occurs explicitly in a number of texts. In 2 Chronicles 25:20 Amaziah would not listen to the words of Joash because, literally, 'it was from God'. Similarly, Eli's sons will not listen because[59] God desired to kill them. In Ezekiel 38:10 God says of Gog that 'thoughts will come into your mind' to go against Israel and other nations, though in verse 16 it is God who is bringing him against Israel. God may even be seen to be the indirect cause of sin when he incites David to count the people (2 Sam. 24:1). Interestingly, the Chronicler tells us that it was Satan who incited David (1 Chr. 21:1). Thus God may even be seen to be the cause of actions that are attributed to Satan. As a member of God's divine court even Satan is seen to be under God's sovereign control (Job 1–2).

Perhaps the classic exposition of this theme is found in the story of Joseph. The key to the events of the story is Genesis 50:20,[60] 'you intended evil against me, God intended it for good, in order to preserve many people, as he is doing today'. Hamilton notes that the 'it' can only be the evil of the brothers, or the implied plans of the brothers.[61] Even though the brothers were bent on evil

---

[59] The causality is clearly expressed here with *ki*.
[60] C. Westermann, *Genesis 37–50: A Commentary*, 204–5.
[61] V.P. Hamilton, *Genesis 18–50*, 706.

God was behind all their plans. Thus the psalmist writes, 'he [God] had sent a man ahead of them, Joseph' (Ps. 105:17, NRSV). Von Rad carefully indicates what is, and is not, deducible from this passage:

> Even when no man could imagine it, God had all the strings in his hand. But this guidance of God is only asserted; nothing more explicit is said about the way in which God incorporated man's evil into his saving activity. The two statements 'you meant . . .' and 'God meant . . .' are ultimately very unyielding side by side.[62]

God's complete sovereignty and human freedom are affirmed. Neither is compromised, or in the words of von Rad, yields.

If we have interpreted these verses correctly and they are what Pinnock describes as 'pan-causal', then 'openness is in deep trouble'.[63] Pinnock denies that 'pan-causal' texts exist, but such a denial runs against a great deal of the Old Testament. If we consider God's words to the nations in Amos 1–2 God again and again tells of what he will do against them: 'I will send a fire . . . I will break the gate bars . . . I will cut off . . .' Yet it is other nations, and in particular Assyria, who will be the instruments of God's judgement. This idea is found throughout the so-called 'oracles against the nations', which are found in almost every prophetic book in the Old Testament.[64] God may even use the nations against Israel, as he threatened to do in Deuteronomy 28:49. Thus in Isaiah 10 God calls Assyria 'the rod of his anger' (v. 5) whom he brings against Israel, even though this is not what Assyria has in mind (v. 7). A similar thing is affirmed of Sennacherib in Isaiah 37:26 (= 2 Kgs. 19:25): God determined long before that he would use him to destroy many cities. In Habakkuk God rouses the Chaldeans against his people (Hab. 1:6). When Judah goes into exile it is because God has expelled them, even though the immediate cause is Babylon (Jer. 52:3). It is God too who uses Cyrus to bring his people back from exile (Is. 44:28; 45:1,13), but it is God himself who is said to have brought the people back (Jer. 29:10,14).

---

[62] G. von Rad, *Genesis*, 427.
[63] *Lecture 11.*
[64] See esp. Is. 13–23; Jer. 46–51; Ezek. 25–32.

Secondly, God knows not only the past and the present, but also the future. The Old Testament, however, expresses the vastness of God's knowledge in the context of the engagement between God and humans, and not in more abstract terms. Thus the most detailed expression of God's knowledge is found in very personal terms in Psalm 139. Nothing is hidden from God's eyes, not even the psalmist's thoughts. God knows his words before he speaks them (v. 4). The psalm even suggests that the psalmist's life was ordained for him: 'In your book were written all the days that were formed for me, when none of them as yet existed' (v. 16, NRSV).[65] At the very least, together with Job 14:5 and Psalm 69:28, it suggests that God has ordained the length of his life. Jeremiah too is personally aware of God's knowledge of him before he existed: 'before I formed you in the womb I knew you' (Jer. 1:5, NIV).

Undoubtedly the strongest evidence for God's foreknowledge has often been thought to be prophecy. Prophecy though is not an impersonal prediction of the future, but a personal engagement between God and his people, via the prophet, seeking an appropriate response whether that is faith, repentance, humility or whatever. Thus prophecy is not purely foretelling, but also forthtelling. However, Pinnock argues that prophecy is not based on God's knowledge of the future. Instead, it can be explained in one of three ways: 'the announcement ahead of time of what God intends to do, conditional prophecies which leave the outcome open, and predictions based on God's exhaustive knowledge of the past and the present'.[66] Pinnock's attempt to have a wider understanding of prophecy, particularly its conditionality, is to be welcomed, but his rejection of God's foreknowledge is not supported by the Old Testament.

The element of foretelling is present in prophecy. The false prophet may be recognized because his word about the future is false: 'If a prophet speaks in the name of YHWH but the thing does not take place or prove true, it is a word that YHWH has not spoken' (Deut. 18:22). The same point is made by Micaiah in 1 Kings 22:28 and in Ezekiel 13:6. Similarly, in Jeremiah 28:9: 'As for the prophet who prophesies peace, when the word of that prophet comes true, then it will be known that YHWH has truly sent the

---

[65] This verse poses considerable difficulties to translators.
[66] 'God Limits', 158.

prophet'(NRSV). Thus the true prophet is known because the word he speaks comes true.

It is God's knowledge of the future that is the basis of his challenge to the other nations and their gods in Isaiah:

Set forth your case, says YHWH;
bring your proofs, says Jacob's king
Let them bring them, and tell us what is to happen . . .
Tell us what is to come hereafter,
that we may know that you are gods. (Is. 41:21–3, NRSV)

Let all the nations gather together,
and let the peoples assemble.
Who among them declared this,
and foretold to us the former things? (Is. 43:9, NRSV)

Who is like me? Let them proclaim it,
let them declare and set it forth before me.
Who has announced from of old the things to come
Let them tell us what is yet to be.
Do not fear, or be afraid;
have I not told you from of old and declared it? (Is. 44:7, NRSV)

Who told this long ago?
Who declared it of old?
Was it not I, YHWH? (Is. 45:21, NRSV)

Through this challenge God emphasizes the reliability of what he has said in the past, and his trustworthiness for the future. Again, YHWH's knowledge of the future is given to Israel so that she might trust in YHWH, the faithful God, not as an end in itself. Isaiah intends to show Israel that YHWH is the only God, and all the other gods are worthless. Therefore it would not be too much to argue that in Isaiah 41 divinity is proved by knowledge of the future.

Numerous prophecies indicate that God has revealed the future to his prophets. Joseph's dream shows that the brothers will bow to him (Gen. 37:5–7), a volitional action on the part of the brothers. In Genesis 40 the baker and cupbearer dream about their future. In Genesis 49 Jacob makes certain predictions about his sons,

including that Judah will have the sceptre. In Exodus God tells
Moses that Pharaoh will not let Israel go (4:23), and when Pharaoh
does harden his heart we are repeatedly told, 'as YHWH had said'
(e.g. 7:13; 8:15). Balaam prophesies David's rise and subjection of
Moab and Edom (Num. 24:18). Moses predicts the exile and the
return (Deut. 30). A man of God prophesies the destruction of
Eli's family (1 Sam. 2). A man of God from Judah predicts that
Josiah will tear down the altar at Bethel over 250 years later (1 Kgs.
13:2; cf. 2 Kgs. 23:15–18). Ahijah's words are fulfilled through
Baasha (1 Kgs. 15:29). Many more examples could be adduced, especially from the so-called Deuteronomistic History (Deuteronomy to 2 Kings) which has a well-known belief in the fulfilment of
the prophetic word.[67]

Pinnock, however, challenges us with those texts where God
uses 'if' or 'perhaps'. Our interpretation of 'God's repentance' also
belongs here. Pinnock argues that 'in saying "perhaps" God also indicates that he does not possess complete knowledge of the future'.[68]
Clearly, such verses (e.g. Ezek. 12:1–3; Jer. 22:4–5) stand in considerable tension with those that indicate God knows the future.
However, as we have already seen when God speaks about the future it is always to seek an appropriate human response. Thus these
verses, like the whole of the prophetic phenomenon, indicate that
the relationship God has with Israel is genuine, and that human
response is important.

Those texts where God uses 'if' or 'perhaps' *might* indicate that
God's knowledge is limited and Pinnock argues that they do.
However, these verses do not speak directly to the question of
whether God knows everything; rather they show that Israel's response to God's word is important and their relationship with God
is genuine. The flow of Pinnock's argument here is important. He
argues from biblical texts which do not speak directly to the question of divine knowledge, and then reads texts which do speak
directly to the question of divine knowledge in the light of these
texts. This is an exegetical manoeuvre of dubious legitimacy.

---

[67] Many scholars would argue that these prophecies were *ex eventu*. Even if
this were so we could still say that the authors of these texts believed that
God knew the future.
[68] 'Systematic', 122.

Prophecy, then, is an extremely complicated phenomenon in the Old Testament.[69] The tensions that exist between divine knowledge of the future and prophecy's conditionality, that is between the elements of foretelling and forthtelling, are very difficult. It cannot be denied, however, that many Old Testament passages view God as knowing the future and revealing it to his prophets, but always to seek an appropriate response.

Thirdly, in Daniel and Isaiah God is seen to have a divine plan. Since Albrektson's seminal *History and the Gods* Old Testament scholarship has accepted that generally the Old Testament does not speak of a divine plan, in the sense of a blueprint for history.[70] The prophets had an idea of a divine *purpose*. However, Daniel and the apocalyptists had an idea of a divine blueprint for history, and it is possible that this is the sense of Isaiah's use of 'plan'.[71] Taken as a canonical whole might it not then be legitimate to read the references to a divine plan, or divine plans, in the history books and the prophets in the light of Daniel and Isaiah? Even if we do not, openness theism still has problems with the divine blueprint for history that is found most clearly in Daniel 7–12.

Fourthly, the Old Testament presents God as both a king and a judge. Pinnock too argues that God is a king and a judge, but the meaning of these two metaphors is redefined within the light of the metaphor of God as parent. Pinnock, however, claims that the Old Testament supports his understanding of God as a king and judge in this way. Thus on God as king Pinnock and Brow write, 'when creative love theists think of monarchy, we do not picture an all-determining power but a Davidic king who protects and shepherds his flock and delegates power to others'.[72] On God as judge 'judgment has mostly to do with ruling and saving. Remember how God raised up "judges" to deliver Israel.'[73]

---

[69] This is seen nowhere more clearly than in recent discussions on true and false prophecy. See e.g. D.W. van Winkle, '1 Kings XIII: True and False Prophecy', 31–43.

[70] B. Albrektson, *History and the Gods*, 68–97.

[71] J. Jensen, 'Yahweh's Plan in Isaiah and in the Rest of the Old Testament', 443–55.

[72] *Unbounded*, 29.

[73] Ibid. 73.

The picture of God as king in the Old Testament cannot be reduced to the idea of a shepherd king, although this is an important
part of the picture and emphasizes God's care and concern for his
people. However, there are other aspects to God as King. God as
judge is part of the metaphor.[74] As a king he is the one who makes
commands which must be obeyed. He is a warrior, an image which
is problematic for most Christian presentations of God, but it seems
to me more difficult for openness theism than for others. He is also
rich, a builder, wise and lives forever.[75] Unfortunately some of these
themes receive little or no reflection in Pinnock's writings,
especially God as judge, warrior, or the one who commands.

The reduction of God as judge to one who rules and saves on the
basis of the judges in the book of Judges is incredibly problematic.
The use of 'judge', *šôpēṭ*, in the book of Judges is far from straightforward, and many scholars have tried to elucidate the book of
Judges use of the term.[76] Whitelam argues that it is likely that the
root *špṭ* 'bore the sense "to govern", as well as "to judge", particularly in the earlier period'.[77] However, *špṭ* is primarily used in the
Old Testament of humans and of God with a judicial sense. Thus
Pinnock interprets a common Old Testament word through its
most difficult, and unusual, usage.

The Old Testament presents God as a judge who has a court in
which he judges both divine beings and humans (Ps. 82:1,8). In
Amos 1–2 and the other oracles against the nations God is seen as
the one who judges the nations and punishes them for their evil.
God's judgement is said to be impartial (Deut. 10:17), but it also involves unilateral action on behalf of the poor and weak (Deut.
10:18).[78] The legal operations in ancient Israel were quite different
to those in a modern society, and Pinnock is right to suggest we
need to have a biblical picture of God as judge. The idea of God as
judge in the Old Testament has judicial aspects, but also sees God as
intervening on behalf of the poor and needy ('salvation').

---

[74] M.Z. Brettler, *God is King: Understanding an Israelite Metaphor*, 44–5.

[75] See Brettler, *God*.

[76] See J.A. Soggin, *Judges*, 2–4, and K.W. Whitelam, *The Just King: Monarchical Judicial Authority in Ancient Israel*, 51–9, for discussion.

[77] Whitelam, *Just King*, 58.

[78] For the sense of 'doing justice' in these verses see M. Weinfeld, *Social
Justice in Ancient Israel and in the Ancient Near East*.

Before we leave the subject of God as king and judge in the Old Testament we should notice the agreement there is among many Old Testament scholars that the predominant metaphor for God in the Old Testament is that of king. Marc Z. Brettler writes, 'it [God is King] is the predominant metaphor used of God in the [Hebrew] Bible, appearing more frequently than metaphors such as "God is a lover/husband" (e.g. Jer. 3; Ezek. 16 and Hos. 2), or "God is a father" (Deut. 32:6; Isa. 63:16; Jer. 3:19)'.[79] Brettler is supported by many other Old Testament scholars.[80]

Fifthly, there are certain aspects of the Old Testament's presentation of God that Pinnock does not explore. Though Pinnock spends a great deal of time on the Trinity he has no reflections on what it might mean that God is one, which Trinitarianism presupposes. Yet the affirmation 'YHWH, our God, YHWH is one' (Deut. 6:4, NIV) provides the justification for the 'greatest commandment' (Mk. 12:29) and in a transmuted form has affected Christianity's central creeds: 'We believe in one God the Father Almighty.' Further, the Old Testament has things to say about the implications of God's oneness, especially in Deuteronomy and Isaiah 40–55. This neglect may, perhaps, be because the themes of sovereignty and election with which God's oneness is so often linked are not conducive to Pinnock's theology.

Interestingly, God's holiness is barely mentioned in Pinnock's recent works. God commands Israel to be holy because 'I am holy' (Lev. 20:26). In what ways is 'I am holy' any less of a significant statement about God's character than 'God is love'? Indeed, in Amos 6:8 God swears by himself, and in Amos 4:2 God swears by his holiness. This suggests that '*holy* as applied to Jehovah is an expression that in some way describes Him as God'.[81] The avoidance

---

[79] Brettler, *God*, 164.

[80] E.g. 'the metaphors that appear to dominate Israel's speech about Yahweh may be termed images of governance' (Brueggemann, *Theology*); on sovereignty Miller writes, 'a basic theme of the Old Testament, if indeed not *the* basic theme' (P.D. Miller, 'The Sovereignty of God' in D.G. Miller [ed.], *The Hermeneutical Quest: Essays in Honor of James Luther Mays on His Sixty-Fifth Birthday*, 129; his italics); and Gibson: 'The leading image of God in the Old Testament is undoubtedly of him as king' (J.C.L. Gibson, *Language and Imagery in the Old Testament*, 121).

[81] A.B. Davidson, *The Theology of the Old Testament*, 155.

of God's holiness by Pinnock is possibly because it in many ways provides a counter theme to a great deal of what openness theism says.[82] It encompasses themes of God's otherness, his sovereignty, his moral purity and his uncompromising response to human sin. It is perhaps important, then, that Pinnock's recent work *Flame of Love* has an overwhelming preference for 'the Spirit' or 'Spirit' in contrast to the New Testament's preference for the 'Holy Spirit'.[83]

The idea of a single 'root metaphor'

My essay has tried to show that the portrayal of God in the Old Testament is extremely rich and complex, with numerous tensions. This should not surprise us, or unduly concern us. Christian theology has always affirmed that God is *incomprehensible*, not in the sense that he can never be understood, but in the sense that he can never be *fully* understood. We have also shown that many aspects of God as he appears in the Old Testament do not fit with Pinnock's picture of God. We have also shown that some of the important metaphors the Old Testament uses cannot be redefined in the light of one metaphor. Therefore, I will conclude by questioning the whole idea of a single 'root metaphor'.

Pinnock's arguments are similar to those of T.E. Fretheim, whose book *The Suffering of God* has so influenced Pinnock.[84] There are, however, fundamental differences between the two. Where Pinnock speaks of 'root metaphor' Fretheim speaks of 'controlling metaphors'.[85] For Fretheim controlling metaphors 'function to delimit metaphorical possibilities', that is, they indicate inferences from metaphors of God that are inappropriate. Such an inappropriate inference would be that because kings die, God, the heavenly king, must be mortal. Fretheim wants Old Testament scholarship and the church to hear voices in the text that it often ignores – such as God's suffering, his vulnerability, possibility of change – and to emphasize their importance. Fretheim argues convincingly that

---

[82] See Brueggemann in J.G. Gammie, *Holiness in Israel*, ix.

[83] Pinnock, *Flame of Love: A Theology of the Holy Spirit*, passim.

[84] Pinnock describes Fretheim as 'my favourite biblical scholar', and *The Suffering of God* as 'an incredible book' (Pinnock, *Lecture 11*).

[85] Fretheim, *Suffering*, 11.

people operate with a limited number of metaphors when they think of God. This often works to subordinate or block out other metaphors. This has happened with legal metaphors which have been predominant in the church. For Fretheim, 'it is not a matter of exchanging one metaphor for another, but of evaluating our operative metaphors and working to extend that list'.[86] It is only in this way that we can avoid an unbalanced view of God. It is for this reason that Fretheim speaks of plural 'controlling metaphors', in sharp contrast to Pinnock's singular 'root metaphor'. Pinnock's arguments then are only superficially similar to those of Fretheim. Unlike Fretheim, Pinnock *does* want to exchange a model of God as Judge with one of God as Father. Rather than metaphors being kept in constructive dialogue, Pinnock gives one dominance and redefines all other metaphors in the light of it. Ironically, it is exactly this that Fretheim is protesting against.[87]

The quest for a 'root metaphor' for God is one that Pinnock shares with some other systematic theologians.[88] It is a quest which runs counter to the direction of much current Old Testament theology. At this point Old Testament scholarship may constructively question the direction of some developments within systematic scholarship. Thus Brueggemann writes:

> The other temptation to theological closure is reductionism, the temptation to reduce metaphors about Yahweh to a few or a single one. Such reductionism, as in finding the 'right' noun for Yahweh, in the end is another form of reification. Against such reductionism, the testimony of Israel practices a determined pluralism in its nouns for Yahweh. As Brian Wren has urged 'many names' for God because no single name is adequate, so the Old Testament employs many metaphors for Yahweh because no single metaphor can say all that Israel needs to say about their God. The full gamut of nouns for Yahweh contains not only a rich variety, but also a panorama of possibilities, many of which contradict each other. The witnesses in Israel, moreover, do not undertake to harmonize or make all the metaphors fit together. Rather, the rich range of metaphors often stand in tension

---

[86] Ibid. 9.
[87] J. Sanders understands Fretheim better in 'God as Personal' in Pinnock et al. (eds.), *Openness*.
[88] See e.g. V. Brümmer, *The Model of Love*.

with each other, so that one metaphor may say what is left unsaid by another, so that one may correct another, or so that one may deabsolutize another.[89]

Though Pinnock may be correct in thinking that Christians operate with one root metaphor (though I remain unconvinced), both Fretheim and Brueggemann would argue that it is wrong-headed for theology to operate in this way. We need to enlarge the number of metaphors with which we speak about God and keep them in dialogue with each other, not reduce them. Brueggemann would also, I think, question if such an idea were not in fact out of keeping with the pluralistic spirit of our times. Is not the quest for *one* root metaphor, modernism masquerading under the façade of a postmodern interest with metaphor?

Just over a decade ago a Canadian theologian wrote the following wise words:

> We must not seize the sovereignty pole and block out the human free-dom pole, or vice versa, which would violate the Bible's integrity. Theologies which have tended to do this have resulted in really unfortunate positions by way of implication and extension. The biblical balance is what we should strive to maintain in our theology too. The mark of a wise and sound theologian is to let the tensions which exist in the Bible stay there and to resist the temptation to tamper with them. In this particular case, the metaphysical competence of our reason is humbled. I cannot tamper with the data as regards divine sovereignty and human freedom just because it would be easier if one were at liberty to do so.

The Canadian theologian who wrote these words? Clark Pinnock in 1985.[90]

Pinnock's recent work has failed to resist the temptation to let the tensions that exist in the Bible stay there. Instead, he has grasped the pole of human freedom and blocked out sovereignty. He has grabbed the pole of God's love and blocked out God's holiness and justice. This essay has attempted to show the 'unfortunate position' this has placed Pinnock in as regards certain Old Testament affirmations about God.

---

[89] Brueggemann, *Theology*, 231–2.
[90] 'How I Use', 31.

3

The New Testament and Openness Theism[1]
Simon Gathercole

> Some say that we are players,
> some say that we are pawns . . .
>
> Robbie Williams, 'Millennium'

Clark Pinnock's formidable challenge to conventional theism does present some helpful correctives to positions held in some quarters. He has a refreshing approach to theodicy and the problem of evil, asserting the importance of not 'explaining' the origin of evil in such a way as to justify its existence. The presence of evil in the world is not something that can be justified: it must be overcome. To explain rationally its origin would excuse it.

Pinnock's opposition to timelessness is also stimulating. His particular *bête noire* is the view expressed in C.S. Lewis's *The Screwtape Letters*, that God experiences all of history in the same way simultaneously: 'Of the present moment, and of it only, humans have an experience analogous to the experience which our Enemy [God] has of reality as a whole.'[2] Pinnock is right, I think, to challenge this view: it is only part of the truth.[3] A hard view of timelessness sits

---

[1] My thanks to Crispin Fletcher-Louis for reading and commenting on this essay.
[2] C.S. Lewis, *The Screwtape Letters*, 76. If the reader is not familiar with the genre of this book, the reference to 'the Enemy' is explained by the fact that the imaginary author of the 'Letters' is a devil.
[3] Other conventional theists (e.g. Henri Blocher) have also opposed timelessness.

particularly uncomfortably next to the New Testament, where God actually enters into history and experiences reality in time. Of course, God is still 'up there', and remains, on one level, outside time. But can we really believe (if it is possible to ask this kind of question) that at the moment of Jesus' cry of dereliction on the cross, God's 'experience' was the same at every other point in time? Or is the crucifixion as present an experience for him now as it was in the thirties AD, or in 1000 BC? This seems unlikely, though of course we are getting into deep waters. I do not intend in this essay to trespass into the territory of the philosophers and systematicians, still less into what should remain in the realm of mystery.

On very similar grounds, Pinnock is right to question some for-mulations of divine impassibility.[4] It seems likely that God's imma-nence – especially when one considers the incarnation and the indwelling of the Spirit in believers – more than justifies belief in a God who experiences suffering in history. But this is not necessarily incompatible with God experiencing all of reality from beginning to end. It is perhaps possible to talk of 'degrees' of God's experience, when one grants that he does enter history. Again, the moment of the separation of the Father and the Son is a *locus classicus* for the suf-fering of God in history. The groaning of creation, church and Spirit together is another (Rom. 8:22–6). And we should not only talk of God's *suffering* in history: there is perhaps also his pleasure. While we can 'grieve the Spirit' (Eph. 4:30) God also delights in those who fear him (Ps. 147:11).[5]

However, despite these positive contributions, there are serious grounds for criticism of the open view of God from the New

---

[4] An increasing number of conventional theists are sceptical towards impassibility: M. Erickson, *The Evangelical Left: Encountering Postconservative Evangelical Theology*, 99, cites his own *Christian Theology*, 270, as well as W. Grudem, *Systematic Theology: An Introduction to Biblical Doctrine*, 165–6; see also D.A. Carson, *How Long, O Lord? Reflections on Suffering and Evil.*

[5] R. Rice ('Biblical Support for a New Perspective' in C.H. Pinnock et al. [eds.], *The Openness of God: A Biblical Challenge to the Traditional Under-standing of God*, 41–2) uses God's 'excitement' (on the basis of the parables in Lk. 15) as an argument for openness theism, but I hope to have shown that the attribution of emotions to God is not the exclusive preserve of the open view of God.

Testament. Nathan MacDonald has discussed the serious problems with Pinnock's and Rice's reading of the Old Testament texts in *The Openness of God*. It is notable that in Richard Rice's presentation of the open view of God from the biblical data, the Old Testament furnishes much of his evidence for God's knowledge being confined to the past and the present, divine repentance, and so on. The treatment of the New Testament (which takes up only eight pages)[6] focuses rather more on the character of Jesus as one who serves and suffers with others, rather than exerting authority over them.[7] Again, the concern to point out that Jesus is a sympathetic and compassionate friend is an important one. But Rice's language 'rather than' is misleading. Jesus is not portrayed as one who serves and suffers *at the expense of* his authority: the staggering truth is he *retains* his authority. Of course he does not cling on to the privilege of deity so as to abuse it (Phil. 2:6ff.) – he does not perform the magic tricks that the Devil would have wanted him to in the wilderness temptations (Mk. 1:12–13; Mt. 4:1–11; Lk. 4:1–13). But his power over sin is in the authority to forgive (Mk. 2:1ff), his power to perform signs and wonders, his power over nature, and his authority to give commands to people to repent, to believe in him, to follow him, to lay down their lives for him show that Jesus did not *renounce* his power.

This essay aims to deal with four key areas of Pinnock's theology that are particularly important, and which are problematic from a New Testament point of view. The focus is on the doctrine of God, which forms the first and longest section, because it is what shapes the rest of Pinnock's theology. One positive effect of this controversy over the doctrine of God is that God himself is on the agenda of our thoughts. Evangelical theologians have in many quarters been so concerned with (admittedly important) controversies over doctrine of Scripture, the atonement and justification to name but three, that it is a good thing that we are concerned with the God who should be the focus of our thoughts, and the one we seek to know better.

---

[6] Pinnock et al., *Openness*, 38–46.
[7] Rice, 'Biblical Support', 40.

Doctrine of God

The intention of this section (and in fact of this whole essay) is to present the New Testament's vision of God, in interaction with that of Pinnock. Essentially, it will be argued that the New Testament presents a compatibilist view of divine sovereignty and human responsibility, which is a position that Pinnock rejects. By 'compatibilism' I refer to the possibility of divine agency and human responsibility coexisting in the same event: that God's decreeing an action should not be seen as ruling out the possibility of its still taking place according to the desires and action of the human agent.[8]

An important element that goes hand in hand with compatibilism in the New Testament is the twofold nature of God's will. That is, part of God's ultimate purpose contains things which he brings about which are not his *ideal* will, but which do contribute to his *ultimate* will. As we have seen in the Old Testament, for example, God's *ideal* will is that his people dwell prosperously in the land, but in order to bring about his ultimate will, he must bring disaster on them if they disobey and remove them from the land in order *then* to restore them.

As has been noted, talking about God's decreed will and God's prescriptive will does raise important questions, but the Arminian distinction between God's prescriptive and his permissive will is just as problematic: God must still 'decide' to permit something.[9] Patrick Richmond, in his contribution, will discuss the crucial issue of God being responsible for the outcome of any risks he might take. But the chief issue that concerns us here is that Pinnock refuses to accept that 'God's will' is used in different ways in Scripture. There is of course God's prescriptive will: his purpose for humanity which is rejected or accepted by individuals. This is the usage which Pinnock focuses on. But Pinnock takes this to be the only kind of will or purpose. He uses, among other texts, Luke 7:30 ('but the Pharisees and experts in the law rejected God's purpose for themselves', NIV) to assert that God's will is not done all the time

---

[8] I am leaving open the question of whether this is an antinomy which is perhaps impossible to resolve (thus Packer) or whether the tension finds its resolution in God bringing about his decreed will *through* human desires (thus Helm, Feinberg).

[9] D.A. Carson, review of C.H. Pinnock (ed.), *Grace Unlimited*, 177–8.

irrespective of human choices, and that God does not have a blue-print for history.[10]

It is important, however, to recognize instances where Scripture speaks of God's will in a sense which approximates to what has been traditionally understood as his 'decreed will', that is, God ordaining what actually takes place. As 1 Peter makes clear in two places, God's will is often that Christians suffer: and Peter is here talking not just about the general pattern of the Christian life, but of con-crete examples (1 Pet. 3:17; 4:19).[11] Paul often uses God's will to de-scribe not just the purpose of God to conform his people to the image of his Son, but as extending to the realm of his travel arrange-ments. As he left Ephesus, he promised, 'I will come back if it is God's will' (Acts 18:21, NIV). And he tells the Romans twice that he hopes and thinks that it is God's will for him to return to them (Rom. 1:10; 15:32). Elsewhere Paul defines God's will simply in terms of *what happens*: in Romans 9:19 Paul's dialogue partner asks how we can be morally responsible when no one can resist God's will. Again, in Ephesians 1:11, God brings to pass everything ac-cording to the purpose of his will. This verse is debated in *Predestina-tion and Free Will: Four Views of Divine Sovereignty and Human Freedom* by Pinnock and John Feinberg. At the risk of unfairly tak-ing the exegetical high ground over two systematicians, I would say that both have misunderstood the verse. In Paul's statement that 'In him we were chosen, having been predestined according to the plan of him who works out everything in conformity with the pur-pose of his will', (Eph. 1:11, NIV) Feinberg is right to see that God is described as accomplishing 'all things' in this verse.[12] But Pinnock is correct, I think, to say that the verse does not use 'God's will' in the

---

[10] Pinnock, *Grace Unlimited*, 101; 'God Limits His Knowledge' in D. Basinger and R. Basinger (eds.), *Predestination and Free Will: Four Views of Divine Sovereignty and Human Freedom*, 149. In fact, 'the purpose of God' here means purpose in the 'limited' sense of God's purpose in accomplish-ing salvation through Christ. See C.F. Evans, *Saint Luke*, 356: 'here it specifies John's mission and baptism as an indispensable part of the divine plan for Israel's salvation'; cf. also J.B. Green, *Luke*, 22–3.

[11] J.N.D. Kelly, *The Epistles of Peter and of Jude*, 194, notes that 'suffering is providentially ordered'.

[12] J. Feinberg, 'God Ordains All Things' in Basinger and Basinger, *Predesti-nation*, 29–32.

sense of God's decreed will here:[13] in verse 9, 'the mystery of God's
will' was his *purpose of salvation in Christ* (as in Lk. 7:30) which – Paul
says – was what God has now revealed to his people. But Pinnock is,
I would maintain, wrong to conclude that the verse is not saying
what it obviously does say: that God is the one who brings all things
to pass.[14]

For a concrete, practical example, Paul's 'thorn in the flesh'
might be a good starting point. It is of no relevance *what* this thorn
actually was. The point is that 'a thorn was given me in the flesh, a
messenger of Satan to torment me, to keep me from becoming too
elated' (2 Cor. 12:7, NRSV). This thorn or messenger must have
been sent by God: the devil would hardly try to keep Paul humble.
And we see here that the 'torment' that Paul speaks of (hardly something good in itself!) is sent by God for an *ultimate* good: that Paul
should depend on God (2 Cor. 12:9). There are a number of individual examples in John's Gospel, which Carson has discussed,
which are evidence of God's strategy of bringing about something
tragic in order ultimately to bring glory to himself. Two particular
examples will suffice here. First, when the disciples ask him whether
a man was born blind on account of his own sins or because of those
of his parents, Jesus replies, 'Neither this man nor his parents sinned;
he was born blind so that God's works might be revealed in him'
(Jn. 9:3, NRSV). Again, Lazarus' illness 'does not lead to death;
rather it is for God's glory, so that the Son of God may be glorified
through it' (Jn. 11:4, NRSV).[15]

We see this taking place on the larger scale of the canvas of the history of salvation in Christ in the New Testament. One of the most
important examples of this is Paul's description of the function of the
Law in salvation history. It is the apostle's conviction that the Law
was given to Israel not as a means to righteousness, but rather so that it
might show up sin. 'For "no human being will be justified in his
sight" by deeds prescribed by the law, for through the law comes the
knowledge of sin' (Rom. 3:20 NRSV). 'Did what is good [i.e. the

---

[13] 'Pinnock's Response' (to Feinberg), ibid. 58.
[14] E. Best discusses the theme of sovereignty in Ephesians, and relates
God's plan for his people in 1:3–11 to 2:10 where 'even their good deeds
have been predetermined' (E. Best, *Ephesians*, 49).
[15] See the discussion of these texts in D.A. Carson, *Divine Sovereignty*,
127–8.

Law], then, bring death to me? By no means! It was sin, working death in me through what is good, *in order that sin might be shown to be sin*, and through the commandment might become sinful beyond measure' (Rom. 7:13 NRSV). The purpose of God is evident here, as Dunn comments: '[Paul's] main purpose here is rather to emphasize that even the law's being used by sin for death is part of God's fuller and deeper strategy to bring out the character of sin and of its end product and payment – only death.'[16] For Paul, this was God's plan all along: only by reading Paul with a hermeneutic of suspicion could we say that he was engaging in *ad hoc* rationalizations. This role of the Law is vital to his thought. Galatians 3:19 ('Why then the Law? It was added because of transgressions . . .') is a disputed verse,[17] but Romans 5:20 (NRSV) is incontestable: 'But law came in, with the result that the trespass multiplied; but where sin increased, so that, just as sin exercised dominion in death, so grace might also exercise dominion through justification leading to eternal life through Jesus Christ our Lord.' This is a classic expression of the twofold purpose of the Law, and therefore the twofold will of God: the Law comes *so that* transgressions increase *so that* grace will ultimately reign in righteousness. As Stephen Westerholm, Pinnock's colleague, recognizes: 'The thought that God should give the law to make sin worse is indeed striking; it is undeniably Pauline . . . What is new in Paul, as we have already seen, is the insistence that God must have *intended* the law to lead to sin.'[18] But, as Cranfield crucially notes, the ultimate purpose is that grace may triumph.[19] J.D.G. Dunn[20] and N.T. Wright,[21] whose

---

[16] J.D.G. Dunn, *Romans*, 387.

[17] Dunn and Hübner take the polar opposite views: the former that 'for transgressions' means to *deal with* transgressions through the sacrificial system, the latter that it means to provoke transgression.

[18] S. Westerholm, *Israel's Law and the Church's Faith: Paul and his Recent Interpreters*, 178, 192.

[19] See esp. C.E.B. Cranfield, *On Romans*, 15–22.

[20] Dunn, *Romans*, 286.

[21] See N.T. Wright, *Climax of the Covenant*: 'It could even be argued that Romans 5.20 is the climax of the whole Adam-Christ passage, explaining the position of the law within the entire scheme of divinely ordered history' (195). Indeed, while it is somewhat sidelined in Dunn (Rom. 5:20 is mentioned but never discussed in *Theology of Paul the Apostle*), the increase of sin in Israel is a crucial part of Wright's presentation of Paul's theology.

theologies of Paul are radically different from those of Cranfield and Westerholm, also agree that this is what Paul is saying. Whatever one's reading of Paul, then, there can be no disagreement on this point which we saw Dunn describe as 'God's fuller and deeper strategy'. Again, in a climactic statement of similar colour to Romans 5:20, Paul declares in Romans 11:32: 'For God has imprisoned all [i.e. both Israel and Gentiles] in disobedience, so that he might have mercy on all' (NRSV). All this can be summarized under Paul's maxim in Romans 8:28: 'we know that all things work together for good, for those who love God' (NRSV).[22] 'All things' are not, as Pinnock rightly says, good in themselves, but in God's overarching plan they work together for good.

In addition to the distinction between the two 'wills', there are also important New Testament texts which speak of the compatibility of God's action and human action. First, Philippians 2:12–13: 'work out your salvation with fear and trembling, for it is God who works in you, both to will and to work, according to his good pleasure' (NRSV). This is described by Gunther Bornkamm as 'an oddly paradoxical sentence' and by Ralph Martin as 'raising all manner of dogmatic issues to do with justification *sola gratia* and synergism'.[23] Even if it is not interpreted on an individual level,[24] it still talks about God operating within people both at the level of the *desire* (τὸ θέλειν) and at the level of *action* (τὸ ἐνεργεῖν), in accordance with his will. This is in keeping with Paul's theology of the guidance and empowerment of God through the Spirit evident from passages like Romans 8:9, Galatians 5:18,[25] Colossians 1:29.[26] Paul also maintains

---

[22] Though some translations (e.g. NIV) take God as the subject, that is, 'God works all things together for good', which might be more conducive to Pinnock's theology.

[23] R.P. Martin, *Philippians*, 103; the Bornkamm reference (*Der Lohngedanke im Neuen Testament*, 91) also comes from Martin.

[24] R.P. Martin, *Philippians*, 103, and G. Hawthorne, *Philippians*, 98–100, note that it should be taken corporately.

[25] See J.M.G. Barclay, *Obeying the Truth*, 116: 'The Spirit provides all the necessary guidance in the fight against the flesh'; cf. 117: 'all the necessary moral direction without requiring submission to the control of the Law'.

[26] J.D.G. Dunn, *Colossians*, speaks of (on 1:11) 'complete dependence on divine enabling' (73), as well as (on 1:29): 'the balance between human effort and divine enabling' (127).

that the perseverance of Christians can only take place by God exerting his power.[27] These texts bear witness to an extraordinary phenomenon, and one which is most problematic for openness theism. It is that the New Testament describes the motivations and empowerment for the Christian life as brought about by God through the Holy Spirit. In other words, there is a far greater divine involvement in the choices and actions of Christians than Pinnock gives credit for. It is important not to draw conclusions from this that the Bible does not draw: the Christian is by no means *less* free because of the Spirit's work within. Similarly, the condition of the Christian in glory is presumably one of freedom, even though this does not include freedom to sin. Again, God's freedom in being faithful or loving is not libertarian freedom, that is, freedom to act to the contrary: God is *not* free to act unfaithfully or unlovingly. These descriptions of freedom – the freedom of the believer who is led by the Spirit, the freedom of the saints in glory who nevertheless do not have freedom to sin, and the freedom of God who does not have freedom to act against his character – are important theological precedents for compatibilist freedom over against the libertarian model.

In addition to God's action through believers, unbelievers also carry out God's purposes: the events of the Passion must have seemed to the participants as consisting of free actions, yet the Gospel writers see it all as happening according to divine plan. As Peter says, 'For in this city, in fact, both Herod and Pontius Pilate, with the Gentiles and the peoples of Israel, gathered together against your holy servant Jesus, whom you anointed, to do whatever your hand and your plan had predestined to take place' (Acts 4:27–8 NRSV).

Response to Pinnock's arguments against compatibilism

1. Logical contradiction.
Pinnock's first objection to compatibilism which we will assess is that it is *rationally* untenable. This comes in his brief mention of D.A. Carson's *Divine Sovereignty and Human Responsibility*:

> Carson needs to distinguish *contradiction* from *mystery*. A circle is not and cannot ever be at the same time a square. An action is not and

---

[27] See Col. 1:11; Phil. 1:6.

cannot be at the same time determined by God and freely chosen in a significant sense. To say it can be is not mysterious but self-contradictory. Trusting the Bible is not the issue – the issue is whether we wish to attribute nonsense to Scripture in our interpretation of it.[28]

So Carson, according to Pinnock, is using 'mystery' as a cloak for 'contradiction'.[29] According to the Aristotelian principle of non-contradiction, 'X' and 'not X' cannot both be true at the same time in the same way. I would agree with Pinnock that this is an important principle: without it, revelation – to say nothing of the construction of a theological system – is problematic to the point of impossibility. But can Pinnock be so sure that the conditions are such in compatibilism that they constitute a contradiction: that is, does the compatibilist model argue that X and not X are being argued for in the same way at the same time? There are lots of unknowns when we come to deal with God's providence.

It is instructive, I think, to recount here Pinnock's defence of the doctrine of the Trinity. He is articulating the doctrine both in the face of those (some evangelicals) who say that the doctrine is completely indefensible rationally,[30] but also against process theists who maintain that God's eternity and loving character require that the cosmos is also coeternal with him:

> Does the doctrine make any rational sense? People often give the impression that they think it does not. Admitting that it is a mystery, I would contend that the doctrine is rational too, in many ways . . . If God is personal, does he need to depend on a creation to exercise personality? Or, if God is love, does he have to depend on creation to

---

[28] *Openness*, 193, n. 33.

[29] Cf. Pinnock's comments as far back as 1975 on compatibilism: 'There is a theological theory widely maintained in evangelical circles that Scripture teaches on the one hand that God has divinely decreed all that comes to pass, and on the other that man is a responsible moral agent' ('Responsible Freedom and the Flow of Biblical History' in idem, *Grace Unlimited*, 102).

[30] I refer to his horror at Millard Erickson's statement 'Try to explain it, and you'll lose your mind. But try to deny it, and you'll lose your soul' (*Christian Theology*, 342) in C.H. Pinnock, 'The Holy Spirit as a Distinct Person in the Godhead' in M. Wilson (ed.), *Spirit and Renewal*, 34.

express his love? Or, if it is God's nature to communicate, does he have to depend on a creation in order to converse? In terms of intelligibility, it would seem that the Trinitarian model has some advantages over the Unitarian view. So although the doctrine is not rationally derived but based on God's revelation in history, I would never admit the charge that the doctrine is irrational. On the contrary, it seems to possess a superior rationality compared with the alternatives.[31]

Here, it is important to note that Pinnock locates the rationality of the doctrine of the Trinity in its inner-systemic connections. Many Christians would try to defend the Trinity on other grounds: in David Lodge's novel *The British Museum is Falling Down* the Roman Catholic protagonist Adam Appleby is confronted by a sceptical friend on the subject of the Trinity. In the café in the British Library, the friend places a salt cellar in the centre of the table (one), then a pepper pot beside it (two) then the mustard (three). ' "I should have brought my clover leaf with me," said Adam. He spooned some mustard onto his plate, and sprinkled it with pepper and salt. "Three in one".'[32] Pinnock rejects this kind of apologetic, grounding the apologetic for a doctrine in its coherence with the rest of the system. For Pinnock, the mathematical element of the 'problem' of the doctrine of the Trinity is an irrelevance: it finds simple resolution in the communion of love within the Godhead that did not wait until creation for love to find expression.

When we come to compatibilism, the resolution of the tension by Pinnock and other openness theists makes much more 'mathematical' sense: it 'adds up'. God provides for human freedom by limiting his own power. The more freedom allowed to humanity, the more delegation of God's power is required: they must adjust in mathematical proportion. But as Pinnock knows from his formulation of the Trinity, there is more to doctrine than math(s): 'What a colorless notion of unity we work with if we cannot think beyond mathematical oneness.'[33] Mysteries find their *justification* in biblical exegesis, and their *explication* in thinking about their inner-systemic

---

[31] C.H. Pinnock and D. Brown, *Theological Crossfire: An Evangelical/Liberal Dialogue*, 64–5.

[32] D. Lodge, *The British Museum is Falling Down*, 59.

[33] 'The Holy Spirit', 40.

coherence, and the practical way in which God deals with the world.

C.S. Lewis discusses a similar example, again in *The Screwtape Letters*, where according to the diabolical economy, love is a logical impossibility because the interests of one person can never be exactly the same as another. God must, then, have some ulterior motive for loving humans other than just *love*. According to Screwtape, love doesn't make sense: mathematically, it doesn't add up:

> My good is my good and your good is yours. What one gains, another loses . . . 'To be' *means* 'to be in competition'. Now the enemy's philosophy is nothing more nor less than one continued attempt to evade this very obvious truth. He aims at a contradiction . . . The good of one self is to be the good of another. This impossibility he calls *love*.[34]

Lewis is highlighting here (in one sense) how *illogical* love is: it does not make 'sense' that our sacrifice for another can actually be *our* highest good as well. But love, like the Trinity, makes considerable sense according to the logic of faith. There is no reason why the issue of power should not be an analogous case. Pinnock needs to explain why the mystery of compatibilism is necessarily of a different order to the mystery of love, or of the Trinity, with which we are so familiar in Christian theology.

2. God's will being done in sin and perdition.

This leads into the next objections of Pinnock to compatibilism, which are closely related to each other. The first Pinnock describes in this way. He acknowledges the view of compatibilism – though the *word* was not widely used in theological discussion at the time – and cites John Gerstner's defence that 'it is possible for God to predestinate an act to come to pass *by means* of the deliberate choices of individuals'.[35] Pinnock's objection to this is not philosophical: he says that rationality cannot solve the problem either way. His objection is theological and moral: 'It is surely blasphemous to maintain, as this theory does, that man's rebellion against God is *in any sense* the product of God's sovereign will or primary causation.'[36]

---

[34] Lewis, *Screwtape Letters*, 92.
[35] 'Responsible', 101.
[36] Ibid. 102.

(a) God's judgement issued in 'giving over'
Crucial for Pinnock is a doctrine of human activity which is unin-
hibited by God's intervention at the level of the will. But one New
Testament passage which is extremely problematic for this thesis is
Romans 1:18–32. Here, God's wrath is at work in the world in the
present, and Paul gives three examples of the way this takes place.
Each is described as God drawing a certain action out of sinful humanity which fits – in a kind of poetic justice – with the spiritual attitude of the actor. This is described in terms of God 'giving over'
the person to a certain kind of sinful action. Here, human activities
are not described as being unambiguously free, autonomously decided upon by the agent in question: they are the clear result of the
direct judgement of God. This is antithetical both at the level of detail and also at the level of *tone* to what Pinnock claims throughout
his work, but it is clearly what Paul is saying. 'They exchanged the
glory of the immortal God for images . . . therefore God gave them
up in the lusts of their hearts . . . to degrading of their bodies' (vv.
23–4, NRSV.); 'they exchanged the truth about God for a lie . . .
God gave them to degrading passions' (vv. 25–6, NRSV); 'And since
they did not see fit to acknowledge God, God gave them up to a de-
based mind and to things that should not be done' (v. 28, NRSV).

So, to return to Pinnock's objection to compatibilism with
which we started: that, contra Gerstner, it is impossible for God to
predestinate an act to come to pass *by means* of the deliberate choices
of individuals. Pinnock's view is profoundly problematic, because
we see in Romans 1 evidence not of predestination specifically, but
very clearly of what is in some sense divine causation. And yet the
actions in view are clearly actions which would have been felt to be
free, and are also actions which are subject to the judgement according to deeds which Paul goes on to outline in Romans 2: in
other words, the person is morally accountable for them, even
though God gave the person over to those actions.

(b) Hardening texts
It is not merely actions, however, that can be attributed to God's
judgement. The New Testament can also talk of God taking action
in hardening the hearts of individuals (and groups). MacDonald has
dealt with the considerable number of 'hardening' texts in the Old
Testament, and there is no softening of this hardening theology in

the New Testament. In two places in particular, this Old Testament theology is drawn on directly. First, Jesus in his parable discourse in Mark 4 draws directly on the commissioning of Isaiah in Isaiah 6, where he is commanded to go and preach *in order to harden the hearts* of the recipients of the message. And Jesus, in a programmatic statement in response to the disciples' question of why he taught in parables, answers: 'To you has been given the secret of the kingdom of God, but for those outside everything comes in parables, in order that [Is. 6:9] *they may indeed look, but not perceive, and may indeed listen, but not understand, so that they may not turn again and be forgiven*' (Mk. 4:11–12; cf. Mt. 13:11, NRSV).[37] Another quotation from Isaiah 6:10 comes in John 12:39, where God is described as the one who 'blinded their eyes'.

Second, Romans 9. This is a peculiar chapter, and might well seem to be one of the more 'extreme' passages about God's sovereignty in the New Testament. But it is particularly appropriate to discuss here because it deals with roughly the same arguments that are involved in the debate between openness and compatibilism. And, by virtue of the literary genre of Romans 9:19ff., we even have it cast in the form of a debate. First, Paul gives his example of Jacob and Esau, which is the basis of his distinction between Israel according to the flesh and Israel according to the promise (*not all Israel are Israel*). The paradigm of Jacob and Esau works because it is Esau who should have had the birthright, yet Jacob was actually chosen: not merely because of his trick, but because of God's prior election 'before the twins were born or had done anything good or bad' (9:11, NIV). Paul then answers a possible objection to the statement that 'Jacob I loved, but Esau I hated' (9:13, NIV): the objection that God might be unjust in doing this (9:14). For Paul, this is of course impossible, God after all has mercy on whomever he pleases:

---

[37] 'In other words, the parables are purposely meant to blind those outside from "seeing" the mystery of God's Kingdom that is now revealed in the miraculous healings and exorcisms of Jesus . . . so that they may fulfil the tragic role within God's mysterious salvific plan of those who fail to "convert" and "be forgiven" ' (J.P. Heil, *The Gospel of Mark as Model for Action*, 100).

For he says to Moses, 'I will have mercy on whom I have mercy, and I will have compassion on whom I have compassion.' It does not, therefore, depend on man's desire or effort, but on God's mercy. For the Scripture says to Pharaoh: 'I raised you up for this very purpose, that I might display my power in you and that my name might be proclaimed in all the earth.' Therefore God has mercy on whom he wants to have mercy, and he hardens whom he wants to harden. One of you will say to me: 'Then why does God still blame us? For who resists his will?' But who are you, O man, to talk back to God? Shall what is formed say to him who formed it, 'Why did you make me like this?' Does not the potter have the right to make out of the same lump of clay some pottery for noble purposes and some for common use? What if God, choosing to show his wrath and make his power known, bore with great patience the objects of his wrath prepared for destruction? (Rom. 9:15–22, NIV)

Because of the nature of the subject matter here, there are a number of issues in this passage that pertain directly to openness theism. First, 'it does not depend on desire or effort'. That is, the recipients of God's mercy are not recipients because of their 'will' (οὐ τοῦ θέλοντος). On the contrary, it is God's mercy, which is purely his decision. Second, it raises the issue of Pharaoh being 'raised up' so that God's power might be displayed. The 'power' here is unquestionably the power of the signs and wonders that God performed to save his people, and which were a direct consequence of Pharaoh's stubbornness. Just as God has mercy on whomever he pleases, so he hardens whom he wills in 9:18 (ὃν δὲ θελει σκληρύνει). Third, it gives a guideline to the theologian who is approaching such difficult issues as these. In 9:19, Paul's dialogue partner asks how moral responsibility and accountability can still be realities if God's sovereignty is so strong. Paul replies not with a counterbalancing statement on the nature of freedom, but rather: 'Who are you, O man, to talk back to God?' (9:20, NIV) Pinnock dismisses compatibilism as contradictory nonsense, but there is a serious warning here: these truths about election and sovereignty must be treated with fearful (understood correctly) reverence. Fourth, this passage even forces the Christian to contemplate the meaning of verse 22. I do not say this lightly, and neither do I see it as integral to the argument, but Calvin's 'dreadful decree' of double predestination which includes the reprobation of the wicked should at least be considered on exegetical grounds, and not ruled out *a priori*.[38] Perhaps Paul himself is hesitant to come to the conclusion of reprobation with any certainty, hence his prefacing the statement with 'What if . . . ?'

Whatever is the truth on this last issue, it should not distract from what is clear. The New Testament describes the 'will' or 'plan' of God in different ways. As MacDonald argued in the previous essay, Pinnock tends towards a reductionistic approach, and does not do justice to the diversity of the evidence, which in this case includes a 'purpose' of God which is specifically God's activity in Christ, a 'purpose' which is his ideal will for people in individual situations, but also a purpose or will that is coextensive with what actually takes place. These statements about the twofold will of God cohere well with the evidence for compatibilism above. Neither the logical nor the moral objection which Pinnock makes is compelling. The logical basis finds parallels in other areas of theology, and even Pinnock's own theology. Pinnock's moral objection, opposing the idea that 'man's rebellion against God is *in any sense* the product of God's sovereign will' is clearly in sharp contrast to what the New Testament actually says. It seems that rebellion can be *in some sense* the product of God's sovereign will: we must be permitted to make an appeal to mystery, rather than jettison such a considerable amount of New Testament evidence.

Anthropology, creation and fall

Pinnock has a few key starting points for his doctrines of humanity, sin and freedom. In 'Responsible Freedom and the Flow of Biblical History', he presents a picture of Adam living in fellowship with God, and 'enjoying free will in the fullest sense, acting without any coercion'.[39] Crucially for Pinnock, humanity is given the power of self-determination because freedom is the condition of a real loving relationship, and seems to be 'the necessary prerequisite to a deeper knowledge of God'.[40]

---

[38] 1 Pet. 2:8 also provides a parallel.
[39] 'Responsible', 98.
[40] Ibid. 99.

According to Pinnock, the fall of Adam is the knock-down argument 'that the course of history is not laid out in advance as a kind of inflexible blueprint'.[41] Or again, 'The Fall demonstrates conclusively that God's will is not something that is always done regardless.' Pinnock rejects in the strongest possible terms that the Fall might have been part of God's purpose and plan:

> The Fall simply cannot be interpreted deterministically without con-
> tradicting the character of the God of the Bible and making him the
> cause of sin. Boettner's sentiments must be completely repudiated
> when he writes: 'Even the fall of Adam, and through him the fall of the
> race, was not by chance or accident, but was so ordained in the secret
> counsels of God.'[42]

As far as New Testament theology is concerned, Pinnock's position is nonsensical. If the Fall was not a part of God's plan, then the coming of Christ and his saving work cannot be either. Pinnock comes close, I think, to admitting elsewhere that the coming of Christ was not an integral part of God's original purpose: 'I think we can say that God made humanity in such a way that it would be possible for him to assume our nature *should that be required*'[43] (emphasis mine). The seriousness of the claims that Pinnock is making here should be evident to any Christian who reads the New Testament. Even on Pinnock's understanding of corporate election, what can Ephesians 1:3–11 mean but that Christ was from before the beginning of time to be the agent of God's salvation? Peter says the same: that Jesus was 'chosen before the creation of the world'.[44]

The second element of Pinnock's theological anthropology which is open to criticism from the New Testament is his presentation of the nature of human freedom. The nature of the freedom of Adam before the Fall – although I think there is a lot of truth in Pinnock's description of Adam's perfect fellowship with God – is very difficult to formulate because of the paucity of information that

---

[41] Ibid. 100.
[42] Ibid. 101. The quotation is L. Boettner, *The Reformed Doctrine of Predestination*, 234.
[43] 'The Role of the Spirit in Redemption', 60.
[44] 1 Pet. 1:20.

we have. But it has to be said that there is a qualitative difference between 'freedom' pre- and post-Fall. Pinnock tends to blur the distinction.[45] The language of the New Testament on the question of
human capacity, post-Fall, is often metaphorical, but is also expressed in the strongest possible terms. The passages which come
closest to being general statements of human sin in the Old Testament (e.g. Gen. 6:5, and the sources of Paul's texts in Rom.
3:10–18) are more than matched in the New. Jesus assumes that
people are 'evil' in Matthew 7:11, and the phrase 'slaves to sin',
which is a very common metaphor, is attested in numerous different places (Jn. 8:34; Acts 8:23; Rom. 6 passim). Paul asserts that all
are naturally 'under sin' (Gal. 3:22) and 'dead' (Eph. 2:1). These
three images all come together in Romans 7: 'sold into slavery under sin' (7:13); 'our sinful passions, aroused by the Law, were at
work in our members to bear fruit for death . . . Who will deliver me
from this body of death?' (7:5,24, NRSV). If they do not have the
Spirit, they cannot 'accept the things that come from the Spirit of
God, for they are foolishness to him' (1 Cor. 2:14, NIV).

These ingredients all point to the complete picture of a humanity which is in need of divine revelation in order to accept the message of the gospel. Those without the Spirit cannot accept the
truth of God and the gospel, just as the unregenerate person 'neither does, *nor can* obey God's Law' (Rom. 8:7; emphasis mine).
The metaphor of death in Ephesians 2:1 is of course a metaphor, as
Pinnock has pointed out. But a metaphor for what? Ernest Best argues convincingly that it refers to 'realized death', that is, the reality in the present of the eschatological condition of death which is
the judgement of God on sin.[46] In biblical terms, the only solution
to this is God's activity: the renewal of the person by the Spirit
(Ezek. 37:1–14; Rom. 1:4; Tit. 3:3–6). It is the burden of Paul in
particular among the New Testament writers that the reception of
spiritual truth, and obedience to God is only made possible by the
special work of the Holy Spirit. But this burden is no Pauline in-
novation: when Jesus tells the disciples that it is easier for a camel to

---

[45] Pinnock's theology of a thoroughgoing immanence of the Spirit also
similarly blurs the distinction between the Christian and the non-
Christian which he explores in his works on pluralism.
[46] E. Best, *Ephesians*, 79.

pass through the eye of a needle than for a rich man to enter the Kingdom, the response is incredulous: 'Who then can be saved?' But Jesus affirms 'What is impossible with men is possible with God' (Mt. 19:26/Lk. 18:27).[47]

Pinnock's objections to traditional formulations of freedom and fallenness have led to problematic exegesis of New Testament texts, and I would argue, the theological absurdity that we saw at the beginning of this section.

Soteriology

'Getting in'

The starting point for Pinnock's critique of traditional soteriology is the claim that causal and relational models of salvation are mutually exclusive and incompatible. Pinnock is open about the fact that this is an assumption, though he would of course maintain that it is a biblical one, based on the character of the God of love. Salvation, he argues, cannot simultaneously be something brought about unilaterally by God and also be a real relationship, which must be freely entered into. I will argue here that Pinnock's objection is neither rational nor biblical.

First, the rational level – and here I am thinking not in terms of a pure, timeless rationality, but a kind of pre-modern rationality which is the rationality of the biblical world. Pinnock's concern is that any doctrine of salvation must describe a process whereby the two parties enter into relationship by choice. That is not to say that there is a completely symmetrical relationship between the activity of God and the activity of humanity: of course God has created us, has redeemed us, and offers us reconciliation. It is only then, for Pinnock, that the human response is required.

But this model of relationships freely entered into by the choice of both participants is a rather modern, humanistic model. In general terms, it is not 'ancient', and in particular, it is not biblical. Purely on the level of experience it does not wash. Pinnock's root metaphor for the relationship between God and his people is that of God as a loving

---

[47] Compare the strong language Jesus uses in Jn. 6:63.

heavenly father who has a close intimate relationship with his children, where he is aware of their needs, provides for and protects them.[48] So far, so biblical. But anyone from any culture must recognize that *the relationship between father and child is not one freely entered into by the choice of both participants*. At birth, the child is 'thrown' into the world unconsulted and presented – without any discussion on the matter – with two parents! Similarly, Adam (and therefore humanity as a whole) becomes a child of God by virtue of creation (Lk. 3:38): not through his own choice at all, but only through God's decision to create. And our regeneration is often described as a 're-creation' or even just as 'creation'.[49] The question of what happens *subsequent* to entry into relationship with God – whether people then have the freedom to reject it – will be dealt with later. What should be obvious, however, is that the creation of the relationship could be brought about unilaterally by God: there is no *a priori* reason why it is impossible.

Again, in our culture, marriage and friendship are often described in terms of being relationships freely entered into, but in the biblical world, marriages were usually not like this. They were arranged, as in most pre-industrial cultures. In both Jewish and Graeco-Roman culture, the woman had little if any say in the matter, and even for the male partner, the arrangement was often a *fait accompli*.[50] Even friendship in the Graeco-Roman world (*philia*) was based on mutual obligations and a complex network of social ties, rather than on personal affection – not that that was unimportant.[51] Sociability, outside the high echelons of society, took place within the context of those

---

[48] C.H. Pinnock and R.C. Brow, *Unbounded Love: A Good News Theology for the 21st Century*, 29: 'Jesus' metaphor of the Father who loves us unconditionally is the central image in creative love theism, rather than Judge or sovereign, and it controls the meaning of these other metaphors.'

[49] The analogy of creation and salvation comes in Gal. 6:15; Eph. 2:10; 4:24. The image of 'new creation' comes in 2 Cor. 5:17 (amplified in 4:6); Jesus uses 'new birth' in Jn. 3; Paul talks of *palingenesia* in Tit. 3:5.

[50] See e.g. S. Treggiari, *Roman Marriage: Iusti Coniuges From the Time of Cicero to the Time of Ulpian*, 165.

[51] 'The appellation or categorization *philos* is used to mark not just affection but overridingly a series of complex obligations, duties, and claims' (S.D. Goldhill, *Reading Greek Tragedy*, 82).

with whom one had a common profession:[52] the vast proportion of people did not have time to engage in a lot of activities with other friends. The modern concept of friendship as relationship freely entered into is dependent, again, on modern concepts of leisure time where one has time and opportunity to 'choose' friends. When Jesus describes his disciples as friends rather than servants,[53] it is because he has revealed to them what he is doing rather than kept it secret and remained private and aloof.

From his own perspective, Pinnock has defined the biblical models of the parent-child relationship and the friend-friend relationship in the light of the God of love. And the results seem so attractive that anyone disagreeing might well seem like a spoilsport. But Pinnock is actually articulating modern constructs, rather than biblical ones: and they are so attractive because they do tap into what most people today know (or think they know) about relationships. The alternative – a relationship brought about unilaterally, or brought about by force of social factors – Pinnock presents as 'engineered', something closer to rape than real relationship.[54] But it is vital that our reading of the Bible is not finally conditioned by modern presuppositions.

One of Pinnock's objections to a hard view of human sin and the need for divine grace is that it makes a nonsense of all God's appeals to people to turn to him, or follow him. It would mean that God is saying, 'Follow me', 'Turn away from sin', etc., and in the next breath, 'But of course you can't.'[55] So let us examine some New Testament texts which treat the issue of soteriology. First, Pinnock is right to affirm that Jesus offers in his preaching the possibility of forgiveness, and indeed commands repentance. There is of course

---

[52] In the Roman world, the *collegium* was one of the most important social units in this regard. Those of a certain profession – who would also for this reason probably live in close proximity with each other – would gather probably monthly for social reasons. See R. MacMullen, *Roman Social Relations, 50 B.C. to A.D. 284*, esp. Appendix A, 129–37; also F. Meijer and O. van Nijf, *Trade, Transport and Society in the Ancient World: A Sourcebook*, and van Nijf's other works on this subject.

[53] Jn. 16:15.

[54] Though, rather bizarrely, Pinnock begins *Flame of Love: A Theology of the Holy Spirit*, 9, by encouraging us to pray that the Spirit 'ravish' us.

[55] This is of course rather a loaded way of presenting the issue.

no sense of the message only being presented to the elect. Those who hear the message should respond, and are accountable to God if they do not. But there is an important sense in which this is in tension with God's initiative in conversion. Carson has dealt with the numerous texts in John's Gospel: no one can come to Jesus unless the Father draws them (6:44); believers are those whom the Father has 'given' to Jesus (Jn. 17); the disciples are disciples not because they chose Jesus, but because Jesus chose them (15:16) and this choosing does *not* include Judas Iscariot (13:18) and so on.[56] A similar pattern could be constructed from Matthew's Gospel:

> At that time Jesus said, 'I praise you, Father, Lord of heaven and earth, because you have hidden these things from the wise and learned, and revealed them to little children. Yes, Father, for this was your good pleasure. All things have been committed to me by my Father. No one knows the Son except the Father, and no one knows the Father except the Son and those to whom the Son chooses to reveal him. Come to me, all you who are weary and burdened, and I will give you rest. Take my yoke upon you and learn from me, for I am gentle and humble in heart, and you will find rest for your souls. For my yoke is easy and my burden is light.' (Mt. 11:25–30, NIV)

This is an important passage because it expresses very clearly the teaching of Jesus that God's initiative comes not only in creation and the cross, but also in the work of revelation by the Father and the Son, and the Father's *concealment* of the truth from the 'wise and learned'. It teaches very strongly the impossibility of salvation without the special revelation that comes – as we saw in Romans 9 – by the Son's choice: 'no one knows the Father except the Son and those to whom the Son chooses to reveal him' (Mt. 11:27, NIV).[57] Matthew also records Jesus' saying that Simon Peter was blessed

---

[56] For divine initiative in salvation in the Gospel of John, see Carson, *Sovereignty*, esp. 181–92.

[57] On the 'hiddenness' of the truth from the wise and learned, it is not just that the revelation 'is hid' from the wise because of their pride (W.D. Davies and D.C. Allison, *Matthew*, 274–6). D.J. Harrington is closer: 'What God has hidden from them is the significance of Jesus's deeds and the presence of God's Kingdom in his ministry' (*The Gospel of Matthew*, 167).

because of his acknowledgement that Jesus was the Messiah, 'for this was not revealed to you by man, but by my Father in heaven' (Mt. 16:17, NIV).[58] Again, Jesus' saying that 'many are called, but few are chosen' (Mt. 22:14, NIV) defines specifically the work of God in salvation as not merely confined to the sphere of accomplishing reconciliation in Christ, and making the universal offer (in this verse, the *calling* element): people are also 'chosen'. The 'passive of divine action' corresponds to what some theologians have named 'effectual calling'. A similar distinction comes in Romans 11:5, where Paul distinguishes between the election that *the people of Israel as a whole* enjoyed under the covenant, and the election of the *remnant*, which is, literally, 'according to the election of *grace*' (κατ' ἐκλογὴν χάριτος). Returning to Matthew 11:25–30, the beauty of this passage is that a strong view of the sovereignty of God is unselfconsciously juxtaposed with a wonderful description of the comfort that Jesus offers and his gentleness in his dealings with humanity. This is one of Pinnock's strengths: he does challenge those who have a rather impersonal view of God, which focuses on his sovereignty *at the expense of* his love. But the answer to this is to hold together in our minds the picture of God painted in these verses, rather than throwing the biblical baby out with the Platonist bathwater. The statement that 'God is love' (1 Jn. 4:16) cannot be used as a filter through which one can remove these affirmations of God's choosing those to whom he reveals his salvation.

The Pauline corpus has more of an emphasis on predestination and the whole sweep of God's plan than on the sovereignty of God in conversion as it is described in the teaching of Jesus in the Gospels. Pinnock and Rice object strongly to the traditional doctrine of predestination on the grounds that *individual* election also implies *individual* non-election. Election, says Pinnock, must be corporate: a reference to the group who conform to God's plans for his people.[59] But there are two principal grounds for objection to this view of predestination. First, one could criticize it on logical grounds.

---

[58] As Davies and Allison note, flesh and blood 'came to be a technical term in Rabbinic texts meaning "human agency" in contrast to divine agency' (*Matthew*, 623).

[59] Based principally on H.H. Rowley, *The Biblical Doctrine of Election*, 1950.

Granted that in much traditional theology there is an emphasis on the individual that is somewhat foreign to the actual biblical writings, this has led to a considerable swing of the pendulum in the opposite direction. On this model, there is such a focus on community that it is forgotten that a community must actually contain real *people*. In Pinnock's scheme, 'the elect' is an empty set, with no actual members when God designs his purpose for them. Second, it is very difficult to avoid the fact that there are specific references in the New Testament to elect people. It seems almost glib to point out that Paul tells his Roman readers (Rom. 16:13) to 'greet Rufus, chosen in the Lord' (ἀσπάσασθε Ῥοῦφον τὸν ἐκλεκτὸν ἐν κυρίῳ). But more substantially, there is clear reference in Acts to occasions where those whom God has elected are the ones who come to faith. In Pisidian Antioch, Paul and Barnabas address Jews and Gentiles, and some Gentiles respond to the message: 'When the Gentiles heard this, they were glad and honoured the word of the Lord; *and all who were appointed*[60] for eternal life believed' (Acts 13:48, NIV).[61]

There is also another ingredient to election which implies the personal dimension: God's strategic emphasis in electing the poor and disadvantaged in order to display his power. Paul and James both highlight God's *tendency* (which is by no means a rule, of course) to choose 'the foolish things of the world . . . the lowly things of this world and the despised things' (1 Cor. 1:27–9), 'those who are poor in the eyes of the world' (Jas. 2:5). The reference in James is particularly interesting from a compatibilist viewpoint. He balances the 'choosing' element alongside the importance of the human response: 'Has not God *chosen* those who are poor in the eyes of the world to be rich in faith and to inherit the Kingdom he promised to *those who love him?*' (Emphasis mine.)

The second objection to the Reformed view of predestination is that it refers not primarily to human destiny but to a call to service –

---

[60] F.F. Bruce, *The Acts of the Apostles*, argues that 'appointed' (τεταγμένοι) refers to inscription of names in the heavenly book of life (275).
[61] There is possibly a similar reference in Acts 18:10. But it is not certain whether God is saying here that Paul is secure in Corinth because there are many of God's people who are yet to come to faith under Paul's ministry, or that Paul still has a lot of work to do with the believers there.

to the *role* of the elect in God's saving work.[62] This is true in some descriptions of 'calling' in the New Testament – Paul being chosen as apostle to the Gentiles, for example. But it is a reductionistic oversimplification: by no means all (or even most) of the passages discussing election talk in this way. It is lacking from Ephesians 1:3–11. And in Romans 8:28–39 where it is perhaps present in a similar form to that which Rice is describing – the people of God being predestined to be conformed to the likeness of his Son – it is still *applied* by Paul in the direction which Rice and Pinnock oppose. Paul uses the doctrine of predestination as an assurance to believers all through the passage, the climax being that nothing can separate us from the love of God that is in Christ Jesus (Rom. 8:39). In 1 Corinthians 1:26–31 there is no mention of the role in God's saving purposes, and the rhetorical thrust is the humility that the doctrine of election necessitates. In John 6 and John 10, there is again none of the emphasis that Rice notes; rather the force is Christological. The emphasis is on *who* is doing the electing. The concept functions in a much more complex way than Rice appreciates.

But to return to the broader issue of salvation, it can be concluded that causal and relational models of salvation need not be seen as incompatible. There are many analogies for human relationships where the relationship is created 'causally' but is none the less relational for that. I hope to have demonstrated that the New Testament presents salvation in terms that do not enable the evidence for God's initiative in salvation (not merely at the occasion of the cross, but also at the occasion of conversion) to be so easily overlooked.

'Staying in'[63]

The main purpose of the section above has been to demonstrate the unilateral character of the creation of the relationship that exists between God and Christian believers. The question then becomes:

---

[62] As with the first objection, based on H.H. Rowley.
[63] With apologies to E.P. Sanders. As should be clear, this heuristic taxonomy of 'getting in' and 'staying in' is in no way dependent on his description of the patterns-of-religion of Judaism, Jesus and Paul being 'covenantal nomism' (*Paul and Palestinian Judaism*, and *Jesus and Judaism*).

But do God's children not have the ability to reject that father–child relationship? Can they not 'run away from home' like the prodigal? This question has largely been answered by the passages presented above (referring to the Spirit's empowerment to obey, etc.) in arguing for a compatibilist answer to this question. But these passages that speak of the work of the Spirit sustaining obedience need to be set (albeit far too briefly) in their biblical–theological context, which will show God's active role more clearly.

First, one needs to consider the Old Testament evidence. Under the old covenant, the Law is given to the people of Israel, and if they obeyed it, they would receive life from God (Deut. 30). This was because 'life' was precisely what humanity had *lost* at the Fall: Adam was told that if he disobeyed he would 'surely die' (Gen. 2:17), which is what happened. Humanity is thus now subject to death; but if the people of Israel obeyed Torah, then this process would be reversed. However, the Torah did not solve the problem of the heart, and did not supply any transforming power, as can be seen from the continuing disobedience of Israel throughout the Old Testament. Paul formulates this narrative pattern into a theological statement in Romans 8:3: the law was powerless to lead to life because of the weakness of the flesh. As Romans 7:10 puts it, 'the very commandment that promised life, proved to be death' (NRSV) or 'the very commandment that was intended to bring life actually brought death' (NIV). Hence, the coming of Jesus brings *life*, the very thing that the Torah was powerless to do (Rom. 8:3). But it is not just the creation of the relationship. When the Old Testament prophets talk of the new covenant which God is going to bring about, they talk about it as consisting of *a new obedience which is the work of God himself.* Jeremiah 31:31–4 for example talks not just about forgiveness of sins (v. 34). There will be a crucial difference between the old covenant and the new:

> 'It will not be like the covenant that I made with their ancestors when I took them by the hand to bring them out of the land of Egypt – a covenant which they broke, though I was their husband,' says the Lord. 'But this is the covenant I will make with the house of Israel after those days,' says the Lord: *'I will put my law within them, and I will write it on their hearts . . .'* (vv. 32–3, NRSV emphasis mine)

This is significant because it speaks of *God's* work of empowering – having the Law in one's heart is not merely a cognitive matter, but is concerned with obedience – in contrast with the covenant-breaking disobedience of Israel's ancestors. God had told the Israelites to keep the Law in their hearts (Deut. 6:6), but they did not.

'Circumcision of the heart' functions in the same way as 'writing the Law on the heart' in biblical theology. First, under the old covenant, God instructs his people, 'circumcise your hearts, therefore and do not be stiff-necked any longer' (Deut. 10:16; also Jer. 4:4, NIV). However, even under the old covenant, it is envisaged that Israel will not do this: when all the blessings *and curses* of the covenant have fallen on Israel, then God will restore them and 'the Lord your God will circumcise your heart and the hearts of your descendants, so that you will love the Lord your God with all your heart and with all your soul in order that you may live' (Deut. 30:6, NIV). Again, God himself needs to do the work. And the New Testament describes God doing this by the Holy Spirit (Rom. 2:29), just as it is the Spirit who gives life to the dry bones in Ezekiel 37. It is the Spirit whose work is actually effective in bringing about the obedience of Christians in the passages discussed above in the context of compatibilism. For this reason I am surprised at the popularity of Pinnock's theology among charismatics and Pentecostals. For all Pinnock's frequent talk of (the) Spirit in his work, the emphasis is only one of statistical frequency: the work of the Spirit is, in my view, significantly diluted. The 'Spirit who comes with power'[64] we see working with such force in the Bible has become for Pinnock a 'gentle divine persuasion operating in the world', or 'the serendipitous power of creativity'.[65] Pinnock does speak of the power of the Spirit, but at far less length.

The problem with the traditional theology of attributing our perseverance to the work of God is that it can breed presumptuousness and immorality: if we know we are saved, we can do whatever we like. But anyone who did display this attitude would show that they did not really know God at all. This theology in which God

---

[64] See the stunning descriptions of the Spirit coming in power in Judg. 14:6,19; 15:14; 1 Sam. 10:6,10; 11:6; 16:13, etc. These texts are not mentioned in Pinnock's *Flame* (his theology of the Holy Spirit).
[65] 'Role', 52–3.

empowers and preserves believers can never be used as licence to presume that we are secure if we are not living as Christians. The Bible always maintains that our perseverance is both the work of God *and* something we are responsible for: as we saw earlier: 'work out your salvation with fear and trembling, for it is God who works in you, both to will and to work, according to his good pleasure' (Phil. 2:12–13, NIV).

New Testament use of the Old Testament

One of the greatest weaknesses of openness theism is the *ad hoc* nature of the New Testament's use of the Old Testament, according to Pinnock and those who share his doctrine of God. This is grounded in the denial of foreknowledge: only the very broad outlines of Christ's redemptive work are 'planned' by God, and the precise details of the life and death of Jesus are not foreseen. This means that the Gospel writers are drawing creatively upon the Old Testament in the interpretation of Jesus' ministry, and imaginatively appropriating the texts of their heritage, rather than drawing on the intrinsic 'meaning' of the Old Testament texts. I will argue here that this is a dangerously misguided approach to the question of how the New Testament approaches the Old Testament.

First, it is necessary to discuss one vital New Testament passage which is often ignored on this subject – 1 Peter 1:10–12:

> Concerning this salvation, the prophets who prophesied of the grace that was to be yours made careful search and inquiry, inquiring about the person or time that the Spirit of Christ within indicated when He testified in advance to the sufferings destined for Christ and the subsequent glory. It was revealed to them that they were serving not themselves but you, in regard to the things that have now been announced to you through those who brought you good news by the Holy Spirit sent from heaven – things angels long to look into (NIV).

For many evangelical scholars, it is a given that the historical–critical 'meaning' of a text is its primary meaning, and that any fuller sense in which the text has a subsequent eschatological fulfilment is a supplement to that primary meaning. It is – in this view – at best a secondary meaning, and at worst a cavalier appropriation or even manipulation of the 'original' meaning of the text. This approach is a symptom of the 'selling-out' of evangelical biblical studies to the academy in some quarters. But what this verse clearly teaches is that the prophets knew *precisely* that they were speaking 'into' the Messianic age: 'they were serving not themselves, but *you*'. Here the prophets were consciously looking beyond their own age into the eschatological age of the Messiah, not merely talking about events in their own lifetimes that then, in a secondary sense, came to refer to Jesus.[66] The reason that this is such a strange verse is that it cuts right against the grain of the historical-critical method. This is not to deny that the historical-critical method can be useful, but merely to note its limitations in deciding what is in the mind of the author, especially when the inspiration of the Spirit comes into the picture! Pinnock seems to succumb to a privileging of the historical-critical method even as he is criticizing it: he still calls the historical-critical meaning of the text the 'first horizon',[67] and so does not do justice to the *canonical* meaning of the text (which will include historical-critical observations), which is the real first horizon. As the Reformers (and now Brevard Childs) argued, the *sensus literalis* included the meaning of the text in the context of the Bible, as distinct from the allegorical meaning. 'Calvin spoke of Christ when expounding the Old Testament because for him this *was* the literal meaning of the text.'[68] When we come to interpret the Old Testament, our first horizon must include the *theological* meaning of the text in its full biblical context. From this point of view, even the concept of the *sensus plenior* might be misleading if it implies that the 'fuller' canonical sense is somehow bolted onto an 'original' historical-critical one.

In his discussion of the New Testament use of the Old Testament, Richard Rice comes to some extraordinary conclusions. He takes up three hard cases for openness theism: the hardness of Pharaoh's heart, Judas's betrayal of Jesus and Peter's denial. 'All of them fulfilled predictions and the first two, at least, seemed to be part of a

---

[66] Paul is perhaps making a similar point (though not as strongly) in Rom. 15:3: 'For whatever was written in *former* days was written for *our* instruction . . .'

[67] 'Role', 497.

[68] P.R. Noble, 'The Sensus Literalis: Jowett, Childs, and Barr', 1.

prior plan. Was their occurrence therefore inevitable? Not necessarily.'[69] He asserts that it is logically possible that these represent *conditional prophecies*. But: (1) this does no justice to the portrayal of
God's active role in hardening Pharaoh's heart in Exodus – to say
nothing of Romans 9; (2) Rice's argument that the betrayal of Judas
does not do justice – as we will see later – to the way the New Testament authors saw the Old Testament passages they were using to be
speaking *directly* about the events about which they were also writing; (3) Jesus' statement about Peter's denial in Mark 14:30 is hardly
cast in terms of a conditional prophecy – rather it is a foregone conclusion: 'Truly I tell you, this day, this very night, before the cock
crows twice, you will deny me three times' (NRSV). The timing and
the number of denials is so precise that it must have been based on
foreknowledge: and its fulfilment comes with exact precision: at the
moment of Peter's third denial, the cock crowed for the second
time (Mk. 14:71–2). Rice's concluding remark that 'although certain things did (and do) happen in harmony with divine predestination, this does not mean that these events could not possibly have
failed to occur'[70] seems incongruous in the light of these three
examples which he fails to explain adequately.

This passage from 1 Peter is particularly helpful because it is a
programmatic statement about the nature of prophecy in general.
But we can also see the same pattern at work in individual references
to *prophecies*. To take the well-known quotations in Matthew 1–3,
there can be no doubt that Matthew thought that these Old
Testament texts were originally written about Jesus.[71] The words,
for example, in Matthew 3:3 – 'this is the one of whom the prophet
Isaiah spoke' – clearly presuppose that Isaiah was *genuinely* writing
about John the Baptist. Again, with the fulfilments in Matthew 2:15
and 2:18 this fulfilment takes place on a typological level as well as
the plane merely of predictive prophecy.

---

[69] Rice, 'Biblical Support', 55.

[70] Ibid. 56.

[71] See R. Hays, *The Moral Vision of the New Testament*: 'One effect of this
Matthean narrative technique is to highlight the "scripted" character of
salvation history; nothing is random or uncertain, for all events are under
the authority of God's providence' (96). Contra J. Sanders, *The God who
Risks: A Theology of Providence*, 94.

Again, from the words of Jesus himself in Luke 24:26–7, the same attitude comes through very clearly: ' "Was it not necessary that the Messiah should suffer these things and enter into his glory?" Then beginning with Moses and all the prophets, he interpreted to them the things about himself in all the Scriptures' (NRSV). From these verses, it can be seen that Jesus thought that the passages which he then explained to the disciples (whichever they were) had been written *about himself.* Luke 24:44 is the same: 'Everything written about me in the Law of Moses, the prophets and the psalms must be fulfilled' (NRSV).

In the fourth Gospel, Jesus says very plainly it is hard to come to any alternative reading of the text that Moses wrote about him: 'If you believed Moses, you would believe me, for he wrote about me. But since you do not believe what he wrote, how are you going to believe what I say?' (Jn. 5:46–7, NIV). Those who define 'what Moses wrote' in historical-critical terms are in danger of approximating to the view of these persecutors of Jesus: that the Old Testament is not intrinsically Christological, but that Christological interpretations are secondary, derived by (at best) creative, Spirit-inspired, imaginative exegesis, or (at worst) sleight of exegetical hand. New Testament scholars should have the same courage and conviction that the biblical authors themselves had: that the Old Testament, in its constituent parts as well as in its entirety, always was about our Lord Jesus Christ. Openness theists frequently give a very different explanation of the underlying approach to the Old Testament seen in these texts – from Jesus, John the Baptist, Matthew, Luke and John the evangelist – from the authors themselves, particularly when one considers the general principle outlined in the passage from 1 Peter 1:10–12.

Finally, it must be concluded, that since the *authors* of the Old Testament texts knew what they were looking forward to, it must *a fortiori* be the case that God had planned both the history and the theology of the Old Testament as predictive of the person and work of Jesus. Openness theists are not willing to take the text at face value and really identify with the authors. It is at this point, where scepticism towards the text is most stark, that openness theists seem to have more in common with the liberal, historical-critical tradition, than with evangelical theology. This question of the relationship between the Old Testament and the New Testament comes down to whether we accept what the New Testament actually says.

Conclusion

Many of the problems with the open view of God should have become evident. In particular, it can be seen that Pinnock's arguments that compatibilism is either a logical, theological, or moral impossibility are not persuasive. The agency of God and human agency can coexist in peace. And especially when one places this New Testament evidence in conjunction with what MacDonald has observed from the Old Testament, we are forced to conclude that human responsibility in no way diminishes divine control – to say nothing of foreknowledge. The implications of Pinnock's doctrine of God for his anthropology, namely that human freedom compels an understanding of God's limiting his knowledge of the future, leads (very logically) to the position that the coming of Christ is not an integral, original part of God's purpose, and requires that all the soteriological language of 'choice', 'election', 'predestination', 'revealing', 'hiddenness', 'hardening' and the like, be radically reinterpreted. Pinnock often gives the impression that the handful of references to divine control need to weighed against the hundreds of appeals which give the impression that obedience is a matter of free choice. It is hoped that, together with MacDonald's evidence from the Old Testament, these references to divine initiative in salvation cannot be merely reduced to scattered exceptions. They are part of the fabric of biblical theology.

4

Clark Pinnock's Response to Part 1

I am grateful to the editors and essayists for giving serious attention to my work and for allowing me an opportunity to respond to their assessment. They have all treated me respectfully, even though some think that I have fallen into error and doubt my evangelical credentials. The dialogue can be hard-hitting at times but it is appropriate, given the fact that weighty matters are under discussion. At least the dialogue never devolves into diatribe. Readers should be aware that there are numerous ways to go after large questions concerning God's nature and how God works in history in addition to those represented here. That rich diversity will obtain long after I am gone. Therefore, they might think of this book as a primer to stimulate them to explore an even fuller range of alternatives. Besides Calvinists and Arminians, there are evangelicals who are Molinists and Thomists and Barthians. We can all celebrate the growing maturity and sophistication in evangelical systematic theology as it comes of age. I am content if I have made a helpful contribution to that.[1]

The book begins with the most important question in my opinion – is the openness model of God biblical? Tradition and

---

[1] In order to fill in gaps, let me refer to three books which present my understanding more fully. For input on this theological maverick: Barry L. Callen, *Clark H. Pinnock: Journey Toward Renewal* (Nappanee, IN: Evangel, 2000); for a fuller presentation of the openness model: C.H. Pinnock, *A Most Moved Mover: Theology of Divine Openness* (Carlisle: Paternoster Press/Grand Rapids: Baker Book House, announced for 2001); and the most scholarly work from the openness perspective: John Sanders, *The God who Risks: A Theology of Providence*. Let me also add that xxxx

philosophy are important but of the greatest importance is Holy Scripture and whether the model is consonant with this the primary standard of theology. Space forbids my doing full justice to all that is in these two essays but let me do what I can. Its strength biblically lies (I think) in the way it lifts up the personal nature of God. Central to Scripture is Yahweh's desire for loving relationships and a people with whom to establish a covenant. God does not create a world in which to exercise total control but a world in which loving relations are possible, mutual and reciprocal relations, give and take relations. Far from a totally unchanging and all-determining Absolute, God is a personal agent, who creates, acts, wills, plans, loves and values in relation to covenant partners. He is presented to us as the father of children, nurturing, raising and calling them to participate in an open future with him. It is not the picture of the domination of a creator over creatures but the picture of a parent wanting fellowship with created persons. The openness model of God is difficult to counter because it corresponds so well to what readers of the Bible already know and experience. In fact, a common response to it (I have found) is: 'That's nothing new – I've always thought that.' This is humbling to one who has worked hard to bring the model to the attention of the public but gratifying too. The response suggests we may be onto something.

The first essays examine the biblical foundations of the openness model of God. On the one hand, they are not in agreement with me but (on the other hand) they are not in agreement with each other either. MacDonald insists that we affirm both human freedom with moral responsibility and exhaustive divine sovereignty on the grounds that the Bible requires it, even though it feels like a contradiction. (Note: I assume that MacDonald holds to libertarian freedom, though he doesn't actually say so, on the ground that he finds real tension between the two poles of sovereignty and freedom. If he held to compatibilist freedom like Gathercole, there would be no tension and his appeal to accept it would then be confusing.)

---

[1] (*continued*)   the ideas being debated here are not mine alone but are advocated by many respected authors outside the 'evangelical openness circle' such as John Polkinghorne, Richard Swinburne, Keith Ward, Peter Baelz, J.R. Lucas, Vincent Brümmer, Hendrikus Berkhof, and H.D. McDonald.

Gathercole and I do not accept that a contradiction or antinomy exists because, in Gathercole's case, he opts for deterministic freedom, which is (by definition) 'compatible' with all-controlling sovereignty, while I opt for non-determinist (or general) sovereignty which is 'compatible' with libertarian freedom – both tactics eliminate a contradiction.

I appreciate the fact though that MacDonald recognizes the importance of the personal metaphors of Scripture and takes them seriously as reality-depicting. This is refreshing because defenders of exhaustive sovereignty tend not to do so because they cannot. They are compelled to put them down to anthropomorphic or accommodational language because such metaphors rule out exhaustive sovereignty. MacDonald however wants to hold on to the truth of the personal metaphors, which imply real interactive relationships, alongside belief in all-controlling sovereignty which creates a contradiction. He would like me to affirm that God controls every event (on the one hand) and that humans are free (and responsible) for what they do (on the other hand). My difficulty in doing so is that, although paradoxes (things that puzzle) cause me no problem and mysteries (things that go beyond my ability to comprehend) are delightful, contradictions are another story because they require one to give up on the goal of intelligibility which theology is oriented toward. (Recall Anselm's motto – 'Faith seeks understanding.') Therefore, I prefer, along with Gathercole, to question the exegetical basis of the supposed contradiction rather than try to choke it down. I wonder how many other contradictions MacDonald entertains.

In reference to Gathercole, let me make two points – why I do not think his endorsement of compatibilist freedom is a good idea and what my view of general sovereignty is. First, as regards human freedom, if he is right that what we say and do flows from predestined conditions in our makeup, then I cannot take seriously even his argument for it, because (to me) a rational argument implies that both parties are seeking the truth regardless of what their pre-existing brain states happen to be. I want to hear what he thinks the truth is on the basis of evidence, not what he has been pre-programmed to think. Compatibilist freedom spells the end of rational thought and is most unattractive too when it comes to moral and spiritual matters. Were our actions causally determined, no one would be morally responsible and no relationship of love involving free consent would be possible. Determinist freedom is freedom only in name. It is an invention designed to give the appearance of freedom in a context of theological determinism, which allows no true freedom.

Second, as regards divine sovereignty, the Bible presents God creating a world populated with creatures who are free to love him. God could have created robot beings completely under his control who could say yes to God but never no. But instead God chose to make non-robotic creatures capable of loving relationships. He gave them the capacity to choose and respects their choices even when they disappoint him. Even when they sin, God does not give up on them but responds in order to redeem the situation. God remains faithful to his original purposes, while adjusting his plans to take into account the decisions of his creatures. Out of love for them, he even becomes one of them and dies for them, that they may share eternally in his love. God is sovereign over his sovereignty and what a glorious kind of sovereignty God has freely chosen to exercise! God according to exhaustive sovereignty seems intent on being a bully, to which I could submit but which would not inspire admiration in me and certainly not love.

For my part I understand God's sovereignty in the context of covenant relationships. God is described as the husband of Israel and the church is called the bride of Christ. Such imagery speaks of relationships of mutuality and reciprocity. It is a sovereignty in the context of love where tenderness not control is the order of the day. The purpose is not manipulative relations but true fellowship, not impersonal relationships but personal, not I-it but I-thou relations in which the free assent of both parties is essential. A man can woo a woman but cannot compel her to love him in return. Imagine being married to a partner who loved out of conditioned responses! God is the initiator and the major player in these situations but desires our genuine participation. God does not want to dance alone or dance with a mannequin. It is personal fellowship that he values most. God is free to choose the kind of relationship he wants and it seems that he has chosen personal not manipulative relationships. God is not bound to act omnicausally but free to work non-coercively in relation to a significant creation. God graciously limits himself in order to give us room to be and freely enter the divine communion.

I have not done justice to all that these authors have had to say in defence of exhaustive sovereignty but have tried to describe the forest, if only a few of the trees.

Both MacDonald and Gathercole, and (in Part 2) Richmond and Gray, focus on the omniscience of God and the fact that, in my view, the future is partly settled in God's mind and partly unsettled. Although I consider the view biblical, critics often consider it the Achilles heel of the openness model. A simple way to explain my understanding is to refer to the Lord's interaction with king Hezekiah on the matter of the timing of his death (2 Kgs. 20:1–7). God had announced that the king would soon die but the king prayed and the Lord added fifteen years to his life. (Evidently the initial prediction had been conditional without the point being made. One wonders how many other prophecies are conditional without the point being made?) At any rate, the date of the king's death was shifted from being near to more remote in time. Obviously this date was not a fact settled in God's mind – it could have occurred at one time or another, depending on circumstances. The biblical narrative is replete with examples like this which indicate that the future is partly settled and partly unsettled. How else could God be said to regret how things turn out or alter what he said he would do? What could it possibly mean to say that God tests people to see what they would do if he already knows it? How could he speak in conditional terms if the future is entirely settled? Why would he use misleading terms like 'if' and 'maybe' and 'perhaps' in regard to the future? If God has exhaustive foreknowledge, there are only certainties and no maybes. Jeremiah portrays God as a flexible potter who, if one thing doesn't work out, can go back to the drawing board and try something else (18:7–10). Obviously the future is not a fixed entity in God's mind – things can go one way or another. Is this a weakness in God? I think not. Flexibility is a sign of strength not weakness. It is a beautiful thing that God adjusts to changing circumstances as a responsive being. MacDonald cites Isaiah against my interpretation but nothing in Isaiah contradicts it. God is not appealing to a crystal ball when he declares what will happen in the future – he is announcing his purposes and intentions for the future. Aspects of the future are settled because God will see to it that they take place but that in no way denies that there are other aspects of the future which are not settled.

The implication of much biblical material is that the future is not completely settled in God's mind and not exhaustively foreknown. If it were, it would make no sense for the Bible to say that God was happy about this or disappointed about that, or that God regretted a situation and changed plans. The Bible views the future as (to some degree) settled and to that extent known and (to some degree) unsettled and to that extent unknown or known as unsettled. There is a great deal of biblical support for the proposition that the future is partly open and partly settled and we have no right to be sceptical of it as several authors in this book are, just because it does not agree with the older thinking. How (I often wonder) could God have made it any clearer that the future is not entirely settled?

Ironically, openness theists get accused of being philosophically biased when we question exhaustive divine foreknowledge. Critics say that our belief in libertarian freedom contributes to it, whereas we actually question it because we think it is unbiblical. More likely it is that traditionalists reject the scriptural teaching because of their philosophical presuppositions. Let me explain. Believing that God must be unchanging in every respect, they also believe that his knowledge of the future must be unchanging. Given their assumptions, they cannot accept the biblical teaching that the future is partly settled and partly unsettled, however clear it may be.

It is not dishonouring to say that God does not know every detail of the future. To say God cannot know the unknowable is not different from saying that God cannot do the undo-able. Insofar as the future is unsettled and not yet entirely definite, God knows it truly – that is, God knows it as unsettled and not yet definite. If God knew the future as completely settled, when it is not, he would not know it truly. The issue here is not about God's knowledge as much as it is about the nature of the future itself. The past is definite and settled but the future is not. The future contains both definite things (like the things God pledges to do) and possible things (like how many will respond to the gospel). Some things may go one way or the other and God is well aware of that. If God does not know something in the future, it is not because his knowledge is deficient but because there is nothing to be known as yet about that something. The key question really is: has the future been exhaustively settled from all eternity or is it partly open? It is a fundamental issue to most of this book.

Sometimes I am disappointed by critics of the openness model who say that we are driven in our thinking by modern assumptions and do not even try to establish a biblical basis. MacDonald and Gathercole do not make this accusation but subject our claim to be biblical to reasoned critique. I thank them for that and say in words like St Paul's: 'Think over what the other person is saying, for the Lord will give us understanding in all things' (2 Tim. 2:7).

Part 2

5

Openness to the Bible? A Traditional Challenge to Clark Pinnock's Understanding of God

Patrick Richmond

In *The Openness of God: A Biblical Challenge to the Traditional Understanding of God*, Professor Clark Pinnock and his co-authors offer a multidisciplinary critique of such classical doctrines as God's comprehensive foreknowledge, impassibility and eternal immutability. These doctrines are revised in the light of certain biblical texts and a model of divine-human relationship that involves significant freedom from God. I am grateful to Clark Pinnock for this stimulating contribution to discussion about the Christian doctrine of God, but I will argue that the traditional approach has more to be said for it than he often suggests. Specifically, I argue that the tradition is not simply a Hellenistic corruption of the Bible. There is biblical support for key elements of the traditional understanding. Straightforward appeal to texts suggesting God's ignorance, repentance and emotions generates undesirable inconsistencies with other biblical material. God himself provides a model of freedom different from the open choice between good and evil and the open view of providence risks undermining confidence in God.

Is the tradition corrupted by Hellenism?

Pinnock and his collaborators explain the genesis of the traditional doctrine of God in terms of the excessive Hellenization of biblical religion. The personal, dynamic thought of the Bible was infected in the Patristic period by the theological virus of pagan, Greek metaphysics. The impersonal, static, all-determining God of Greek philosophy corrupted the Christian doctrine of an emotional, open God.[1]

Three caveats ought to be lodged immediately.

Biblical thought cannot be neatly separated from Hellenism

Hebrew culture was infected with Hellenism centuries before the New Testament was written. Alexander the Great conquered the Persian Empire and, after his death in 323 BC, his territories were carved up. Judea thus found itself under Greek influence. Diaspora Jews constituted an important minority in Egypt, eventually occupying two of the districts in Alexandria. Evidence suggests that these Jews quickly abandoned Aramaic in favour of Greek. The most decisive step was taken with a translation of the Old Testament into Greek, the Septuagint (LXX), the project beginning around 270 BC and continuing perhaps over a century.

The tradition of allegorical interpretation of passages in the Old Testament deemed offensive to Greek tastes can be traced back as far as Aristobulus, an advisor on Jewish affairs to Ptolemy VI (180–145 BC). The philosophical theology of Philo of Alexandria (30 BC to AD 50) is but the climax of Jewish moves to view the Scriptures through a Hellenistic lens. After a bitter struggle with the Ptolemies, the Seleucids gained control over Judea in 198 BC. Antiochus IV (176–65 BC) provoked the Maccabean revolt by his policy of radical replacement of Judaism by Hellenism. However, the revolt was not so much a rebellion against Hellenism as against paganism. The subsequent Hasmonean dynasty accepted many of the non-religious elements of Hellenism. The Hasmonean ruler Aristobulus called himself 'a lover of Greek culture'. The Romans who conquered Palestine likewise sought to spread Greek culture. Philo praised Augustus as one who 'Hellenized the outside world in its most important regions'. In Palestine Hellenization transformed the areas around Judea, such as the Decapolis, and urban centres. Gadara, a city in Transjordan produced Mennipus the Satirist,

---

[1] E.g. C.H. Pinnock et al. (eds.), *The Openness of God: A Biblical Challenge to the Traditional Understanding of God*, 8–9 and 101.

Meleager the poet and Philodemus the Epicurean philosopher. Herod the Great encouraged the process of Hellenization, writing his autobiography in Greek and establishing classical games, a theatre in Jerusalem, an amphitheatre in the plains and building the temple in Jerusalem in a lavish classical style. After an exhaustive examination of the evidence Martin Hengel concludes that Palestinian Judaism was just as much Hellenized as that of the Diaspora.[2]

Acts 6:1f. describes Hellenists among the earliest Christians and it was the Hellenists, including Stephen and Philip, who took the lead in spreading the gospel to the Gentiles (Acts 11:19–20). The most obvious effect of Hellenization is indicated by the fact that the New Testament was written in Greek.

Moreover, most of the citations of the Old Testament in the New Testament are from the Greek Septuagint. Sometimes the Septuagint translation is essential for the meaning of the New Testament text, such as when Matthew claims that Mary fulfils the prophecy that a virgin shall conceive and bear a child (Mt. 1:23 citing Is. 7:14, LXX). The Hebrew text speaks of a young woman, not a virgin. In Matthew 10:28 Greek ideas of the separability of the soul and body seem in evidence. John's Gospel begins by mentioning the Logos, a term of great significance in much Greek cosmological speculation, and John's sharp dichotomies between flesh and spirit, above and below, and earthly and heavenly may reflect popular Platonism.

Paul was born in Tarsus, a city noted for its Stoic philosophers. Though Paul rejects the more florid displays of Greek Oratory (1 Cor. 2:1–4), his letters nevertheless used several rhetorical devices and he meets his sophistic opponents (in 2 Cor. 10–13) by using their techniques and procedures. He frequently uses illustrations from Greek athletic contests. In his famous speech before Stoics and Epicureans at Athens he quotes Aratus (Acts 17:28), in 1 Corinthians 15:33 he quotes Menander's line 'bad company is the ruin of good character', and in Titus 1:12 we find a quotation from Epimenides. In Romans 1:23 and in 1 Timothy 1:17 we find God in terms of 'invisibility' and 'immortality', terms indebted to Hellenism rather than to the Hebrew Old Testament. Broad parallels have often been noted between New Testament and classical

---

[2] M. Hengel, *Judaism and Hellenism*, and M. Hengel, *The 'Hellenisation' of Judea in the First Century after Christ*.

household codes. The influence of Hellenism is clear in the letter to the Hebrews, with its excellent Greek, rhetorical techniques, dependence on the Septuagint and distinction between worldly shadows and heavenly realities. Although it is possible to dispute dependence on specific Hellenistic sources in each case, overall it seems certain that Hellenism has influenced New Testament thought. We may thus argue that the use of Hellenistic thought is biblical.

Hellenism cannot explain the development of the traditional doctrine of God

Stoics, Aristotelians, Platonists and Epicureans all had very different views of God and providence. Indeed, the doctrine of Cicero, who argued that God could not foreknow future free choices, is strikingly like that of Pinnock. The Church Fathers therefore needed to be selective in appropriating philosophical ideas and could not agree with them all. Furthermore, as Sanders accepts, the Fathers did not completely sell out to Greek philosophy.[3] They held on to such doctrines as the resurrection of the body, the incarnation and the Trinity, even though such doctrines drew universal scorn from pagan philosophers. They were quite capable of resisting the philosophers when they wanted, making their acceptance at certain points all the more significant. Thus any claim that exposure to Hellenism would inevitably lead to doctrines of a changeless God knowing the future should be rejected, since Hellenistic philosophy presented a range of positions on the nature of God, foreknowledge and free will. Furthermore, the Fathers were quite capable of digging in their heels over apostolic doctrine, whatever Greek philosophers argued.

There is a danger of the genetic fallacy

Where an idea comes from does not determine its truth value. The fact that an idea has its origins in Hellenistic philosophy does not mean that it is false. As we have noted, Cicero argues, like Pinnock, that God could not foreknow future free choices. If the fact that an

---

[3] J. Sanders, 'God as Personal' in Pinnock et. al., *Openness*, 60.

idea had a classical genesis ruled it out then this would be a serious problem for Pinnock himself! Therefore, rather than rooting about for the origins of ideas we must concentrate on whether the ideas themselves are any good. We must investigate whether there are any good arguments in favour of the traditional position, regardless of whether the tradition contains ideas present in Greek philosophy.

Should we take all biblical descriptions at face value?

Biblical language does sometimes describe God as seemingly igno-rant of the future, repentant and emotional. Why does the tradition tend to interpret such language metaphorically rather than literally? Part of the reason is that this biblical language seems inconsistent with the incorporeality of God and more elevated conceptions of his greatness, knowledge, power and providence. I shall attempt to argue that even Pinnock does not take all of the biblical descriptions of God literally, and therefore cannot insist on literal interpretations in criticizing the tradition. When we look at biblical descriptions of God, we find that many are clearly anthropomorphic, talking of his face (Ex. 33:20,23; Is. 63:9), eyes (Heb. 4:13), nose (Deut. 33:10), mouth (Deut. 8:3), ears (Is. 59:1), lips (Job 11:5), tongue (Is. 30:27), neck (Jer. 18:17), arms (Ex. 15:16), hand (Num. 11:23), finger (Ex. 8:19), heart (Gen. 6:6) and foot (Is. 66:1). The Bible likewise de-scribes God's actions anthropomorphically. He is portrayed as smelling (Gen. 8:21), tasting (Ps. 11:5), sitting (Ps. 9:7), rising (Ps. 68:1), walking (Lev. 26:12), wiping away tears (Is. 25:8), and sing-ing (Zeph. 3:17). Such examples could be considerably multiplied. If a simple appeal to proof texts were all it took to establish the falsity of the doctrines of foreknowledge, impassibility and immutability, then it seems we would also have to abandon God's incorporeality, the doctrine that a body is no part of God's essential being.

According to many texts, God has a body. If quoting proof texts is sufficient, then God has a body. If we doubt that God has a body, then we must doubt that quoting proof texts is sufficient. Of course, there are texts which assert that God is invisible (1 Tim. 1:17), spirit (Jn. 4:24), and present everywhere (e.g. Ps. 139; Acts 17:28, from Aratus; together with Paul saying of Christ that 'in him all things hold together', Col. 1:17). Such texts seem to deny that God is essentially corporeal and bodily, though even here some might find room for debate. If we follow the traditional interpretation of these texts and accept that God is essentially incorporeal, assuming a bodily appearance for the purposes of appearance to human beings, then we must reject a literal interpretation of anthropomorphic texts about God. As Rice says, 'most Christians rightly construe such descriptions as symbolic and deny that physical form and features characterize the divine being itself'.[4] We will also become wary of taking literally other descriptions of God that include or imply his corporeality. Indeed, considering how widespread anthropomorphic descriptions of God are, we may become wary of taking literally descriptions of God that make him like a man if there is reason to doubt that they should be so interpreted.

Rice's case for interpretation at face value

No doubt fearing that such an inductive argument from anthropomorphic texts will then be deployed against descriptions of God's repentance and colourful emotional life, Rice attempts to argue that descriptions of God deciding, acting and feeling should be taken at face value.[5]

First, Rice says, 'If human beings and God have nothing whatsoever in common, if we have utterly no mutual experience, then we have no way of talking about God and there is no possibility of a personal relationship with him.' This suggests that traditional interpretations imply that we have nothing in common with God. However, traditional interpretations allow similarity and analogy. God is conscious, is fully aware of and intensely concerned with the world, has wisdom and will, intentionally causes effects in the world and has reasons for causing these effects. In such ways God is like us, and biblical descriptions communicate this to us. Biblical language helps us relate personally to God without always being metaphysically precise or literal.

Second, Rice argues that the frequency with which descriptions of God's thoughts and feelings appear in Scripture means we should

---

[4] Ibid. 34.
[5] Ibid. 35.

take them at face value. If this were a good argument then the amazing frequency with which descriptions of God's body parts and bodily actions appear in Scripture would mean that we should take such descriptions literally. Rice doesn't take such descriptions literally and so it seems that this is not a good argument. The frequency of such language suggests that it is useful and important, but not that it is literal.

Third, Rice argues that the strategic significance of the passages where we find descriptions of God's thoughts and feelings suggests that we should take them literally. Certain passages have a defining function, indicating what it is that makes God God, or distinguishing God from other things, such as false gods and human beings. This argument is also unconvincing; Rice himself must allow that strategically important, definitive passages can employ non-literal language. So, to give an example that Rice himself cites, and describes as 'an important confession of faith' we find:

> My father was a wandering Aramean, and he went down into Egypt …
> Then we cried out to the Lord, the God of our Fathers, and the Lord
> heard our voice and saw our misery, toil and oppression. So the Lord
> brought us out of Egypt *with a mighty hand and an outstretched arm*, with
> great terror and with miraculous signs and wonders. (Deut. 26:5–10
> NIV; emphasis mine)

As Rice says, 'worshippers would recite these words as they offered the first fruits of their harvests to God. The setting underscores the importance of the words. It shows that the Hebrew people identified God by his actions. They understood who he was in light of what he had done.'[6] Yet it is clear that this defining passage makes use of anthropomorphic language to describe God's action, language that Rice does not take literally. Likewise, in the New Testament we find 'God is light' (1 Jn. 1:5), a passage similar in structure to 'God is love' (1 Jn. 4:16) which Rice takes to be definitive.[7] The image is taken up in the Nicene creed which describes Jesus Christ as 'light from light'. Such texts are clearly important, definitive passages yet they use metaphorical language. There can be no barrier against using figurative

---

[6] Ibid. 36.
[7] Ibid. 18.

language, even in important, definitive, credal statements. So it seems that Rice does not argue effectively against interpreting language about God's inner life and actions metaphorically. If taking such language at face value generates inconsistencies we may reasonably explore figurative interpretations.

God's greatness

In describing how the Fathers interpreted Scripture, Sanders frequently notes that they interpret things in the light of what is appropriate given God's greatness and perfection.[8] Though Sanders generally seems not to approve of this, one can argue that there is nothing unbiblical about such interpretation. Psalm 145:3 declares, 'Great is the Lord, and greatly to be praised; there is no end of his greatness.' (see also Pss. 48:1; 96:4, NRSV) Hasker accepts that the assumption that God is an absolutely perfect being is proper and correct.[9] God is deserving of absolute, unreserved and unconditional worship and devotion. If we were to discover that God was in some significant way deficient or imperfect our worship would be tinged with disappointment and regret. Such worship is not an expression of the sort of devotion that Jesus enjoined in his command to love God with all of our heart and soul and strength and mind. It is therefore a reasonable presupposition of the Great Commandment that God is worthy of unlimited worship and devotion and is thus of unsurpassable greatness.

If the ascription of unsurpassable greatness to God is to mean anything then we must have some idea of what unsurpassable greatness means. Since knowledge and the ability to achieve one's good purposes seem to be intrinsically admirable and great-making qualities, the burden of proof seems to be on those who argue for limits on God's possession of these qualities, particularly in the light of biblical evidence suggesting that God's knowledge and effective power are not limited in the way that Pinnock claims. Admittedly, our views of greatness are fallible and may be tainted by sin, but there is a similar problem in interpreting all Scripture: our interpretations too are fallible and may be tainted by sin. Furthermore, there

---

[8] Ibid. 74–87.
[9] Ibid. 131.

are several, mutually supportive, ingredients generating the traditional doctrine of God. Ideas about God's greatness interact with other biblical themes and traditional interpretations to produce the final product.

God's knowledge

In their essays, Nathan MacDonald and Simon Gathercole offer considerable evidence from the Old and New Testaments which suggests that God knows future choices of his creatures. Such concepts of divine knowledge were present in intertestamental Jewish texts (Susanna 42; Judith 9:5–6) and were accepted as Christian orthodoxy. In contrast, Pinnock appeals to texts suggesting that God does not know the future.[10] However, on closer examination, it seems that these texts suggest that God does not exhaustively know the *present*, contrary to other verses (e.g. Heb. 4:12–13) and Pinnock's own understanding of omniscience, whereby God knows everything about the present and past. So, for example, Moses said that God was testing the people in order to know whether they actually love him or not (Deut. 13:3). However, if God knows the present then he knows whether the people presently love him or not. He does not need to see the people's actions in order to know the state of their hearts and minds. Indeed, on Pinnock's libertarian understanding of freedom, the people might fail the test and disobey, even though they do indeed love God. Given a libertarian understanding of freedom there must be the possibility of choosing otherwise. If the people's love guaranteed that they obey God then on Pinnock's view they would not be free.

Pinnock also appeals to God's expression of frustration with Israel's wickedness: 'nor did it enter my mind that they should do this abomination' (Jer. 32:25; also Jer. 7:31 et al.). Such texts are difficult to take literally, even on Pinnock's premises, for, even if God did not expect the people to do this abomination, it must have entered his omniscient mind that they *might* do it. Indeed, he would have known the precise probability that they would do it. There are several other biblical examples where God appears to have limited knowledge of the present. In Genesis 3:9 God asks where Adam and

---

[10] Ibid. 123.

Eve are. In Genesis 11:5 he comes down in order to see the city of
Babel. And in Genesis 18:20 he goes down to see if Sodom and Go-
morrah are as bad as the outcry suggests. All of these texts suggest
that God is limited in his present knowledge. They therefore must
be interpreted non-literally by Pinnock and his allies, further
strengthening the argument that it is inconsistent to insist on a literal
interpretation of texts suggesting divine ignorance of the future
when even Pinnock must interpret several texts about God's
knowledge in the traditional way, that is, non-literally.

God's repentance

Proverbs 19:21 claims that 'The human mind may devise many
plans, but it is the purpose of the Lord which prevails.' Psalm 33:11
suggests that 'the plans of the Lord stand for ever, the purposes of
his heart through all generations'. Many verses talk about plans and
purposes that God has had from eternity, from before the
foundation of the world (Mt. 13:35; 25:34; Eph. 1:4,11; 3:9,11; 2
Tim. 2:19; 1 Pet. 1:20; Rev. 13:8). These plans include the redemption wrought by Christ, which Paul seems to think is greater
than the universal sin and death brought by Adam (Rom.
5:15–18). It therefore appears problematic to take at face value the
statement that God was sorry or repented that he made humanity
upon the earth (Gen. 6:6), as Pinnock does,[11] for it suggests that
God's purposes have not prevailed, and that the situation is
irredeemable.

Belief in the unsearchable greatness and wisdom of God
generates further problems with God literally repenting that he had
made humanity, even if one accepts Pinnock's view that God is ignorant of the future. Being sorry for what one has decided to do
suggests that the previous decision was unwise. Even if the result of
a decision turns out worse than one expected, due to factors beyond
one's control, one could still know that the original decision was a
good and a sensible one to make given what one knew at the time,
and that in the same situation one could legitimately make the same
decision again. Repenting of his decision suggests that God realized
he should not have made it. This seems particularly implausible

---

[11] Ibid. 117.

given that God was able to redeem the situation, as he did through the Ark and the subsequent salvation wrought by Jesus Christ.

Literal repentance seems even more problematic given the evidence produced by Nathan MacDonald and Simon Gathercole from the Old and New Testament that suggests that God does indeed know the future. A God who thus foreknows the future is hardly apt to become sorry later for what he has done, given that he foresaw what would happen from the beginning.

Arguably, in the interests of overall consistency, it is reasonable for the tradition to seek to interpret God's repentance figuratively, in a way that does not imply literal change of mind and purpose. Are there any other indications that this is a reasonable strategy, besides our general awareness of the use of figurative descriptions of God and his actions, noted above?

Perhaps: two other descriptions of God's repentance, his repentance from destroying Israel in response to prayer (Ex. 32:14) and from destroying Nineveh in response to penitence (Jon. 4:2), suggest that God's repentance need not be interpreted as a straightforward change of mind and purpose. In these cases there is a difference between what God had threatened to do and what God subsequently does, just as there would be if God had literally changed his mind and purposes. However, more general statements about God's purposes to punish sin but spare the penitent and respond to prayer (e.g. Jer. 18:7–10) indicate that we should take the initial statement about what God will do as being implicitly conditional. Thus we should interpret his statement of intent to punish as being a statement that God will punish *unless* there is repentance or effective intercession. Therefore, when God says he will punish Nineveh this should be interpreted as a conditional statement: he will punish unless they repent. On this interpretation God's initial statements can be said to be true without accepting that God literally changed his mind or spoke falsely. As noted in Nathan MacDonald's article, God is apparently *inviting* repentance or prayers by his threatening declarations of intent to Moses (Ex. 32:9–14) or to Nineveh (Jon. 3:4). Perhaps even Pinnock could allow that God issued his threats because he wanted to change the situation and avoid the need for destruction. If this is correct then the subsequent statements that God repented need not to be interpreted as straightforward changes of purpose. This gives us reason for thinking that he cannot consistently object outright to less straightforward interpretations of God's repentance.

Language about repentance may then be interpreted as a vivid metaphor. Rather than indicating a change in God's purposes, it may be an imaginative way of expressing his concern to change from his earlier activity. For example, his creative activity towards humanity is supplanted by destructive activity in the flood, and his threatening activity to Israel and Nineveh is changed for better things. Interpreting God's repentance more figuratively is arguably more consistent with biblical concerns taken as a whole.

God's emotions

When we look at the texts to which Pinnock and his collaborators appeal in establishing God's emotions we find that they are full of figurative language. What is more, these descriptions of God often involve *explicitly* corporeal language about God. For example:

> When Israel was a child, I loved him . . . It was I who taught Ephraim to walk, I took them up *in my arms* . . . I led them with chords of human kindness, with bands of love . . . *I bent down* to them and fed them . . . How can I give you up, Ephraim? How can I hand you over, O Israel? . . . *My heart recoils within me*; my compassion grows warm and tender. (Hos. 11:1,3,4,8, NRSV; emphases mine)

Here the description of Israel as a child is clearly metaphorical and the language about God's action is anthropomorphic. Significantly, even the description of God's emotion describes him with a heart within his body. Similarly, anthropomorphic descriptions of God's heart occur elsewhere, as in, 'Is Ephraim my dear son? Is he my darling child? For as often as I speak against him, I do remember him still. Therefore *my heart yearns* for him' (Jer. 31:20), and 'The Lord was sorry that he had made humankind on the earth, and it grieved him *to his heart*' (Gen. 6:6).

So it seems that biblical language about God frequently uses anthropomorphic idioms, and this is true not least in descriptions of God suffering emotion. If God does not literally have a heart within him, must he literally have emotions? As well as descriptions of God's emotions which *explicitly* mention body parts, Pinnock should consider whether literal emotions *implicitly* require that God have bodily sensations and feelings. This is because real emotions and feelings involve changes and sensations in one's body, and because we have little idea of what feelings and sensations would be like without an apparent bodily aspect. Emotions activate the involuntary, autonomic nervous system. For example, anger unconsciously raises heart rate and blood pressure, reduces blood flow to the gut, increases it to the brain and muscles, affects glandular secretions and releases stress hormones such as adrenaline. This in turn sensitizes our muscles, making them ready for action. This is why we feel 'pumped up' and tense when we are angry and have sensations in our stomachs and in our hearts. Quadriplegics incapable of these bodily effects do not experience proper anger. They have to make a conscious effort to act as if angry. If God's anger lacks such autonomic, bodily changes and sensations then it is not literally anger.

Moreover, we can give little or no clear content to any sensation or feeling without granting it some apparent bodily aspect. We have feelings *in our bodies*. What is it like to have a sensation or feeling that does not appear to be associated with some part of one's body? What would it be like to feel anger or grief with no body and no nervous system? We have no positive idea, let alone experience, of what is being claimed here. It is therefore no coincidence that biblical language often talks of God's body parts, such as his heart, in connection with his emotions, for it is in association with our body that we experience emotion and sensation. If God lacks an autonomic nervous system and a mammalian physiology then it seems that emotions are transplanted into a context in which they make little literal sense. God lacks the bodily equipment in which to locate literally heart-rending grief or hot-blooded anger. We cannot give any clear content to language about his emotional feelings and sensations. He lacks the very things which cause, constitute and characterize human experience of anger and grief.

Another problematic feature of real emotions is their involuntary, reflex nature. One cannot just choose to have an emotion. Emotions by their very nature happen to one involuntarily and move one from without, as the etymology of the word suggests. They interfere with one's freedom and rational decision-making processes. Emotions disturb deliberation and reduce self-determination, sweeping one along on tides of passion. We recognize that emotions diminish our responsibility, as in crimes of passion and fits of jealousy. However, God is meant to be the only wise God (Rom. 16:27), the God of peace (Phil. 4:9; 1 Thess. 5:23) and free to do as he pleases (Dan. 4:35; Pss. 115:3; 135:6), and therefore free to act justly and rationally. If God's emotions conflict with his wise and free decisions then they seem to reduce his greatness and leave him struggling with himself, an object of pity rather than awe. on the other hand, if God's emotions are somehow always in perfect harmony with his rational self-determination and purposes then they are motivationally redundant and make no difference. God will not be moved by them because he is already sufficiently moved by his rational self-determination. In a perfectly rational agent emotions would seem to be at best an ineffective complexity and at worst a serious interference and flaw.

Perhaps aware of this problem of passion, Rice quotes Heschel favourably, where he distinguishes pathos, 'the result of decision and determination, from passion, an emotional convulsion that takes possession and drives someone blindly'.[12] However, it must be noted that this involves non-literal interpretation of the Bible, which seems to describe God suffering passion. On the very next page Rice cites God's 'fierce anger' (Ex. 32:12). Revelation speaks of the 'fury' of God's wrath (Rev. 14:10; 16:19; 19:15). We have already heard Hosea 11:8–9 talking of how God's heart 'recoils' within him and his emotional inability to give Ephraim up. All of these descriptions sound like passion rather than something decided and determined upon. Once again it seems that even believers in an open God do not take biblical descriptions of God straightforwardly.

The New Testament continues the use of metaphorical or figurative language about God. In Romans Paul describes the Spirit joining in with our suffering, 'groaning with sighs too deep for words' (Rom. 8:23). Few would insist that the Spirit himself literally groans or sighs; rather the Spirit is involved in making *our* yearning sighs acceptable prayer to the Father. We may therefore interpret the injunction not to grieve the Spirit (Eph. 4:30) as a vivid warning not to do the things God dislikes. It perhaps also suggests

---

[12] Ibid. 26, citing A.J. Heschel, *The Prophets*.

that the indwelling Spirit makes *us* grieve at sin. For all these reasons, drawing metaphysical conclusions from literal interpretation of such texts seems problematic.

All of this is *not* to argue that descriptions of God's emotions tell us nothing. As well as their bodily and physiological elements, emotions also have a cognitive component. For example, we judge that something is offensive or unjust in becoming angry at it, and we judge that someone is miserable and in need of support and comfort when we feel pity. Passion additionally implies deep concern and strong motivation. One gets emotional about things one cares strongly about, and when one is moved emotionally one is powerfully motivated to act. Furthermore, when we know that someone is suffering from an emotion we have some idea of how they are motivated to act. In the same way, when we are told that God is angry at sin we know that he is greatly concerned about sin and is powerfully motivated to punish. When he feels pity he totally understands and cares about our wretchedness, and is strongly motivated to help. Ascribing passion to God thus vividly conveys the depth of his awareness, concern and motivation, in addition to his cognitive judgement of the situation.

Rice complains that such philosophical interpretations of biblical language are laboured.[13] However, many attempts to translate the Bible into philosophically precise prose are laboured. It would be commonly conceded that the Bible speaks of the sun rising (e.g. Gen. 32:31) or standing still (Josh. 10:13), whereas a scientific description would note that the sun is relatively static. Reduction of metaphor into precise prose is frequently dissatisfying. The tradition need not deny the value of the metaphor.

Pinnock asks how God can be loving and not pained by evil?[14] This question apparently presupposes that God's love is the same as ours, whereas reflection suggests that it is analogous to ours.[15] Pinnock accepts 'the mystery of God's inner life' and that God

---

[13] 'Biblical Support for a New Perspective' in Pinnock et al., *Openness*, 49.
[14] Ibid. 118.
[15] For Thomas Aquinas's account of analogy and metaphor in talking about God, and his account of God's love in terms of benevolence and will to create good, see B. Davies, *The Thought of Thomas Aquinas*, chs. 4–5.

cannot experience physical pain.[16] Unfortunately, it is hard to know what God's purely mental pain is meant to feel like, once all bodily sensation and imperfection is subtracted. Traditionally, God's universal love involves benevolence, a will to bestow good gifts irrespective of merits, rather than anthropomorphic psychology. God cannot take pleasure in evil or misery, but must desire to avoid it, disapprove of it and be dissatisfied with it. However, any finite dissatisfaction with creation would seem to be infinitesimal compared with God's satisfaction and infinite delight in the unlimited good of his own existence and the great good of creation overall. Moreover, given a traditional doctrine of Providence, all evil is ordained by God only as logically necessary for great good.[17] For example, sin is logically necessary for the full display of grace and just judgement and the eternal celebrations of these in the coming kingdom. Therefore, God's dissatisfaction with evil is voluntarily chosen by him as part of a compensating good, rather than a suffering inflicted from without. The dissatisfaction will be more than compensated by his satisfaction in the great goods for which the evil is necessary.

Again, the claim that the divine nature is without emotion or suffering does not mean that God does not understand or care about our suffering, or that Jesus, God incarnate, cannot sympathize with us in our weakness. Christ's human nature literally suffered, body and soul, and God, the standard of reality, counts this suffering as God's own. The omniscient deity does not need to be affected by suffering, for he eternally knows and understands it. He is perfectly aware of and absolutely concerned with everything that happens. Indeed, Christ counts the persecutions and hardships of his people as his own (Mt. 25:40; Acts 9:5). Not one sparrow falls to the ground without God's will and the very hairs of our heads are numbered (Mt. 10:30–31). All things work together for good for those who love God (Rom. 8:28). Therefore, any suggestion that the traditional doctrine makes God 'aloof and impassive'[18] is misleading, falsely implying as it does that God is unconcerned with his world and lacks motivation to change it. The divine nature is impassable in

---

[16] Pinnock et al., *Openness*, 119.

[17] Sadly, there is no room to offer a full account of how and why God might ordain evil. For the beginnings of such an account from a Calvinist perspective see P. Helm, *The Providence of God*, ch. 8.

[18] E.g. Pinnock et al., *Openness*, 119.

that it lacks suffering, not that it lacks concern, understanding or motivation.

Why should the Bible portray God in human terms?

We have seen reasons, such as biblical testimony to God's greatness, incorporeality and knowledge, not to interpret biblical descriptions of God's humanlike ignorance, repentance and emotions straight-forwardly. Why then does Scripture abound with such language?

The early Fathers generally agreed with Philo that the Bible describes things in an everyday way, using the idioms and understandings of the common people rather than philosophically precise language. For example, Origen explains such language as God's parental accommodation and condescension to his people. Origen notes passages of Scripture which compare the relationship of God to a father with his growing child, such as Deuteronomy 1:31 and 8:5.[19] He argues that when God becomes involved with the affairs of humans he takes on the ways and the speech of humans. When we talk to a two-year-old, we use baby language for the child's sake, because if we were to keep to adult speech and talked to children without coming down to their way of speaking and thinking then they would not be able to understand. Thus, when speaking to little children, we use a childish or babyish form of speech. We make up childish names for activity and play little games to persuade them to behave correctly. When we play and converse with them we act as if we had far less knowledge and ability than we really do, so as to help them participate. When we praise or scold them we exaggerate our tone of voice and facial expressions to help convey approval or disapproval of their actions. In the same way, God deals with us as if he had far less knowledge and ability than he really does so as to help us to understand and respond appropriately. He speaks in terms of human emotions and feelings in order to convey to us his concern and the importance of our actions and to help us to respond appropriately. This is not deceit but condescension to our human limitations and way of thinking.

---

[19] *Homilies on Jeremiah* 18:6 in M. Wiles and M. Santer, *Documents in Early Christian Thought.*

If God spoke in a way that conveyed his full knowledge and power this might well confuse people with all of the philosophical puzzles and paradoxes that debates about predestination, fatalism, free will and foreknowledge have so often engendered. If one had to have a grasp of such difficult concepts in order to read the Bible or hear God's word then few indeed would benefit from it.

Thus Origen argues, and the tradition has generally followed him. We may also see God's condescension in his appearing in human form and his assumption of flesh at the incarnation. Human language, appearance and nature are not essential to God, but he takes them on in order to reveal himself to us in a familiar and accessible way.

This is not to say that no cognitive or propositional meaning may be gleaned; descriptions of God's emotions convey God's intense concerns and motivations. Positive emotions, like joy, convey what God values and is motivated to promote, and negative emotions, like anger, convey what things he finds offensive, unsatisfactory and is motivated to destroy or punish. However, such intellectual deductions need not be the primary purpose of such language. The primary purpose may be practical, to help us relate appropriately to God. The Israelites were not expected to do philosophical theology so much as to do the will of God. As 2 Timothy 3:16–17 teaches 'All Scripture is God-breathed and is useful for teaching, rebuking, correcting and training in righteousness, *so that God's servant may be thoroughly equipped for every good work*' (emphasis mine). The revelation of God may thus be more concerned with right response by the many than with metaphysical abstraction for the few.

Eternity and timelessness

The idea of divine timelessness, present without past or future, was used by Philo[20] and is present in the Apostolic Fathers as early as Ignatius (d. *c.* 107).[21] It became the dominant, though not the only, understanding of divine eternity in Christian tradition. It finds

---

[20] Philo, *On the Immutability of God*, 32, cited in *Openness*, 70, 183, n. 37.
[21] Ignatius, *Epistle to Polycarp* 3:2 and *Epistle to Ephesians* 7:2, cited in *Openness*, 73, 184, n. 43.

scriptural support in John 8:58, 'before Abraham was, I am',[22] suggesting an eternal divine present; 2 Peter 3:8, 'With the Lord a day is like a thousand years, and a thousand years are like a day', suggesting that God does not experience our passage of time; together with claims that God does not change (Mal. 3:6; Jas. 1:17); is always the same (Ps. 102:27; Heb. 13:8); and is called a Rock (e.g. Is. 44:8), an image of stability. Some of these texts are particularly concerned with God's moral constancy, but Pinnock holds that the Bible requires a stronger concept of God's immutability than this, stating that God is 'from everlasting to everlasting', 'changeless in nature and essence'.[23] Eternal timelessness offers a simple, unifying explanation of these otherwise disparate features of God's nature.

Further support comes from the idea of God's limitless greatness and perfection. It is arguably better for God to enjoy a timelessly eternal existence, in which he limitlessly possesses all of his blessedness and causal activity *at once*, rather than watching it be washed away for ever in the river of time. If God is in time then he may *remember* his past pleasures and actions, but he no longer experiences, possesses or does them in fact. A memory of happiness is not the same as actually being happy. Remembrance of doing good is no substitute for doing it. Time carries away things of great value. Pinnock's open God does not possess his future kingdom or glory except in hope, and indeed does not even know the future, but is constantly learning new things. Plausibly, it would be greater for God not to lose his valuable past, nor need to wait for the knowledge and fulfilment of the future. A God of unsearchable greatness, worthy of unconditional worship, awe and admiration may well be one who is timeless, limitlessly possessing the whole of his precious life all at once, eternally.[24]

Pinnock offers several objections to the idea of divine timelessness.[25] First, he thinks it is hard to form any idea of what timelessness

---

[22] Note also Ps. 90:2,4 (LXX 89:2,4), 'before the mountains were born or you brought forth the earth and the world, from everlasting to everlasting you are! . . . For a thousand years in your sight are like a day that has just gone by, or a watch in the night.'

[23] Pinnock et al., *Openness*, 117, 118.

[24] This idea is developed and defended at greater length by Brian Leftow, 'Eternity' in P. Quinn and C. Taliaferro (eds.), *A Companion to Philosophy of Religion*, 257–63.

[25] Pinnock et al., *Openness*, 120–21.

might mean, since all of our thinking is temporally conditioned. This seems overstated. Timelessness means that God's conscious- ness is without change or succession. We are sometimes conscious without being conscious of the passage of time. If we imagine a se- quence of events laid out in our minds, as in frames of a feature film, and subtract any idea of beginning and end, we get some idea of what it might be like timelessly to will a succession of temporal events to be. Certainly it is hard to imagine how God's timeless, in- tentional causation is causally related to the actual succession of temporal events, but then many causal relations are hard to imagine, such as how mind and brain interact, or how God and matter inter- act. Difficulty in imagination is not the same as meaninglessness, and unless there is some actual inconsistency then an omnipotent God can will a temporal sequence of events to be. The fact that our thinking is temporally conditioned helps to explain why the Bible uses temporal language. It would be tiresome and difficult to be always translating our normal speech into timeless talk.

This helps answer Pinnock's second objection to the idea of di- vine timelessness, based on biblical history describing God making plans and carrying them out, experiencing temporal passage, in- volved in temporal events and facing an open future.

The force of this appeal to temporal descriptions of divine action is reduced once we accept that many divine actions are described figuratively, as noted above. Genesis 1 says that God made a dome that separated waters under the dome from the waters above it, and fixed the sun, moon and stars in it. Genesis 8:2 tells us that, at the end of the flood, 'the fountains of the deep and the windows of heaven were closed'. The Bible says that God laid the foundations of the earth upon the waters, so that it could never be moved (Ps. 24:2; 93:1; 96:10; 136:6; Job 38:4). Clearly, quite apart from argu- ments about six-day creation and the evolution of species, insisting on a literal interpretation of biblical language about God's activities will generate considerable problems apologetically. The Bible por- trays God in an anthropomorphic way that helps us to relate to him correctly, even if we are philosophically unsophisticated. Language of God's future and past existence conveys the fact that his existence is without beginning or end, and that he is present by his knowledge and power at all times. Talk of plans carried out conveys the idea that God acts purposefully, with wisdom and knowledge, as people who plan do, not in a random, ill-considered or *ad hoc* fashion. Language of temporal involvement conveys God's awareness of all time and his causation of events in time on account of other events. God's saying, 'perhaps they will . . .' (Jer. 26:3; Ezek. 12:3; etc.) conveys the importance of choice; his people must choose, and they cannot take for granted that they will choose correctly.

Pinnock's third objection is that timelessness seems to undermine our worship of God; we praise him not because he is beyond time and change, but because he works redemptively in time. However, we can praise God because he is changeless ('Immortal, invisible God only wise . . . We blossom and flourish as leaves on the tree, and wither and perish; but nought changeth thee'); and divine timelessness does not deny that God causes redemptive, saving effects in time, merely that God himself is in time.

Pinnock's fourth objection is that timelessness would mean that God would not experience or know the world as it actually is. This seems not to be a significant imperfection or weakness for 'knowing the world as it actually *is*' is a tensed statement, picking out the state of the world at the time it is uttered, read or written. Though there is no particular time that 'it actually is' for a God beyond time, God can know the state of the world at any time that temporal beings might pick out. The timeless God can perfectly know each and every space and time, and that they are temporally sequential, and would know what it was like *for us* to experience time, for he would comprehend all our conscious states. His comprehension of all times at once would not limit his ability to cause effects in time, for the times he comprehends are the times he has ordained. God is thus not limited in his wisdom, understanding or effectiveness. He is ignorant only of a fact that for him is logically inapplicable and useless and can only be known by creatures possessing merely a momentary fraction of their life at once. Pinnock, who thinks that God does not know what we would do in hypothetical situations or in the future is in a poor position to criticize the tradition for making God thus ignorant.

Finally, Pinnock complains that a timeless God would be cut off from the world and have no real relationship with people. Once again this seems a misunderstanding; the timeless God would be perfectly aware of the whole world through all time because he is ordaining the existence of the whole world, including its people at all times. The whole world is thus open to God's knowledge and power. Perhaps Aquinas's talk of God's relations to creatures being merely notional in God is misleading. However, it is not denying the reality of the relationship. It merely means that all talk of relationship, change and causation in connection with God is based on changes and effects in creatures, never on changes and effects in God.[26] It is not meant to deny God's knowledge of creation or his power over it. Pinnock's talk of a static, immobile, inert deity[27] also seems misleading. God is not in space and so cannot be static or immobile in any sense that implies fixity of position or lack of power. God cannot be inert in terms of idleness or inactivity because he is eternally active, causing every aspect of space and time to exist.

Pinnock also gives the impression that he thinks the traditional view of God makes God insensitive or unresponsive.[28] However, if God knows everything then he can intentionally cause any effect he wants at any time subsequent to, or even before, our actions. God causes this effect in perfect knowledge of and *in order to* meet our need. Our prayers therefore have effects. Though it is true that our prayers cannot *change* God's knowledge and action, this is merely because he *eternally* knows and causes effects because of our prayers, not because our prayers are somehow irrelevant to him. In the same way, God can take pleasure in us and we can bring him glory. He knows us completely, he is concerned for us and acts to save us. However, he is not indebted to us for this pleasure, for it is ultimately a result of his own generosity and grace. Thus, though it is true that divine eternity and immutability mean that we cannot cause any changes in God, this does not mean that we are unimportant to him. Rather, we are unchangeably known and loved by him.

Must the libertarian view of free will constrain our doctrine of providence?

Nathan MacDonald and Simon Gathercole argue that there is considerable biblical evidence suggesting God's providential

---

[26] See B. Davies, *Thomas Aquinas*, 75–9, for discussion of notional and real relations.
[27] E.g. Pinnock et al., *Openness*, 117, 121.
[28] Ibid. 103.

knowledge and control of future choices. However, Pinnock holds an incompatibilist, libertarian view of freedom that demands an absolute possibility of choosing good or evil. He is therefore led to marginalize or reinterpret such biblical evidence. In support of libertarianism Pinnock appeals to our sense of making choices between real options, which he believes would be illusory if the future is preordained.[29] However, our sense of choice admits of less metaphysically sweeping interpretation. It involves being aware of more than one attractive course of action and selecting among them on the basis of our own considered, intelligent preferences and priorities. Our options can be real in the sense that they really attract us, and we really would do them if we chose. Pinnock would probably insist that we sense nothing preventing us from choosing either option, but it seems very doubtful that we could sense God's foreordination, since it operates without exerting force on us. Even if our choices were predetermined by the state of our mind, brain and surroundings there is reason to doubt that we would sense this. Neurophysiology recognizes all sorts of unconscious processes conditioning action.[30]

Introspecting the moment of choice is difficult, because choosing requires attention to one's options rather than attending to the experience of choosing. It attempts detached observation of a process in which one is deeply involved. Retrospective memory is reconstructed from what was registered at the time, and psychological studies show that we have a very unreliable idea of what our reasons were.[31] It therefore seems doubtful that we could sense predetermining factors by introspection. If the decision-making process is 'chaotic' and non-linear then tiny differences in initial conditions will produce dramatic differences in outcome: the now famous butterfly over Beijing causing thunderstorms over New York. Imperceptible variations in our mind and brain could therefore lead to significantly different decisions. It therefore seems that we would not expect to sense if our decision were predetermined by some combination of mind, brain, and situation, let alone by

---

[29] Ibid. 123.

[30] See e.g. V.B. Brooks, *The Neural Basis of Motor Control*.

[31] See e.g. R. Nisbet and T. Wilson, 'Telling More Than we Can Know: Verbal Reports on Mental Processes', 231–59.

divine foreordination. Foreordination need not mean that 'human freedom is an illusion, we make no difference and are not responsible'.[32]

Though *libertarian* freedom may strictly be illusory, we remain free from blind forces and desires that compel us to act against or apart from our intelligent preferences. Our deliberation, selection and action still makes an essential causal difference to what would happen without it, generating physical force without itself being forced. We still act for reasons and can therefore give a response to those who call us to account for our actions. Authorities can still judge people according to their intentions and whether they paid enough respect to God and neighbour and punishment can still remove unfair advantages and satisfactions gained through wrong choices and deter wrongdoing. Pinnock and his co-authors object to such compatibilist views and offer comparisons with puppets, ventriloquists' dummies, robots, coercion, or manipulation in such views of freedom.[33]

However, even within a Calvinist framework, such comparisons seem flawed. Puppets, dummies and robots are lifeless, mechanical and insentient, lacking consciousness, reason, choices and feelings. Coercion implies use of force, duress or violence. Manipulation connotes exploitation, lack of respect and unfair influence or pressure. In contrast, humans are living, conscious agents endowed with intelligence and power that they exercise in the light of deliberation and reason, on the basis of their own intelligent preferences, purposes and priorities. God does not need to use coercion or manipulation; being omnipotent he can create and sustain the cosmos such that it operates according to its own powers, principles and proclivities, without his needing to exert any force, pressure or unfair influence on it at all. Pinnock will find the predictability of our responses troubling, but those who know us well can usually predict what we will do; this is what is meant by a 'stable relationship'.[34] God can predict our behaviour, not because we are boring or shallow, but because his knowledge is deep. The relationship is not equal, but

[32] Pinnock et al., *Openness*, 121.
[33] Ibid. 114; Hasker, 'A Philosophical Perspective' in Pinnock et al., *Openness*, 143, 145 and 146.
[34] See Helm, *Providence*, 152.

the Trinitarian God is not lonely or in need of equals. Furthermore, the Trinity offers a non-libertarian model of freedom.

Is the libertarian concept of significant freedom consistent with Christian concepts of God?

Significant libertarian freedom involves being free to choose *against* what one believes to be right and best. Pinnock and many other Christians argue that such freedom is necessary or supremely valuable. However, there is reason to doubt this. While there is reason to want to be free to choose against blind, irrational or evil motives, wanting to be free to choose against right reason, as the libertarian seems to do, looks unreasonable.[35] Can Christians consistently hold that such freedom is necessary or of supreme value? This is not the freedom we usually ascribe to God. He is usually portrayed as always acting for good reasons, and being free from any tendency to choose against what is right. Therefore it seems doubtful that significant freedom is of supreme value. If such significant freedom is so valuable or necessary, then it seems surprising that Jesus does not have it.

Traditionally Jesus is not able to sin: 'The Son can only do what he sees his Father doing, because whatever the Father does the Son also does' (Jn. 5:19). Jesus seems to offer a different model of human freedom from the libertarian freedom to sin, independent of God. Likewise, valuing a chance of rejecting communion with God seems perverse. Many Christians do not really want the possibility of rejecting God.[36] Claims that real love requires the possibility of rejection appear to contradict Pinnock's own Trinitarian doctrine: 'God exists as diverse persons united in a communion of love and freedom. God is the perfection of love and communion.'[37] The Trinity seems to provide an alternative model of love and freedom to the libertarian one, a model without the possibility of rejection and wrongdoing, making one wonder whether Pinnock's theology is consistent at a crucial point. It thus seems questionable whether

---

[35] See S. Wolf, *Freedom Within Reason*, 55.
[36] D.R. Griffin, *God, Power and Evil*, 106 and 156, notes that Luther and Barth did not want it.
[37] *Openness*, 108.

libertarian concepts of freedom should govern the interpretation of biblical evidence.

Problems with the open view of providence

Pinnock is led to deny that God has comprehensive knowledge or control of future choices by his libertarian view of freedom. God's knowledge and effectiveness is limited by the unpredictable freedom he grants his creatures. God needs to take risks in governing the world.[38] This risk-taking picture has its attractions. We sometimes admire people who take risks above those who play it safe. We may also want to deny that the worst events in history, such as Hitler's rise to power and the subsequent extermination of the Jews, could be accepted by God as part of his plan. It may seem attractive to see such atrocious events as the results of God's risky plans going wrong. However, there is an anxiety that God has opened himself to such failure as to become a poor basis for faith and hope, and that the risks he takes look unnecessarily reckless.

Is the open God a secure basis for faith and hope?

In general, it does not seem that the open God could be very certain of what his creatures will do. From a libertarian perspective it seems very implausible that in every situation we are highly likely to choose in a certain way. Often our significant decisions seem much more open and finely balanced. Furthermore, if we are meant to find the picture of a risk-taking God attractive, then the idea that God has set things up so that most decisions involve little risk will not be attractive. If God is practically certain of how we will respond in every situation then the element of risk is practically eliminated. We get a picture very like that in traditional views of providence wherein God has risk-free control. God's acceptance of appalling evils then becomes magnified to nearly the same proportions as the open view finds objectionable in traditional views.

For these reasons it seems that Pinnock believes that God is often uncertain of how we will likely choose, and the risks are sometimes

---

[38] Ibid. 125.

significant. This seems to fit better with experience, where some of our decisions are made in circumstances which make them all but inevitable, while others are made under conditions which appear to leave the outcome very open. If this is correct then the probability of God guessing correctly what will happen will become very low as the number of choices multiplies. Plans depending on the decisions of many people are therefore unlikely to work. God will thus have to override or bypass people's freedom to frustrate him in order to guarantee things in the longer run.

However, unless Pinnock is prepared to accept God's overriding of people's freedom *to reject him* – saving them coercively, as it were – it does not seem that he can guarantee any person's salvation. Unfortunately, saving people is arguably one of God's most pressing priorities, especially on Pinnock's premises. He seems to apply the everlasting, irrevocable love that God has for his elect people, Israel, to people generally.[39] If God fails in his purpose to save anyone it seems that he will be left grieving irrevocably. He will have failed everlastingly. The chance of his saving everyone seems minute, depending as it does on so many free choices, and this virtually inevitable failure seems harmful to Christian hope. God's inability to guarantee anyone's salvation also seems to mean that believers cannot have confidence that God can keep them from falling or will complete the good work he has begun in them.[40] There is an extra condition, the co-operation of our free will, and this is essentially unpredictable and unreliable, generating anxiety.

Furthermore, the choices to believe and to remain faithful are morally significant, since there is considerable temptation to do otherwise. Unfortunately, on Pinnock's premises it seems that choosing rightly is not something you can thank God for, since God cannot control the way you choose. We therefore cannot thank

---

[39] Ibid. 108.

[40] Cf. Phil. 1:6; Rom. 14:4; Jude 1:24; Jn. 6:38–40; 10:27–9. Pinnock thinks it is nonsense for God to warn us not to fall away even though it is impossible that true believers do so (*Openness*, 115). However, from the fact that it is impossible to fall away *given warnings* one cannot conclude that it would be impossible *without* warnings. One therefore cannot conclude that warnings are unnecessary. Warnings may play a role in causing backsliders and those considering apostasy to remain faithful, without implying that God cannot guarantee salvation.

God for a crucial element in our salvation, the only element that cannot be taken for granted given God's love. The problem extends more corporately, in that the Bible claims that 'all Israel will be saved' (Rom. 11:26–7) and that the gates of Hades will never prevail against Christ's church (Mt. 16:18). However, it does not seem that God can guarantee this. Indeed, all Israel may reject him or the church may apostatize. Hasker argues that such complete failure is possible, but unlikely, just as it is possible but unlikely for all the air molecules in the room randomly to concentrate in one corner of it.[41] However, this analogy is flawed. Air molecules repel one another at close range, and their independent movements tend to cancel one another out. Human choices depend heavily on others. If few people believe and are saved then it becomes harder for others to believe and be saved. A study of the alarming swings in intellectual and sartorial fashions should show how easily led we all are. Human choice, and the existence and extent of the community of salvation, is therefore less reliable than the behaviour of air molecules, again suggesting that God's plans cannot inspire total confidence.

How attractive is the risk-taking view?

Few would deny that it is sometimes necessary to take risks in order to achieve worthwhile ends, and that risk-taking can be courageous. On the other hand, there are several problems with the view that God is choosing to take risks with our eternal salvation. First, the more that is at stake, the less desirable it is to run risks with it. If we can achieve the same or a similar goal without risking serious loss then we will usually do so. Second, we are especially concerned to reduce risks for other people who depend upon us. For example, parents of dependent children should take special care to avoid risks to their children's well-being. Third, we are more willing to tolerate evil if we are confident that a good outcome is guaranteed. For example, parents might put their child through painful medical treatment if they are confident that it will work, but if the risk of failure is large they will probably hesitate to go ahead.

---

[41] Ibid. 154.

These points suggest that it is not attractive to have God risking the eternal life of his darling children in a context in which they are likely to suffer significantly. God is taking the risk that many, perhaps even most of his creatures will use their freedom to ruin their own lives and the lives of others. Judging by the history of the twentieth century, with such evils as Nazism, Stalinism and the killing fields of Pol Pot, it seems that God has chosen a plan involving a significant risk of horrific, institutional evil and genocide. Even if he has not chosen the specific atrocities that occur, he has chosen a world order that makes the occurrence of atrocities practically certain. We are faced with a God who is accepting the practical certainty of atrocious evil for many of his children, and significant suffering for almost all, yet who does not guarantee that everything will be all right for them in the end. Pinnock might reply that God is not an overprotective parent and that parents take risks with their children's safety so as to allow them to grow into mature, independent adults. However, parents *must* run these risks. Few find the risks attractive.

Pinnock can hardly suggest that the risk of failures is an attractive feature. The risks are a reason not to govern the world in the way Pinnock envisages, even if we grant the value of libertarian freedom and an undetermined choice of whether to accept God or not. God has other options, and can create a world where his children are not at such great risk. God might act in a more traditional way, wherein evil is ordained as logically necessary to eternal good, and his elect children are guaranteed to come to eternal glory. God would thus pass up any value there is in libertarian freedom but he would also avoid horrendous risks, risks that we might expect a wise and loving parent would hesitate to take, given the choice. Frustratingly, there is not space to defend such views properly here, but I hope that I have said enough to indicate why I think Pinnock ought to be more open to the tradition and the Bible.

6

Beyond Arminius: Pinnock's Doctrine of God and the Evangelical Tradition
Tony Gray

Clark Pinnock's theology, classified as either 'openness theology' or 'free-will theism', has brought a major challenge to traditional evangelical theology. Pinnock has been seen as something of an innovator as he recasts the doctrines of God and salvation, to name only two areas.[1] His discussion of the doctrine of God has been set against the background of the classical theological debate between Calvinists and Arminians. It has generally been accepted that both those in the Calvinist and Arminian camps belong to the group known as evangelical, even though there are strong disagreements between them. This essay aims briefly to explore the historical background behind the theology known as Arminianism, focusing on its view of God's foreknowledge and sovereignty. It will then pinpoint to what extent Pinnock has stepped beyond Arminius and Arminianism, and the implications for an evangelical understanding of God's foreknowledge.

Historical perspectives

Calvin and Arminius

John Calvin (1509–64) stands out as one of the pivotal figures of theological history. Bringing together the work of pastor,

---

[1] See in this volume Daniel Strange's contribution on Pinnock as an evangelical maverick.

theologian, reformer and leader, Calvin influenced not only a city but also a whole religion. His *Institutes of the Christian Religion* began as six chapters in 1536, but by the time it appeared in its fifth edition it had seventy-nine chapters. The doctrine of predestination has become, for many, a chief characteristic of Calvin's theology.[2] It must be born in mind that the word 'predestination' was only first used by Calvin in the 1539 *Institutes*, and a number of scholars have argued that predestination was not the central or organizing point of Calvin's theological system.[3] Although the details of this discussion need not detain us here, the significance of it for the later understanding of Calvinism and its relationship to Arminianism is important. Thus McGrath helpfully concludes:

> Far from being a central premise of Calvin's theological 'system' (a quite inappropriate term, in any case), predestination is thus an ancillary doctrine, concerned with explaining a puzzling aspect of the consequences of the proclamation of the gospel of grace. Yet as Calvin's followers sought to extend and recast his thinking in the light of new intellectual developments, it was perhaps inevitable (if this lapse into a potentially predestinarian mode of speaking may be excused) that alterations to his structuring of Christian theology might occur.[4]

Jacob Arminius (1560–1609) was a Dutch theologian educated at Marburg, Geneva, Leiden and Basel. From 1603 until his death he was professor at Leiden, and he reacted against the French Protestant theologian Theodore Beza.[5] Arminius became known

---

[2] Timothy George notes how in 1844 Alexander Schweizer made the claim that predestination was the centre of Calvin's theology, and since 'has become part of the common caricature of the Geneva reformer' (*Theology of the Reformers*, 232).

[3] See ibid. 232–4, and A.E. McGrath, *A Life of John Calvin*, 166ff.

[4] McGrath, *A Life*, 169. Whatever the precise truth in this statement, it becomes clear that during the history of these debates what Calvin or Arminius themselves explicitly believed matters less than what their names come to represent.

[5] Biographical information can be found in C. Bangs, *Arminius: A Study in the Dutch Reformation*. An assessment is given by C. Cameron, 'Arminius – Hero or Heretic?', 213–27. For a more in-depth and critical study, see R.A. Muller, *God, Creation and Providence in the Thought of Jacob Arminius*.

for his understanding of predestination and free will. Although believing in predestination, he was against the idea that God determined the destiny of humans prior to the Fall. This position implied that the coming of Christ was only a second-best plan, because there then exists no link between God's decision of who would be chosen, and the coming of Christ to remedy the Fall. Arminius argued that God predestines people based on his *foreknowledge of whether they will accept or reject Christ. This is God's foreknowledge.* The opposing position argued that God's election takes place before the offer of God's grace in Christ, rather than the other way round. It is a completely free act through which God graciously saves, an act not dependent on the human choice of individuals.

Arminius's writings, for example *On Certain Articles to be Diligently Examined and Weighed*, reveal the strength he felt his position to have:

> 9. ON PREDESTINATION TO SALVATION, AND ON DAMNATION CONSIDERED IN THE HIGHEST DEGREE:
> It is a horrible affirmation, that 'men are predestinated to eternal death by the naked will or choice of God, without any demerit on their part.'

A doctrine of predestination, which holds that God decided at the outset of the world that certain people would be sent to hell, is believed by Arminius to be a horrible decree. This is because, as the following selection demonstrates, predestination is put *before* the creation of the world and God's extension of grace towards it:

> 8. ON THE PROVIDENCE OF GOD
> 1. The providence of God is subordinate to creation; and it is, therefore, necessary that it should not impinge against creation, which it would do, were it to inhibit or hinder the use of free will in man, or should deny to man its necessary concurrence, or should direct man to another end, or to destruction, than to that which is agreeable to the condition and state in which he was created; that is, if the providence of God should so rule and govern man that he should necessarily become corrupt, in order that God might manifest his own glory, both of justice and mercy, through the sin of man, according to his eternal counsel.

It is important to understand clearly how Arminius then views the relationship between God's foreknowledge and the offer of salvation and grace:

15. ON THE DECREES OF GOD WHICH CONCERN THE SALVATION OF SINFUL MEN, ACCORDING TO HIS OWN SENSE

1. The FIRST DECREE concerning the salvation of sinful men, as that by which God resolves to appoint his Son Jesus Christ as a savior, mediator, redeemer, high priest, and one who may expiate sins, by the merit of his own obedience may recover lost salvation, and dispense it by his efficacy.

2. The SECOND DECREE is that by which God resolves to receive into favor those who repent and believe, and to save in Christ, on account of Christ, and through Christ, those who persevere, but to leave under sin and wrath those who are impenitent and unbelievers, and to condemn them as aliens from Christ.

3. The THIRD DECREE is that by which God resolves to administer such means for repentance and faith as are necessary, sufficient, and efficacious. And this administration is directed according to the wisdom of God, by which he knows what is suitable or becoming to mercy and severity; it is also according to his righteousness, by which he is prepared to follow and execute [the directions] of his wisdom.

4. From these follows a FOURTH DECREE, concerning the salvation of these particular persons, and the damnation of those. *This rests or depends on the prescience and foresight of God, by which he foreknew from all eternity what men would, through such administration, believe by the aid of preventing or preceding grace, and would persevere by the aid of subsequent or following grace, and who would not believe and persevere.*

5. Hence, God is said to 'know those who are his;' and the number both of those who are to be saved, and of those who are to be damned, is certain and fixed, and the quod and the qui [the substance and the parties of whom it is composed], or, as the phrase of the schools is, both materially and formally.

6. The second decree [described in sect. 2] is predestination to salvation, which is the foundation of Christianity, salvation, and of the assurance of salvation; it is also the matter of the gospel, and the substance of the doctrine taught by the apostles.

7. But that predestination by which God is said to have decreed to

save particular creatures and persons and to endue them with faith, is neither the foundation of Christianity, of salvation, nor of the assurance of salvation.[6]

A number of important issues therefore characterized Arminius's thought. Firstly, that grace precedes election, such that election rests on a human individual's response to God. Secondly, a Christian person is therefore able to reject God and fall away. Thirdly, that grace, and not predestination, is the bedrock of Christianity. The foundation for these points is the belief that people will be saved because of God's foreknowledge of their response. It is also the case that Arminius's doctrine and his perspectives on God's decrees raises an important question about the relationship between the persons of the Trinity.[7]

In recent scholarship, the question has arisen as to whether Arminius adapted a concept known as Middle Knowledge to aid his case.[8] The elements of this theory will be examined below. Whether this is true or not, the history of theology has often declared that Arminius's theology is, at best, second rate (see the remarks quoted from Ryle and Packer below). Of course, this is partly due to subsequent events, and hence caricatures of his theology have continued ever since.[9]

Arminianism post Arminius

After Arminius's death, Arminianism developed to a position of conditional predestination. Humans are predestined, conditional

---

[6] These quotations are from the Master Christian Library, Version 5, used with permission. © 1997 *AGES Software*. Vols. 1 and 2 tr. from the Latin by J. Nichols, vol. 3 by W.R. Bagnall (italics mine). See also the translation reprinted in G. Olson, *The Story of Christian Theology* (Leicester: Apollos, 1999), 468.

[7] For a discussion of this in relationship to the theology of John Owen, see C.R. Trueman, *The Claims of Truth: John Owen's Trinitarian Theology*, 132.

[8] E. Dekker, 'Was Arminius a Molinist?', 337–52, and Muller, *God, Creation*, 163ff. See also in relation to this Trueman, *Claims*, 115ff.

[9] For a modern defence of Arminius and his views in a historical setting, see G. Olson, *The Story of Christian Theology*, ch. 28.

upon their free choice of Christ. This then relates to the doctrine of the atonement. If Christ died for humanity, did he die just for the elect, or for all? If only for the elect, then the offer of grace to all is nonsense. But if for all, then why is Christ's death not efficacious (why does it not achieve its purpose) for all? For if it were universally applied, then would not all people be saved? Finally, if people became Christians by freely accepting Christ, the Arminians may argue that a Christian could later freely reject Christ and so become lost. These issues became central to later Arminian and Wesleyan thought, but are not the focus of our present concerns.

The Remonstrant articles (1610) encapsulated these thoughts: Firstly, that God predestines according to what he foreknows of a person's free choice. Secondly, Christ's death was for the whole world, every living person, yet only those who believe are saved. Thirdly, a person needs the grace of God to respond. Fourthly, this grace can be resisted by human free will if it so chooses. Finally, it may be that some Christians will not persevere until the end and so will fall away from salvation.

The Synod of Dort (1618–19) attempted to deal with these issues, resulting in a condemnation of the Remonstrant articles and an articulation of what is often known as five-point Calvinism. The Arminian theologians were removed and exiled. An immediate follower of Arminius, Simon Episcopius, realized some of the fear of the anti-Remontrants by developing his theology even further, and questioning the status of the second two persons of the Trinity.[10]

In the line of the Arminian theology developed by the Remonstrants is the work of Hugo Grotius, whose governmental theology

---

[10] For a discussion of the existence of God in Arminian theologians, including Episcopius, see J.E. Platt, 'The Denial of the Innate Idea of God in Dutch Remonstrant Theology: From Episcopius to Van Limborch' in C.R. Trueman and R.S. Clark (eds.), *Protestant Scholasticism: Essays in Reassessment*, 213–26. Interestingly, the issue of divinity in the Trinity had begun to affect Arminius's own theology – see Trueman, *Claims*, 135: 'Owen's formulation, in line with the Reformed tradition and in a manner more perceptive than some of his later critics, points to the fact that it is a christological problem, the relationship between the Son and the Father in the structure of the decree, which lies at the heart of the predestination debate with the Arminians; as a result he develops his theology in response to Arminian assaults in this area.'

of the atonement made him well known. Historically, perhaps the most influential advocate of an Arminian theology was John Wesley. He and his friend George Whitefield famously broke over such theological matters in 1741. Wesley wrote the following as an attempt to define Arminian theology:

> But there is an undeniable difference between the Calvinists and Arminians, with regard to the three other questions. Here they divide: the former believe absolute, the latter only conditional, predestination. The Calvinists hold (1.) God has absolutely decreed, from all eternity, to save such and such persons, and no others; and that Christ died for these, and none else. The Arminians hold, God has decreed, from all eternity, touching all that have the written word, 'He that believeth shall be saved: He that believeth not, shall be condemned;' And in order to this, 'Christ died for all, all that were dead in trespasses and sins;' that is, for every child of Adam, since 'in Adam all died.'
>
> For if God has eternally and absolutely decreed to save such and such persons, it follows, both that they cannot resist his saving grace (else they might miss of salvation), and that they cannot finally fall from that grace which they cannot resist. So that, in effect, the three questions come into one, 'Is predestination absolute or conditional?' The Arminians believe, it is conditional; the Calvinists, that it is absolute.

So Wesley clarifies the key issue that is the subject of our discussion of Pinnock's theology, and his move beyond Arminianism. Wesley was clear that because God possessed foreknowledge of future events, God knew who would respond to his offer of grace, predestination therefore being conditional upon this response. Interestingly, Wesley was also concerned to clarify the use of the terms 'Arminian' and 'Calvinist', a cry that surely speaks into theological debates today:

> Away, then, with all ambiguity! Away with all expressions which only puzzle the cause! Let honest men speak out, and not play with hard words which they do not understand. And how can any man know what Arminius held, who has never read one page of his writings? Let no man bawl against Arminians, till he knows what the term means; and then he will know that Arminians and Calvinists are just upon a level. And Arminians have as much right to be angry at Calvinists, as

Calvinists have to be angry at Arminians. John Calvin was a pious, learned, sensible man; and so was James Harmens [Jacob Arminius]. Many Calvinists are pious, learned, sensible men; and so are many Arminians. Only the former hold absolute predestination; the latter, conditional . . . One word more: Is it not the duty of every Arminian Preacher, First, never, in public or in private, to use the word *Calvinist* as a term of reproach; seeing it is neither better nor worse than calling names? – a practice no more consistent with good sense or good manners, than it is with Christianity. Secondly. To do all that in him lies to prevent his hearers from doing it, by showing them the sin and folly of it? And is it not equally the duty of every Calvinist Preacher, First, never in public or in private, in preaching or in conversation, to use the word Arminian as a term of reproach? Secondly. To do all that in him lies to prevent his hearers from doing it, by showing them the sin and folly thereof; and that the more earnestly and diligently, if they have been accustomed so to do? perhaps encouraged therein by his own example![11]

Wesley's argument with the predestination of Calvinism can be clearly seen in the words of the following hymn that parodies the doctrine:

'Thou hast compell'd the Lost to die;
Hast reprobated from thy Face;
Hast Others saved, but them past by;
Or mock'd with only Damning Grace.

How long, thou jealous God, how long
Shall impious Worms thy Word disprove,
Thy Justice stain, thy Mercy wrong,
Deny thy Faithfulness and Love.

Still shall the Hellish doctrine stand?
And Thee for its dire Author claim?
No – let it sink at thy Command
Down to the Pit from whence it came.[12]

---

[11] All quotations are from the Thomas Jackson edition of *The Works of John Wesley*, 1832.
[12] Quoted in George, *Theology*, 231–2.

Richard Watson, a leading Wesleyan theologian, did not include election in the table of contents of his *Theological Institutes* (1823) because he believed it to be something that had happened after God's act of grace, and therefore not central to theological doctrine. In America, Charles Finney's revivalist theology was thoroughly Arminian, perhaps even more so than Wesley's. Finney, unlike Wesley, questioned the need of God's preparatory grace in the life of the believer to accept God's grace.[13] His writings on religious experience and revivalism have had great impact on practical Christianity ever since, particularly on the theological outlook of William Franklin Graham (see below).

In the nineteenth century there is evidence that at least some Calvinistic theologians accepted Arminians within the evangelical fold. Although they were considered to be erring on certain matters, they could truly be called evangelical. So J.C. Ryle could write the following in defence of Wesley: 'He was a bold fighter on Christ's side . . . he honoured the Bible. He cried down sin. He made much of Christ's blood. He exalted holiness. He taught the absolute need of repentance, faith and conversion.'[14]

Although the debate between Calvinist and Arminian had been at times bitter during the eighteenth century, Bebbington offers the following overview describing the general consensus that was reached within evangelicalism:

> By the beginning of the nineteenth century, however, this debate was dying down. Most Evangelicals were content to adopt a 'moderate Calvinism' that in terms of practical pulpit instruction differed only slightly from the Methodist version of Arminianism. Leading Anglican Evangelicals expressed the view in 1800 that redemption is both general and particular. Arminians were right to stress human responsibility to repent and Calvinists right to stress the need for divine grace. 'I

---

[13] Finney, and his Arminian influence on American revivalism, comes under particular criticism for his view of God's foreknowledge in I.H. Murray, *Revival and Revivalism: The Making and Marring of American Evangelicalism 1750–1858*, 249–50, where Finney is accused of promoting the Pelagian heresy.

[14] J.C. Ryle, *Christian Leaders of the 18th Century*, 104, quoted in J.M. Gordon, *Evangelical Spirituality: From the Wesleys to John Stott*, 220.

frankly confess', wrote William Wilberforce, 'that I myself am no Calvinist, though I am not either an anti-Calvinist' . . . What Evangelicals agreed on seemed of infinitely greater importance than their disagreements, and their pre-eminent ground of agreement was the cruciality of the cross.[15]

Arminianism today

Those within the Methodist and Nazarene denominations, and many charismatic and Pentecostal groups, tend to have an Arminian slant to their theology. However, classification is not so simple – for example, Calvinistic Methodists still exist in some quarters, a number of charismatic groups are strongly Calvinist in their theology,[16] and Pentecostals can also vary widely.[17] Clark Pinnock spoke at a conference in the UK in November 1997 sponsored by evangelical groups including YWAM, Icthus and Pioneer. All of these are well-known groups that practise an Arminian theology. So, for example, the leader of the Icthus churches network, Roger Forster, has written at length on the issue in *God's Strategy in Human History*.[18] This articulates a strong Arminian theology in the face of what he sees as a prevailing Calvinist orthodoxy.[19]

It can be argued that the figure who has done the most to promote an Arminian view of evangelical Christianity is Billy Graham.

---

[15] D.W. Bebbington, *Evangelicalism in Modern Britain: A History from the 1730s to the 1980s*, 17.

[16] E.g. New Frontiers International, headed up by Terry Virgo, publicly endorsed Wayne Grudem's *Systematic Theology* for both its charismatic theology and its Calvinistic stance.

[17] See the fascinating survey of Pentecostal theology up until the early 1970s in W. Hoolenweger, *The Pentecostals*, 291ff. This explores some of the tensions that exist in Pentecostal theology, with an extreme dependence on God to work miraculously in the power of the Spirit when he wills, mixed with a very strong view of the efficacy of petitionary prayer and the role human beings play in bringing God's plans about.

[18] Written with Paul Marston.

[19] It must be said that during the 1997 conference Forster was careful to show appreciation of Pinnock's work, yet wished to encourage people to think deeper and ask more questions, thus perhaps suggesting a degree of distance between his position and that articulated by Pinnock.

A world-renowned evangelist, his teaching and practice have set
the agenda for thousands – if not millions – of Christians world-
wide. Criticized by some conservatives for his techniques and ecu-
menical stance, his practice of inviting his audience to stand, come
forward, and make a decision for Christ appears to be thoroughly
Arminian.[20] Of course Graham is not an academic theologian, and
has never written extensively on God's foreknowledge and predestination. Perhaps like many he could be caricatured as Arminian in
his evangelism (offering the gospel to all such that any who wills
may freely respond) and Calvinistic in his prayer (asking God to in-
tervene directly in the life of human individuals and nations). Yet
his *method* must surely have acted as enormous symbolic approval of
an Arminian approach to theology. It is up to the individual to decide whether they become a Christian or not; it is their free choice
whether to stand at a meeting, go forward, and pray a prayer, or to
stay sitting and ignore the altar call.

A theologian strongly Calvinistic in his approach to theology reflects something of the contemporary consensus view among evangelicals concerning Arminianism. J.I. Packer, who in the article
referred to here offers an extensive critique of Arminian theology,
writes the following: 'Calvinists should therefore approach professed Arminians as brother evangelicals trapped in weakening
theological mistakes, and seek to help them to a better mind.'[21]

What then are the implications of these observations for the theology of Pinnock? According to this historical sketch, evangelicalism has been prepared to accept an Arminian doctrine of God.
More than this, such a doctrine of God has been widely influential
within the movement, and although some (if not the majority) have
asked questions of such a view, it remains an evangelical view. The
question then presents itself as to whether Pinnock has developed a
doctrine of God beyond that proposed by Arminians which may
make him more at home with Pelagian or process theologians.

---

[20] Some of these tensions are explored in 'New Evangelicals, Old Fundamentalists', ch. 13 of the biography of Billy Graham by W. Martin, *The
Billy Graham Story: A Prophet With Honour*, and also at times by Graham
himself in *Just as I Am: The Autobiography of Billy Graham*.
[21] J.I. Packer, 'Arminianisms' in R. Godfrey and T. Boyd (eds.), *Through
Christ's Word: A Festschrift for P E Hughes*, 147.

Critical reflections

Arminian positions

Carl Henry picks out one of the key elements of an Arminian approach to election during his defence of a Calvinistic position:

> Some scholars try to escape the correlation of human choice with divine predestination by grounding the certainty of human acts in divine 'foreknowledge.' Many Arminians affirm merely 'class predestination,' that is, divine election of all believers collectively to God's service; this election they predicate upon divine advance information as to who will believe.[22]

This is the crucial issue that concerns us here. Does God have knowledge of future events or not? Arminius was clear that God does know the future, and it is through this knowledge that he then predestines. A brief excursus on 'Middle Knowledge' will help explore some of these issues.

Middle Knowledge

Middle Knowledge is a concept that arises out of a system of thought known as *Molinism*. Named after Luis de Molina, a sixteenth-century Jesuit theologian, Molinism attempts to steer a middle path between human freedom and the doctrines of providence, foreknowledge and predestination. In his historical context within the Catholic church Molina fuelled controversy the Protestant Reformation had begun in wider circles, but he died before knowing whether his views were to be accepted or not. Pope Paul V decreed in 1607 that neither one side of the argument nor the other could be considered as heretical, thus leaving Molinism as an official possible framework of thought in the Roman Catholic Church.[23]

The model that Molina used to account for the compatibility of human freedom and divine foreknowledge proposed that God possesses three types of knowledge that are logically, rather than

---

[22] C.F. Henry, *God, Revelation and Authority*, 6:85.

[23] See the 'Preface' by A.J. Freddoso, in Luis de Molina, *On Divine Foreknowledge* (Part 4 of the *Concordia*).

chronologically, distinct.[24] Via God's *natural knowledge* he knows all possible worlds and essences. This knowledge is not dependent on God's will; it is essential to his nature; and it is knowledge of what *could* happen. Via his *middle knowledge* God knows all true counterfactual propositions – that is, not just what a created essence could do, but what it *would* do in every conceivable situation. This knowledge is also not dependent on God's will, but is essential to his nature, and it is knowledge of what *would* happen. Via his *free knowledge* God knows all that is in fact true in the actual world. This knowledge is dependent on God's will, but is *not* essential to his nature, and it is the knowledge of what *will* happen in an actual world. 'Between' the second and third categories, God decrees to actualize one of the worlds he knows via his Middle Knowledge. Therefore, the claim is that God is able to create from a position where he knows all possible outcomes of all possible combinations of events. Yet his knowledge is of what free creatures would do in those situations, and so God is able to create a world in which he foreknows all events, while the free will of all created essences is maintained.

Freddoso states clearly the differences between the three 'stages' of knowledge:

> Natural knowledge has among its objects all the *possible* future contingents, whereas free knowledge has among its objects all *actual* or *absolute* future contingents. By contrast, middle knowledge has as its objects *conditional* or *subjunctive* future contingents that stand 'between' the actual and the merely possible. By His natural knowledge God knows that it is metaphysically possible but not metaphysically necessary that Adam will sin if placed in the garden; by his free knowledge He knows that Adam will in fact be placed in the garden and will in fact sin. What he knows by his middle knowledge, on the other hand, is something stronger than the former but weaker than the latter, namely, that Adam will sin *on the condition* that he be placed in the

---

[24] Craig notes how the notion of conceptual, atemporal priority in God's knowledge was not new – both Scotus and Aquinas had used it before. See W.L. Craig, 'Middle Knowledge, a Calvinist-Arminian Rapprochement?' in C.H. Pinnock (ed.), *The Grace of God and the Will of Man: A Case For Arminianism*, 145.

garden. So God has middle knowledge only if he knows all the conditional future contingents.[25]

Molina's account of Middle Knowledge is given in the *Concordia* (1588), in which he demonstrates dissatisfaction with the determinism that was implicit in the Thomist views of his fellow Catholics, and the determinism made explicit by the Protestant Reformers. So Molina defined Middle Knowledge in the following way:

> Finally, the third type is *middle* knowledge, by which, in virtue of the most profound and inscrutable comprehension of each faculty of free choice, He saw in his own essence what each such faculty would do with its innate freedom were it to be placed in this or that or indeed in infinitely many orders of things – even though it would really be able, if it so willed, to do the opposite.[26]

Francisco Suarez, in his two Opuscula (1594–97) also defended Middle Knowledge, but its history from there is less certain. R. Cook points out how Leibniz accepted the idea of 'conditional futures' from Molina,[27] but by far the most interesting modern candidate for accepting Molina's framework is Alvin Plantinga. Plantinga admits that at the time he developed his free will theodicy he was unaware of Molinism, yet he assumed that God knows the truth-value of counterfactuals of human freedom – as Molina's theory of Middle Knowledge also assumed.[28]

At first glance, the advantages of Middle Knowledge seem obvious. Relevant to our discussion of Pinnock is the way in which some have seen a possible reconciliation between the Calvinist and Arminian positions. William Lane Craig has explored this in detail, arguing that, 'With Luther, one could affirm God's infallible foreknowledge of future contingents and, with Calvin, God's sovereign providence over the universe and yet not thereby sacrifice genuine human freedom.'[29]

---

[25] Freddoso, 'Preface', 47.
[26] Ibid. 168 (*Concordia* 4.52.9).
[27] R. Cook, 'God, Middle Knowledge and Alternative Worlds', 296.
[28] J. Tomberlin and P. van Inwagen (eds.), *Alvin Plantinga*, 50.
[29] 'Middle Knowledge', 161.

Craig distinguishes between God's absolute and conditional intentions – God's providence extends to everything that happens,
but God does not positively cause everything that happens. That is,
he permits such events to happen. Molinism is therefore against
Aquinas's use of concurrence in the form of premotion (that is, God
causing a person's free will to choose to perform the action) as it is
deterministic. Instead it argues for concurrence simultaneous to the
decision to act – an influence along with a cause, similar to two men
pulling a boat out of the water at the same time.

Extending providence to predestination, Craig summarizes how
Middle Knowledge can appear to bring the two sides of divine sovereignty and human freedom together: 'it is up to God whether we
find ourselves in a world in which we are predestined, but . . . it is up
to us whether we are predestined in the world in which we find
ourselves'.[30]

Perhaps it allows a way to reconcile a notoriously difficult passage
such as Acts 2:23 where Jesus' crucifixion is attributed to the plan and
foreknowledge of God, yet his crucifiers are still held morally responsible? Robert Cook explores the advantages Middle Knowledge has for the notions of guidance and providence.[31] He argues that
any God lacking Middle Knowledge may in fact offer guidance
which is close to useless – such a God is only dealing in probabilities
concerning what will happen in the future. In the example of a
request from a girl concerning which suitor to marry, a God without
Middle Knowledge cannot give adequate guidance. 'On the other
hand, a being with Middle Knowledge assuredly knows what would
have happened if the girl had married either suitor.'[32]

There are also other scriptural passages of which the concept of
Middle Knowledge is supposed to make sense, most notably the
revelation of the outcome of a hypothetical event to David in 1
Samuel 23:9–13. However, as Cook points out, sense could also be
made out of this situation even if God possessed limited foreknowledge, as God could work out what would happen from the present
trends of the personalities of the people in the situation.[33]

---

[30] Ibid. 157.
[31] 'God, Middle Knowledge', 293–310.
[32] Ibid. 301.
[33] Ibid. 299; see also Carson's treatment of Mt. 11:20–24 in *How Long, O
Lord? Reflections on Suffering and Evil*, 146.

Having explored the details of Middle Knowledge, it must be noted that there remain a number of difficulties that face the doctrine.[34] Their relevance to the question of Arminian theology can then be seen. Is it possible to have knowledge of worlds that might exist? That is, what is the ontological basis of counterfactuals of freedom? More importantly can Molinism ensure that God's election, God's freedom, is not restricted by human beings? However, pursuing these questions here is not crucial, as Pinnock is clear, as we shall see, that God cannot know future free events. As we have seen, even Cook who is sympathetic with Pinnock's theology sees that a God without Middle Knowledge is unable to offer helpful guidance, for example. The alternative he proposes, that such a God could give some guidance based on present trends, is much closer to Pinnock's position, to which we now turn.

Pinnock and the rejection of Arminianism[35]

A number of commentators have already made the charge that Pinnock's theology goes beyond accepted paradigms for evangelicalism precisely because it goes beyond Arminianism. In the conservative paper *Evangelical Times*, Alan Howe writes:

> Pinnock therefore rejects the whole spectrum of views of God, including those of eastern Orthodoxy, Roman Catholicism, Lutheranism, Calvinism, and even Arminianism. What Pinnock and his co-writers are proposing is actually Socinianism, a heresy which arose just after the time of the Reformation and which denied not only God's foreordination and foreknowledge of all things (Calvinism), but also the Arminian teaching that God only foreknows what will come to pass.[36]

Similarly, in the newspaper *Evangelicals Now*, Frederick Leahy writes:

---

[34] E.g. see the exploration of these in T. Gray, 'Hell: An Analysis of the Doctrine of Hell in Modern Theology', ch. 5.
[35] I have begun to develop some of these critical themes in T. Gray, 'God does not Play Dice', 21–34
[36] *Evangelical Times*, April 1998, 12.

Thus we have before us a hybrid theology – ultra-Arminianism grafted onto a Socinian root-stock and planted in the barren soil of human autonomy: an idea dear to the heart of fallen man, the belief that he is independent and self-determining, master of his fate and captain of his soul.[37]

What are we to make of this charge, and of Pinnock's own rejection of Arminianism? He is clear that his theology has no room for a God who preordains anything in what he describes as a Calvinistic way:

Creative love theism is a composite model with the following basic features. First, it celebrates the grace of God that abounds for all humanity. It embraces a wideness in God's mercy and rejects the idea that God excludes any persons arbitrarily from saving help. Second, it celebrates Jesus' category of father to express God's openness and relationality with us. God seeks to restore relationships with estranged people and cannot be thought of primarily as a Judge seeking legal settlement . . . Third it envisions God as a mutual and interrelating Trinity, not as an all-determining and manipulative transcendent (male) ego.[38]

Of course Pinnock goes beyond this. Openness, and most explicitly Pinnock's theology, claims that God has only present knowledge. That is, for a time-bound being to know things in the future is a logical impossibility. God can make an expert estimation of what is going to happen – after all, he is God, has all the resources of the world, and is pretty good at working out what you and I are going to do.

The model most often used to illustrate this point is of a grand-master chess player. If you or I play Kasparov, we stand little chance, for he can work out from all the possibilities within the game of chess what you or I are probably going to do. He has all the experience, all the knowledge of all the possible game plans, and all the expertise, whereas I only know the basic moves. Similarly, God can predict what you or I would do tomorrow, but he does not

---

[37] *Evangelicals Now*, April 1997, 19.
[38] C.H. Pinnock and R.C. Brow, *Unbounded Love: A Good News Theology for the 21st Century*, 8. It is a shame that the authors use such provocative and caricaturing language at the end of this section.

know absolutely, for this would mean that your decision and my decision had been predetermined.

> God knows everything that can be known, just as he can do whatever can be done. But he does not know what is unknowable, and cannot do what is undoable. Future choices made freely are not knowable by any being, for the simple reason that there is nothing yet to be known. Future decisions are future – they do not exist in any sense until they are made. Therefore, it is no deficiency in God's omniscience that he does not know them . . . The Bible presents us with a God who faces the future as an open possibility. Some of it is determined by what has already happened, but much of it is open to God's action and to human freedom. This means that we can be coparticipants in shaping what will occur.[39]

Pinnock wishes to affirm the importance that God gives to human beings, and the respect he grants their free choices. In fact, creaturely freedom is so significant that God may be surprised by our choices. This is a risk. This is a more personal and loving God, who is prepared to take risks with his creation. Thus God is sovereign in much the same way as the grand-master chess player – he will win ultimately, but it may take him a little longer to get there, if we surprise him and do or choose something that God had not anticipated: 'History is not the playing out of a tirelessly fixed decree but a theater where the divine purposes are being worked out by the resourcefulness of God in dealing with the surprises of a significant creation. History is neither random nor predetermined.'[40]

The main contention of the openness view has to do with the relationship between foreknowledge and freedom. Is human freedom infringed because God knows what is going to happen? Some philosophers, for varying reasons, and based on various understandings of God's eternity, deny this. Bruce Reichenbach, who is sympathetic to Pinnock's model of God, strongly disagrees that foreknowledge and freedom are incompatible, as it confuses the fact

---

[39] 'God Limits His Knowledge' in D. Basinger and R. Basinger (eds.), *Predestination and Free Will: Four Views of Divine Sovereignty and Human Freedom*, 97.
[40] *Flame of Love: A Theology of the Holy Spirit*, 56.

that God knows what will happen with the fact that he knows this fact because I choose to do it:

> To argue in this way is to confuse the order of causes (what brings something about) with the order of knowledge (the basis on which we know something). What God knows is the event itself. Thus God will know the event if and only if the event occurs. That is, God will have a certain belief about an event occurring if and only if that event occurs. It is because (in a noncausal sense of having to do with our knowledge) the event occurs that God believes it occurs. But then one cannot turn around and make the event depend on God's knowledge of the event, as the objector does when he says that God's foreknowledge determines, for the foreknowledge depends upon the event, and not vice versa.[41]

Here is an attempt to understand foreknowledge with a strong concept of human freedom from an Arminian point of view. The question for Reichenbach is whether God knows these things within time (and therefore, how can he know events which are, in his definition, radically free, until they occur), or whether he knows them outside time (and therefore his notion of radical freedom may be in trouble).

Whatever the possible responses at this stage, Pinnock is clear in his rejection of Arminianism. Indeed, his rejection of an Arminian position is perhaps more vociferous in his present position than his previous rejection of Calvinism. Although he has many a harsh word to say about Calvinism and the hold he claims it has on evangelical theology,[42] an Arminian position is only Calvinistic theology rewritten.

---

[41] 'God Limits', 110.

[42] 'From Augustine to Arminius: A Pilgrimage in Theology' in idem, *Grace of God*: 'A simple fact, which I did not think much about at the time, was that Calvinian theology enjoyed an elitist position of dominance within postwar evangelicalism on both sides of the Atlantic' (17); 'They pretty well control the teaching of theology in the large evangelical seminaries; they own and operate the largest book-publishing houses; and in large part they manage the innerrancy movement. This means they are strong where it counts – in the area of intellectual leadership and property' (27).

Pinnock beyond Arminianism – process theology?

Does the rejection of God's foreknowledge lead Pinnock into a form of process theology? Openness theologians are keen to avoid the charge of being similar to process theologians – those who identify God with the world, not to the extent of pantheism (where God is the universe), but to the extent of panentheism (where God is the universe and more). They prevent this collapse into process theology by maintaining that although God may change in response to human beings, his essential nature is changeless.[43] So to charge openness with process theology is a mistake. Nevertheless, it is at times a close colleague. Pinnock in the lectures he gave admitted to considering whether there was a time when God was not (a feature common to process thought).[44]

As Donald Bloesch, who is sympathetic to a more Arminian theology, comments:

> These scholars [Pinnock et. al.] plot a middle way between process theism and classical theism, but they are closer in some respects to the first . . . Where open-view theists diverge from process theology is in their affirmation of a real, living God who existed before the creation of the world and who creates out of freedom, not necessity.[45]

Pinnock beyond Arminianism – Pelagianism?

How does Pinnock avoid Pelagianism? In a Pelagian system, predestination and foreknowledge is played down while human will is exalted, such that human beings not only contribute to their own salvation – they are responsible for it. Pelagius himself was driven by concerns of morality, that human beings were free to choose to do the good and hence live moral lives. As De Bruyn notes, 'Pelagius will not in any way compromise the capacity granted to each person to choose between good and evil, because his notion of justice is based on this capacity.'[46]

---

[43] C.H. Pinnock et al. (eds.), *The Openness of God: A Biblical Challenge to the Traditional Understanding of God*, 118.
[44] See C.H. Pinnock, *Theology for Revival*.
[45] D.G. Bloesch, *God the Almighty*, 255–6.
[46] T. De Bruyn, *Pelagius's Commentary on St Paul's Epistle to the Romans*, 23.

How does Pelagius relate this view of free will to God's role in salvation? Pelagius distinguished three elements in the human will:

> Although the fall set in train a habit of sinning, to the detriment of subsequent generations, the created abilities (*posse*) of the will, though overlaid with inveterate custom or obscured by forgetfulness or ignorance, remained as God made them, and needed only our act of will (*velle*) to make the accomplishing of God's will a reality (*esse*).[47]

God's grace does have a role for Pelagius, as God reveals himself both in the law and in the cross of Christ. Although Pelagius emphasized the role of the human will in salvation, he was adamant that the grace of God was central to salvation. Commenting on Romans 11:5–6, Pelagius writes that both Jew and Gentile receive salvation through grace, for 'to bestow gratuitously is called "grace" '.[48]

Although much of what we know of Pelagius's theology has come down to us through the works of Augustine, perhaps the most comprehensive and accessible of his works which can be securely claimed as coming from his own pen is his commentary on Romans.[49] This commentary is heavily influenced by the Eastern theology of Origen, and the theology of Origen known to Pelagius through the writings of Rufinus, which shares a similar view of the human condition. Pelagius wrote his commentary sometime between 405 and 410, and it may be that the resurgence of commentaries on Pauline epistles at the time was occasioned by problems with Manichaeism and asceticism. Certainly in Pelagius's work he constantly attacks the Manichaean understanding of the flesh, affirming instead that human creation is good and able to choose for God. The commentary provides us with sufficient evidence to understand the issues within Pelagius's theology that attracted condemnation.

Denying that human sin is caused by anything other than the free choice of the individual, Pelagius writes concerning Romans 7:15,

---

[47] D.F. Wright, 'Pelagianism' in S. Fergusson and D.F. Wright (eds.), *New Dictionary of Theology*, 500.
[48] De Bruyn, *Pelagius's*, 125.
[49] For an excellent introduction to, and translation of, Pelagius's Romans commentary, see De Bruyn, *Pelagius's*.

'[Sold as if] I were resolved upon sin, so that, should I accept its advice, I make myself its slave, I of my own accord subjecting myself to it' (cf. John 8.34).[50] And on Romans 7:20, 'Sin that lives in me, It lives as a guest and as one thing in another, not as one single thing; in other words, as an accidental quality, not a natural one.'[51]

Pelagius's anti-Manichaean stand is clear in the same context, where he affirms that Paul did not say in verse 18, 'My flesh is not good.'[52]

Holiness of life is both necessary and possible. Referring to Romans 6:4 Pelagius writes:

He shows that we were baptized in this manner so that through the mystery we are buried with Christ, dying to our offences and renouncing our former life, so that just as [the Father] is glorified in the resurrection of the Son, so too on account of the newness of our way of life he is glorified by all, provided that not even the signs of the old self are recognizable in us.[53]

Regarding Romans 6:13 ('Do not present your members to sin as instruments of wickedness'), Pelagius is clear that 'it should be noted that it is through freedom of choice that a person offers his members for whatever side he wishes'.[54]

Faith is persistently seen as the key to salvation. God has only rejected those who do not believe (Rom. 11:1),[55] God would not have given a spirit of stupefaction to people 'if they had wanted to have a spirit of faith' (Rom. 11:8).[56]

Despite the emphasis on human free will, Pelagius was keen to maintain the role of God's grace. He comments on the beginning of Romans 8:29 ('For those he foreknew'): 'The purpose according to which he planned to save by faith alone those whom he had foreknown would believe, and those whom he freely called to

---

[50] Ibid. 103.
[51] Ibid. 104; see also comments on Rom. 5:19, 95.
[52] Ibid. 104.
[53] Ibid. 96.
[54] Ibid. 98.
[55] Ibid. 124.
[56] Ibid. 126.

salvation he will all the more glorify as they work [towards salva-
tion].'[57]

So God foreknew, according to Pelagius, who would be saved.
However, his emphasis throughout is on human ability to make a
right free choice for God. Pelagius does not develop a doctrine of
prevenient grace, thus distinguishing a Pelagian approach from an
Arminian approach. As Strange makes clear in his essay, Pinnock
does develop a doctrine of prevenient grace, which although questionable at various stages, allows him to avoid the charge of
Pelagianism in the way that Arminius does.

> The concept of prevenient grace allows Arminius' soteriology to be
> synergistic (involving both divine and human wills and agencies) with-
> out falling into Pelagianism or Semi-Pelagianism. Unlike the latter,
> Arminius' synergism places all the initiative and ability in salvation on
> God's side and acknowledges the human person's complete inability to
> do anything whatever for salvation apart from the supernatural
> assisting grace of Christ.[58]

In terms of foreknowledge, Pelagius and Arminius have some similarities. Regarding Pelagianism, Pinnock can avoid the charge as he
is keen to affirm God's activity in salvation and our reliance on his
grace, without which we have no hope. Regarding foreknowledge,
however, Pinnock has stepped beyond both Arminius and Pelagius.

Providence, mystery, and evangelical doctrine

What then is the way forward? Concerning the doctrine of God,
and specifically, the extent of God's foreknowledge, Pinnock has
stepped beyond a number of positions. He has denied a Calvinistic
system whereby God predetermines what will happen and therefore foreknows it. He has denied an Arminian (and in this sense, a
Pelagian) system whereby God predestines on the basis of what he
foreknows will happen, for God cannot have certain knowledge of
future free events. In the process he has cut himself off from any

---

[57] Ibid. 113.
[58] Olson, *Story*, 471.

possibilities of a Middle Knowledge system, which may (if the obstacles could be overcome) offer a way forward for an Arminian theology. Yet Pinnock avoids a process theology for he insists on the transcendence of God.

In taking this step of denying God's certain knowledge of future events, Pinnock has stepped beyond the tradition I have outlined. Thus in this sense, and on this particular point of doctrine, Pinnock has moved beyond the evangelical tradition. Pinnock himself may not in fact worry about such a charge. Evangelicals have traditionally affirmed the priority of Scripture above tradition, reason and experience, and if the commitment to *sola Scriptura* takes one beyond these, then the theologian must bow to this authority. However, evangelicals must also consider the role of God in history, and also their understanding of the doctrine of the church. These two points can only be hinted at here. The first may not trouble Pinnock, especially since he is challenging theology on this very point. However, if God is providentially involved in history, and the formation of theology, we must at least ask why he has allowed the prevailing understanding of church doctrine to be that he has knowledge of future events. Admittedly it is possible that this is due to human sinfulness and error. An account must be given of why this is so (and so Pinnock and others offer the account of theology being driven by Greek philosophy, which Richmond replies to in his essay).

The second point is that, whatever the paucity of evangelical reflection on ecclesiology, all evangelicals do have a doctrine of the church at some level. Even as evangelicals we look to history and tradition as a guide and starting point for our reflection. Thus any change in the consensus and any attack on it must be taken extremely seriously. This has been demonstrated in another area where Pinnock has also been involved, concerning the nature of hell. As evangelical theologians tentatively challenged the traditional view and judged it inadequate – proposing the belief that those in hell are ultimately annihilated – for many of them it was a grave step, not to be taken lightly. Whatever our conclusions, this has to be taken seriously when considering Pinnock's challenge to the traditional picture of God as having knowledge of future events. While not ignoring the theological and philosophical problems involved, we may agree with Bloesch when he writes that, 'The core of the problem is the attempt to make the mystery of God's sovereign grace and providence compatible with the biblical affirmation of human responsibility and freedom.'[59]

Is the task of evangelical theologians then merely to throw up their hands and appeal to mystery, hit the panic button when the going gets tough? Certainly non-Christian or non-evangelical critics would make this claim, perhaps arguing then that the God we believe in is inconsistent and illogical. Such claims are in fact hard, if not impossible, to prove. Yet mystery is an acceptable category within theology, and appealed to at a number of crucial junctures. Consider but three vital examples.

Firstly, the Council of Chalcedon set the limits for a Christian understanding of the person of Christ, fully human and fully God. These are the goalposts. A number of the Fathers attempted to clarify the detail, and exclude heresy from truth. Yet the core of Christ's nature, how it actually works, remains a mystery which has been revealed. Secondly, similarly the doctrine of the Trinity remains mysterious. We may set limits by establishing three boundary markers, for example: God is three persons; each person is fully God; there is one God.[60] Again, the inner workings of this Trinity remain a mystery. Thirdly, the doctrine of the atonement remains, at least at one level, mysterious. Granting an understanding of the work of the cross that is penal and substitutionary, *how* this actually works out within the persons of the Godhead remains mysterious.

There of course remain criteria as to why and when the category of 'mystery' is invoked. In debates concerning God's foreknowledge, philosophers of religion resist this category for as long as possible, so that details can be established, and incorrect interpretations ruled out. For an evangelical, once the biblical data has been read, understood, assimilated, and put together, mystery may be a proper response.[61] This must surely be true for all theologians who wish to carry the label 'evangelical'.

---

[59] Bloesch, *God the Almighty*, 256–7.

[60] Wayne Grudem uses these limits in his discussion of the Trinity in *Systematic Theology: An Introduction to Biblical Doctrine*, 21ff.

[61] For an attempt to do this concerning the doctrine of God and God's foreknowledge, see in this volume MacDonald and Gathercole.

At the close of a 600-page account of the history of Christian theology, Arminian theologian Roger Olson argues that Christian theology still faces some major unresolved issues for theological reformers to work on. The major one, of course, is the old debate between monergists and synergists over God's relationship with the world. New light from God's Word on that issue is badly needed as the extremes of process theology and resurgent Augustinian-Calvinism polarize Christian thought as never before.[62] We may disagree with his call for new light from God's word, for surely God's wisdom on this matter has been revealed. Our misunderstanding needs more clarity, perhaps. Pinnock has challenged evangelicals to reconsider some of the most intractable yet vital debates of Christian history. Yet he has concluded with a God who could never be sure that his plans would come to fruition.

Dependent on ideas central to the chess-player analogy, Pinnock admits that God may be surprised. That, although he will ultimately achieve his plans of victory, it may take him a little longer due to our lack of co-operation, or our choosing to do something he had not expected. God does not know what is happening, neither does he ordain what is happening. If God has such limitations, then a number of questions come to mind immediately, questions Arminius and even Pelagius may have shared. How did God ensure that Christ came into the world? If Mary's freedom had objected to being used as God's servant, another servant would have been needed. And if that servant objected, then another. And if not that one, then another. Although it may be unlikely, on the openness model, that all possible Marys would have refused, refusal was still *possible*, and thus it is *possible* that God's plans would ultimately have been thwarted.

Consider another important aspect of theology, the end times. Although it may take longer than God expected to reach the end times, the openness God is confident in his victory. Yet, on the grand-master chess theory, it is *possible* that Kasparov can be surprised, and that even though he is the most resourceful and knowledgeable player in the world, someone could come up with an unexpected move, and throw him off beam. His victory is not assured. What is striking about the analogy of the chess player is that

---

[62] Olson, *Story*, 612.

chess is a closed game – there are not limitless possibilities. Openness theology seems to suggest a limitless amount of possibilities, due to human free choice. As in the chess model, and more so, it is *possible* in the openness model (and it must be possible, otherwise something is set and determined about the future before it has happened, and that conflicts with human freedom) that God's creation would end up in ultimate revolt and never be conquered. Pinnock may reply that God has got eternity to work all this out, so there are no worries. Fine, but it is *possible* that for eternity God would be frustrated. No victory, no final homecoming. If the chess analogy were extended to the idea that it were possible for God to be 'stalemated' by human beings, even a draw in chess (which often happens at the higher levels) is not a victory.

In conclusion, I suggest that although Pinnock raises vital questions for evangelical theology, questions which challenge the prevailing Calvinistic orthodoxy in evangelical theology, he presents a doctrine of God that is thoroughly non-evangelical. For the gospel is good news about what God has done and about what God will do. How can it be good news if God doesn't *finally* know that it will be brought to completion?

7

Clark Pinnock's Response to Part 2

Part 2 examines the relation of the openness of God model to the Christian tradition and raises the possibility that we might have been wiser to have stayed closer to certain older interpretations. Both essayists prefer the more classical model, even if Arminian and not Calvinian, and believe that openness theology is 'thoroughly non-evangelical', in Gray's words. Though this evaluation stings, I take some solace in the fact that the judgement is actually mild in comparison to what is enunciated by certain American critics who declare that we are not Christians at all, not to say evangelicals. In defence of what I have done, I would simply say that my aim has been to point out neglected scriptural truths, which (I think) is a very evangelical thing to do, much like what Luther did in the face of Eck, who said he was not traditional enough.

Richmond's essay typifies the way classical theists think about the nature of God and invites my response. First, I was surprised to learn that he thought that we regard the traditional view as simply a Hellenistic corruption of the Bible. That is an extreme position but not one that I hold though it is one that makes it easier for the critic. Had the tradition uncritically absorbed the motif of a totally unchangeable God and unmoved mover, it could not have proclaimed the reality of the living God of the Bible. Having put the record straight, I find Richmond insensitive to the one-sidedness in the traditional doctrine of God which nevertheless came about as a result of the influence of Hellenistic assumptions about the nature of divine perfection. I refer to the powerful tendency to place God as far away from and as high over us as possible. With all the talk about infinity, immutability, atemporality, impassibility, simplicity,

omnipotence, omniscience, etc. does one not get the impression of
a deity far away, aloof, and cold? We ought to be alarmed when
Aquinas says that God cannot have real relations with the creature
because of the immutability of his essence. He gives the picture of a
God uninvolved in the world, a God who is, in Walter Kasper's
phrase, a solitary narcissistic being who suffers from his own com-
pleteness, and more like a metaphysical iceberg than the living God.

Surely we must register a strong No to this tendency and rejoice
in the glory of the biblical God which lies more in his gracious turning toward us and in his desire to commune with us than in his distance from us. Why is it that, when one reads an essay like
Richmond's, one is impressed how different the traditional formulations of the divine attributes are compared to the perfections of the
God and Father of our Lord Jesus Christ? Richmond seems blind to
the fact that the attempt to harmonize the Greek and the biblical
conceptions of God has led to all manner of abstractions and com-
plications which would not have arisen so readily had we read the
Bible and let it condition our thinking. What astonishes me is that
evangelicals, who make much out of their supposed faithfulness to
the Bible, can so uncritically swallow the pagan legacy of the absolute immutability of God and let it wreak such havoc on the doctrine of God. And the irony of it all is that I am the one whose
orthodoxy is being questioned, when my only slip has been to
prefer the Bible to Plato.

Second, I agree with Richmond that we should not take every
biblical description at face value. (I wonder where he ever got the
idea that we do?) All language about God is metaphorical, human
language. We have nothing else to work with. The truth about God
is mediated to us through metaphors. Where I differ from Richmond is not on the metaphorical character of biblical language but
on the truth these metaphors convey. We should take such expressions as God is a father, God is a king, God is a rock, etc. not literally
but appropriately and seriously. The problem with the tradition is
not that it takes the language metaphorically but that it rejects the
truth conveyed by it. For example, when the Bible says plainly and
repeatedly that God changes his mind and alters his course, traditional theologians reject the metaphors and deny that such things
are possible because of their presuppositions. How could a God,
assumed to be sovereign and omniscient according to classical

definitions, shift from Plan A to Plan B? The Bible must mislead us when it suggests that God could repent – it has to be mere anthropomorphism. Richmond and I agree that the expression 'the arm of the Lord' is a metaphor for God's ability to act. Why then can we not also agree that, since God is said to repent, it follows that God is free to alter his course of action where appropriate and follow a plan different from one previously announced?

Metaphors have meaning and what I want to know from traditional theists is what they think certain of them mean: for example, what does it mean for God to repent, to grieve, to interact, to respond to prayer, etc. It is not a question of taking biblical language literally but of taking biblical language seriously. I was a little disturbed by Richmond's 'higher criticism' of the Bible seen in his sweeping away of so much of what the Bible says. The Bible states that God was sorry that he had made humanity but Richmond insists he could not possibly have done so. Hosea presents God suffering with and for his people but Richmond explains God cannot be feeling grief because he has no physical heart. The gospel presents the incarnate Son of God suffering for us but Richmond knows that he only suffers in his human nature not in his divine nature because of the pagan notion of divine apathy which forbids God from suffering. Only Christ's assumed humanity, not the Trinity, suffers for our sakes in his view. The suffering of the Son apparently does not affect the Father and the Spirit. Richmond entertains the Hellenic-biblical synthesis which requires him to edit the text of Scripture extensively. Notice the irony again – my credentials as an evangelical are being questioned for taking biblical language seriously when the real problem lies in traditional hermeneutics which treats the Bible loosely and forces it onto a Procrustean bed.

Let me refer to the greatness criterion which Richmond advocates. This is the idea that we ascribe to God every attribute of greatness possible. It sounds good but carries a big price. The Bible may speak of God responding to what happens in history but, since this might take away from ascribing immutability to God, we should not follow that line of thinking. God cannot respond to a historical situation if it would mean that God changes in some way. It would not be 'worthy' of God according to the greatness criterion to respond to changing situations. What this means is that the 'real' truth about God is found, not in the biblical metaphors, but in our own criterion of what is 'fitting' for God to be. God's nature must conform to our intuitive notions of what deity should be like. Wherever the Bible does not measure up in its speech about God, we are entitled to invoke the greatness criterion to correct it. If the Bible says God suffers grief, we must take it with a grain of salt, since we know that God cannot suffer. Such language must be an accommodation to our finite minds which assumes that we know God's nature better than the Bible does.

How does Calvin know that God 'lisps' to us, as a nursemaid lisps to a young child? He knows it is lisping because he knows (or thinks he knows) the real truth of the matter, that God cannot repent or be surprised, etc. How does he know that? Because rationally according to his system he knows what the truth about God is and is in a position to judge when the Bible talks in childlike ways. Or, if the Bible presents God as operating in time, he knows from the tradition of timelessness that it cannot be so. Applying the greatness criterion, it is better for God (he thinks) to be timeless and possess his being all at once rather than to be temporal, even if it ruins the biblical concept of God as personal agent.

God's foreknowledge supplies another illustration. The greatness criterion would say that it is better for God to know the future exhaustively than for God to know the future as partly settled and partly unsettled. Thus, even though the Bible indicates in many ways and in many places that the future is partly unsettled, the greatness criterion requires us to opt for a view of the future as completely settled. Why is that, speaking *ad hominem*? What is so great about a God who knows the whole future exhaustively when that threatens the real drama of the creation project? There is (I suppose) an Islamic sort of greatness about it but how much greater is God's knowing certainties and possibilities with the resourcefulness to cope with whatever arises. Would it not seem to require more subtlety and ingenuity on God's part to rule over an open universe than over a determined universe? Am I alone in feeling drawn more to a personal God who invites us to be covenant partners and walk with him into a not yet entirely settled future than to a deity who presents us with an entirely settled future and therefore expects essentially nothing from us? I do not find that adding Plato's notion of perfection to the biblical portrait makes God greater.

Tony Gray affirms the evangelical character of Arminian theology (something which palaeo-Calvinists of my acquaintance are unwilling to do) but is uncertain how to relate my work to it. When I used the expression 'from Augustine to Arminius' in the title of a recent essay, I was not suggesting that I used to be a disciple of Augustine and became a disciple of Arminius, but that I experienced a shift in orientation which these names symbolize. (The issue of foreknowledge has little to do with it.) Augustine stands for theological determinism, while Arminius stands for free will theism. I never accepted everything that Augustine taught (nor do any evangelicals that I know of) and I do not now hold everything that Arminius taught. (I do not agree with his doctrine of election based on foreknowledge either.) I was referring to a shift from non-relational to relational theism, from absolutist to personal categories, from determinism to love.

Nevertheless, divine foreknowledge enters into it and Gray makes much of it. He is right in saying that my denial of exhaustive divine foreknowledge places me beyond what Arminius and most free will theists have said. I have already explained why I do not find the concept biblical – now let me say something more theological. Theologically I consider divine foreknowledge unsuitable and detrimental to relational theism. If we are God's covenant partners and co-labourers, it is important that the future not be completely settled, because that would mean that there is no room for us to participate in shaping the future in the service of God as we are called to do. Positively, an open future means that things can be different on account of our existence. It was not (I think) wise on the part of Arminius to put such emphasis on exhaustive divine foreknowledge, because it gives the very strong impression that history is altogether decided and not something that we are involved in shaping.

Gray is concerned (however) about the fact that Arminians, and virtually everyone else, have held to such foreknowledge literally for ages. One reason for that is the influence of classical theism according to which God is unchanging in every respect, not only his character, but also his knowledge. God cannot learn something he had not known already. God cannot be surprised or change his plans. Otherwise the content of his knowledge would change. Therefore, whatever takes place in history, from events of great significance to the buzzing of a housefly, must take place exactly as God foreknew it. The power of the pagan idea of the absolute unchangeability of God requires a set of unbiblical moves like this one. The reason people have held to exhaustive divine foreknowledge is the same reason they have held to timelessness and impassibility, even though they too are strikingly unbiblical. Let me ask Gray a question: Why do we give such authority to tradition and (in this case) to a pagan philosophical influence, especially in view of the fact that there is not to my knowledge any article of faith about the divine foreknowledge in the tradition? There have, however, always been vigorous debates about it, so let's just continue them and not go hunting for heretics.

I have not transgressed some rule of theological discourse or crossed over some line and placed myself outside the pale. Why can an evangelical not propose a different view of the nature of the future? What church council has declared this impossible? Since when is it a criterion of being orthodox or unorthodox, evangelical or unevangelical? We tolerate all kinds of differences of opinion about important matters – Gathercole himself wants to reopen the discussion of God's timelessness and impassibility – two very ancient theological convictions. I don't think we want (do we?) to shut these discussions down and question each other's orthodoxy on these issues. Gray's spirit, which is charitable, does not worry me but I do worry sometimes when I get the feeling that other critics are trying to marginalize me so that evangelicals won't have to discuss certain issues.

There is another reason too why people have held so tightly to exhaustive divine foreknowledge and Gray illustrates it near the end of his essay when he says that without it God could not be sure that his plans would come to fruition. I detect fear here. Surely God does not require a crystal ball in order to succeed in the work of redemption. He is not so lacking in wisdom, that unless he controls everything, he cannot achieve anything! I myself trust in God, that he can accomplish what he said he would accomplish and I do not need a dogma in my system called exhaustive foreknowledge to make me feel more certain. I have what I consider a very high view of God according to which God is resourceful and wise enough to handle any challenges that may arise from his having created a significant universe.

Part 3

8

In Defence of the Faith: Clark Pinnock and the World Religions

Christopher Sinkinson

Introduction

It is now widely accepted that, historically, Christian theology has failed to deal adequately with the fact that we live in a world of myriad religious traditions. As far as apologetics and polemics are concerned much debate has been carried out with little engagement of non-Christian religions. As Gavin D'Costa notes in an important essay: 'West European theology from the time of the Enlightenment has generally assumed that the integrity and truthfulness of Christianity must be defended and argued for within the public arena peopled by atheists and scientists.'[1] If theology is to be relevant in the future it must have serious engagement not only with secular atheism but also with alternative religious traditions.

It may be shown that much evangelical Christian apologetic has taken place in this rather isolated environment. Apologetics refers to that area of theology concerned to defend the truth of Christianity from the charges of its critics. Many texts on apologetics have strong sections on the objections from Darwinians, Marxists and Freudians but little on the profound objections offered by other religions.[2] This has not always been the case and it would

---

[1] G. D'Costa, 'The End of Systematic Theology', 325.

[2] A striking example might be that of Hans Küng in his *Does God Exist?* Küng would later champion inter-religious understanding within Roman Catholic theology. However, in this lengthy apologetic work originally published in 1978 the debate over God's existence is primarily discussed in the context of western secularism.

certainly be a glaring mistake to make today. For this reason, Clark Pinnock's work as an apologist for his openness model of Christianity is to be commended in attempting to deal with other religions. In various works he has made a robust attempt to relate to the questions raised within a pluralist society. Indeed, part of his apologetic for 'openness' is that he claims to provide a model that will be more successful in making Christianity relevant to non-Christians. Pinnock is clear that apologetics must be carried out in this global context.[3]

In our own times there have been so many Christian responses to religious diversity that there is a need for some way to categorize or catalogue them. The most successful terminology is that of exclusivism, inclusivism and pluralism.[4] Within this threefold typology there is much variation but it is hard to avoid using them as general terms. The exclusivist argues that since Jesus Christ is the exclusive Saviour, only Christianity provides saving knowledge of God. The inclusivist maintains that Jesus Christ is the Saviour but affirms that this saving work may be appropriated even where the name of Jesus has never been heard. In this way, other religions may be included in the saving work of Christ. The pluralist gives up any sense of uniqueness regarding the work of Christ and maintains that most religions provide equally beneficial access to the divine reality. Pinnock has provided helpful discussion of this pluralist account and solid reasons for its dismissal as a Christian option.[5]

However, the inclusivist and exclusivist positions are sometimes divided from each other more by degree than kind. For example, most exclusivists acknowledge that at least some of those who die without any verbal confession of Christ will yet be in heaven. This is particularly so with regard to Old Testament believers, those dying in infancy and the severely mentally handicapped. Paul Helm

---

[3] *A Wideness in God's Mercy: The Finality of Jesus Christ in a World of Religions*, 142.
[4] See esp. A. Race, *Christians and Religious Pluralism* and G. D'Costa, *Theology and Religious Pluralism*. For one attempt to demolish the typology see I. Markham, 'Creating Options: Shattering the "Exclusivist, Inclusivist and Pluralist" Paradigm', 259–67.
[5] E.g. *Wideness*, 134–5; and in D.L. Okholm and T.R. Phillips (eds.), *More Than One Way? Four Views on Salvation in a Pluralistic World*, 60–64.

describes two forms of exclusivism: the opaque and the transparent.[6] Transparent exclusivism (sometimes called restrictivism) argues that anyone who has saving knowledge of Christ will confess this in words – it is transparent who is Christ's. Opaque exclusivism concedes that it is not always visible who has saving knowledge of Christ, perhaps because of ill-health, immaturity or a lack of concepts with which to express that faith. Inclusivism also has variations on the theme. Pinnock describes himself as a cautious inclusivist in order to distance himself from other forms of inclusivism.[7]

Perhaps the line of divide between exclusivism and inclusivism is less to do with the extent of salvation and more to do with how a theologian assesses the value of non-Christian religion. An exclusivist would hold to a much more pessimistic view of alternative religions than would the inclusivist. Therefore, in our assessment of Pinnock's response to other religions we will consider wider issues than simply the extent of salvation. We shall first establish what Pinnock means by 'faith'.

Defender of faith?

Most of Pinnock's printed output has been of an apologetic nature. His defence of the faith has included directly evangelistic titles[8] and works which defend the case for 'openness' theology.[9] *A Case For Faith* is a short and engaging book which presents a series of arguments for the truth of Christianity with a non-Christian reader in mind. Though reference is made to non-Christian religions, the assumed readership is largely secularist. The main arguments of the book are written on the assumption that we have an 'ability to discern the nature of external reality and come to a decision on the basis of factual evidence'.[10] It is interesting to ask whether, in this

---

[6] P. Helm, 'Are They Few That Be Saved?' in N.M. de S. Cameron (ed.), *Universalism and the Doctrine of Hell*, 278.
[7] 'An Inclusivist View' in Okholm and Phillips, *Four Views*, 98.
[8] E.g. C.H. Pinnock, *A Case For Faith*.
[9] E.g. C.H. Pinnock and R.C. Brow, *Unbounded Love: A Good News Theology for the 21st Century*.
[10] *Case*, 121.

work, Pinnock is essentially persuading us of the truth of the *Christian* faith or 'faith' in some more general sense. There are five circles or pillars of evidence that he presents to us. The first three seem to apply to 'faith' in general, of any kind, while the last two are more particular to the Christian faith.

The first circle of evidence is the pragmatic function of faith which makes life possible. There is a basic, human drive for meaning and purpose that sets us apart from the animals. Pinnock notes that 'Religion historically has provided the rationale and has made sense of our existence.'[11] Historically, in the west, this implies the Christian religion but there is no reason to think Pinnock wants to limit his understanding of faith in this way. While the demise of Christianity in the west has left a vacuum in which various forms of secular religions have flourished, including Marxism and Freudianism, such truncated religious systems fail to satisfy the human drive to worship a divine being. It is the 'existence of God' that is required to 'adequately support the meaning of life'.[12] This theistic presupposition is shared among many of the world religions.

The second circle of evidence refers to the felt experience of men and women. Pinnock notes that even secularists have been unable to shrug off the sense of life being more than mere physical existence. At the very least there is a quasi-religious experience of the lack of God in the life of the unbeliever. However, the positive religious experience of God is powerful evidence because it is not restricted to Christian believers: 'All religions emphasize the need to develop and mature in the spiritual disciplines that lead to the knowledge of God.'[13] Pinnock points out that the atheist is not able to claim that Christians alone are suffering the delusion. If it is a delusion then all theistic believers, whatever their religion, are suffering from it. The atheist claim implies that the vast majority of the world's population throughout history has been deluded. Is such a conclusion really credible? For this powerful argument to work there must be some element of 'faith' common to all religions. Pinnock claims:

---

[11] Ibid. 23.
[12] Ibid. 36.
[13] Ibid. 44.

> I think we should regard the great religions of the world as a patchwork
> quilt, combining light and dark colors in various proportions. All
> religions are not true in the same way. Their differences are
> deep-seated and cannot be smoothed over or disregarded. There are
> elements of truth and falsehood, authenticity and deception alongside
> each other in the fabric.[14]

Religions cannot simply be valued according to one standard or
test. There is in each option much to be commended and much to
be denied. However, running through them all is a common element of faith that allows them to be categorized together. Most
strikingly, Pinnock suggests, 'The fundamental questions of life and
death are also engaged there and the quest for salvation pursued.'[15]
Though there may be much disagreement the world religions are
addressing the same fundamental questions, pursuing the same
soteriological goal and share the same basic religious experience of
the divine being.

Trying to identify and describe this common religious experience is difficult but Pinnock believes it can be done. What one finds
is a common, basic sense of the holiness and awe-inspiring nature of
God. In contrast to science, where there is so much disagreement,
we find that religious people 'agree about the greatness and holiness
of God who is absolute and compelling and demands our obedience
. . . the unworthiness of man in the presence of God . . . beyond this
world of sense there lies a mystery . . . it is a mystery that promises
redemption to man'.[16] Pinnock's apologetic case for faith depends
upon this universal or general understanding of 'faith'. The evidence that may be accumulated from the resources of the world religions across world history does provide a powerful critique of the
atheist position. However, these evidences do not set apart one
religion as more likely true than another.

The third circle of evidence also applies to religion as a general
category. It concerns the various cosmological forms of argument
that use the intuition that the universe appears to be designed in
order to point us to a creator God. Christians call this part of the

---

[14] Ibid. 45.
[15] Ibid.
[16] Ibid. 51–2.

general revelation of God's existence in the universe. Such evidences 'incline our minds to consider a God who is moral, personal, powerful, intelligent and the like' but do not provide a revelation of the gospel.[17] This is the fundamental weakness of any natural theology. It can bring us a limited knowledge of God but not necessarily to a saving knowledge of God. However, Pinnock will develop much more on the foundations of natural theology than this, as we shall see.

The fourth circle of evidence concerns the historical facts about Christianity. This includes the evidence that the New Testament is reliable, that Jesus claimed to be divine and, supremely, that he rose from the dead.

The fifth and final circle is the witness of the life of the church to the reality of God working in transforming power within her.

The weight of evidence brought together by Pinnock has a quite general apologetic force. Indeed, the first three circles would be largely of use to many of the world religions. The fourth and fifth relate more exclusively to the Christian faith. For this reason, Pinnock rejects as a pseudo-problem the difficulty presented by pluralism. Stated simply, this difficulty concerns the fate of all those millions who have a faith like that represented in the first three circles, but no saving knowledge of Christ. The classic argument is that, without Christ, the religions of those millions remain damnable. Pinnock points out that this is not the only ancient position held by Christians:

> There is another view, equally ancient and capable of validation from the Scriptures, that holds that God deals with people where he finds them. If he finds them in paganism, as he found Abraham and Melchizedek, he can communicate with them in that milieu. God's revelation of himself is universal and the light is sufficient for those who are chronologically AD but spiritually BC to respond and give themselves to God.[18]

This survey of an apologetic for Christianity is interesting because it establishes that Pinnock has long held a view of the Christian

---

[17] Ibid. 70.
[18] Ibid. 110.

message which affirms 'faith' as a general category of human experience. There is evidence for the particular claims of Christianity but this builds upon more general evidence shared by all the world religions. Taken as a whole, the book is a useful apologetic for religious faith in a general sense. While adherents of other religions would substitute alternative facts for those found in circles four and five much of the argument would be acceptable to them. In this sense, Pinnock has long been a 'defender of faith' as much as a 'defender of *the* faith'.

There are dangers in this apologetic methodology. In particular, it assumes the universal applicability of various terms. For example, the notion of 'salvation' or the 'promise of redemption' from a divine being are assumed to be applicable to common human religious experience well beyond the confines of confessional Christianity. By making these assumptions, Pinnock is able to categorize 'religion' as a common phenomenon. While each religion may itself be a patchwork quilt of good and bad, he is certain that they are all quilts and share the same basic structure, constitution and purpose that quilts have in common. The Buddhist quilt may not be as serviceable as the Christian quilt but they both function as coverings and either are better than none at all! The basic problem we will now develop with reference to Pinnock's more recent work is his failure to provide enough specification for the terms he uses. This is a problem that stems from his commendable apologetic concerns but leads him into serious theological errors.

Identifying religion

Religious studies has been an area of academic scholarship that developed greatly in the last century. Indeed, since the 1940s many theology departments have become departments of 'Theology and Religious Studies' or simply departments of 'Religious Studies'. This shift shows the increasing weight being placed upon the study of religion as a universal rather than simply local phenomenon. The possibility of such a discipline assumes that it is possible to establish what its subject matter should be. However, within the academic discipline there is debate over how we define religion itself.

Some attempts to define religion seek to establish a common essence. This might be a common experience, ethical system or doctrinal claim. Such approaches run into all kinds of problems. It is not clear that there is such an essence to all religions. Certainly, trying to establish a common doctrinal belief is difficult. The Christian belief in the existence of God is simply not shared in any meaningful sense with Zen Buddhism or the religion of Shinto. Attempts to establish a common ethical core are also problematic. It may be true that both Jesus and the Buddha taught us to show love and compassion to those around us. However, this demand is placed in contexts where the very meaning of love and personal identity differ profoundly. The question that such attempts raise is whether we may establish a common meaning to words like 'god', 'salvation' or even 'religion', or whether the words change meaning across cultures. James L. Cox points out that most definitions of religion are either too specific, excluding obvious religious traditions, or too vague.[19] Most scholars use some 'family-resemblance' model of the relationship between religions.[20]

We may now turn to Pinnock in order to establish how he defines 'religion'. His work is certainly not unsophisticated and attempts to establish some common features. Dealing with religions as 'worldviews' Pinnock and Brow identify four basic questions religions answer:

What is the nature of the ultimate?
How may the human predicament be best described?
What is the character of salvation?
How is salvation appropriated?[21]

Pinnock and Brow identify three basic types of religious answers to these questions. The first is that of naturalism which essentially rules out any metaphysical answers. The second is that of monism which identifies ultimate reality with everything there is. The third way of answering these questions is theistic. These religions make a distinction between creation and creator and find the answers in various

---

[19] J.L. Cox, *Expressing the Sacred*, 11.
[20] As John Hick does in *An Interpretation of Religion*, 3–5.
[21] Pinnock, *Unbounded*, 16.

ways in terms of that relationship. These, then, are the three basic religious options. Pinnock and Brow provide reasons for finding the first two religious options deeply dissatisfying but continue to explore the theistic form of religion with reference to the way it explains and empowers love.

Pinnock concedes that even theistic religions cannot be treated as the same in matters of content. However, there is another sense in which they do all share common features. In order to affirm both of these claims, Pinnock uses the account of religion developed by Wilfred Cantwell Smith.[22] This account makes an important distinction between objective and subjective religion. Objective religion concerns the doctrine, scriptures and institutions, while subjective religion refers to personal attitude on the part of the believer.

Smith develops this distinction somewhat differently and to more radical conclusions than does Pinnock. However, outlining Smith's work will help us identify a set of important problems. Smith is a historian of religion and especially of Islam. His historical scholarship has led him to conclude that 'religion' is a very unhelpful term. Indeed, as a way of identifying particular communities it is really only a modern, Enlightenment use of the word. Such use implies that religious communities have a fixed body of belief and practice. In contrast, Smith argues that traditions are in constant flux and process. Therefore, he argues that the term be dropped and replaced by the two terms Pinnock draws upon, 'cumulative tradition' and 'faith'. By the former term Smith means 'the mass of overt objective data that constitute the historical deposit, as it were, of the past religious life of the community'[23] which includes scriptures, buildings, myths and conventions. Historians of religion are primarily concerned with the study of such cumulative traditions. In contrast, faith 'lies beyond that sector of their religious life that can be imparted to an outsider for his inspection'.[24] Smith points out that, in the Christian tradition, the Greek word for 'faith' is a verb

---

[22] Pinnock, *Wideness*, 110–11. For an overview see E.J. Hughes, *Wilfred Cantwell Smith: A Theology for the World*.

[23] W.C. Smith, *The Meaning and End of Religion: A Revolutionary Approach to the Great Religious Traditions*, 156.

[24] Ibid. 170.

rather than a noun. This means that faith is something people do rather than a thing that they have. In this way, faith is profoundly personal.[25] Smith also describes faith as similar to such virtues as courage, enabling him to affirm that 'none of them is an object in the world; they are qualities in persons' hearts and minds'.[26] According to this account, faith is not something that may be objectively stated, discussed or seen as right or wrong. It is a subjective religious quality or piety, valuable wherever it is found. Smith has promoted the view that most of the world's religious traditions are responding in some way to the same, ultimate transcendent reality. Pinnock does not wish to meet Smith at this conclusion but he does use his work to establish the distinction between objective tradition and subjective faith.

Pinnock continues to use the term 'religion' to describe both tradition and faith though he qualifies the word in order to retain Smith's distinction. For example, behind the cumulative traditions Pinnock describes the following subjective reality: 'As subjective, religion is a universal dimension of human life where questions of truth, meaning, and value are asked. It is the sphere of ultimate concern, where people contemplate the highest good and worship God as they understand him.'[27] Pinnock uses this definition of religion as a complementary term for 'faith'. It allows him to distinguish between the conflicting truth claims or ideologies of religions as institutions but identify the common theme of faith in human experience. This distinction is crucial in Pinnock's work as we shall see. For now we may establish that Pinnock uses the term 'religion' in two different senses. The non-generic sense of religion means that which is culturally relative (Smith's 'cumulative tradition'). The generic sense of religion refers to a universally available personal response to God (Smith's 'faith').

It is objective religion that Pinnock describes as a patchwork quilt of good and bad. However, subjective religion is available to all and always good. God is concerned about this subjective religion: 'What God really cares about is faith and not theology,

---

[25] See W.C. Smith, *Patterns of Faith around the World*, 7–16, and *Towards a World Theology*, 113–29.

[26] Smith, *Patterns*, 12.

[27] *Wideness*, 85.

trust and not orthodoxy.'[28] In this way, even atheists may have a faith relationship to God.[29]

The purpose of religion

However, Pinnock is simply not consistent in this treatment of religion. On the one hand, he denies that religions are 'vehicles of salvation'.[30] Presumably this means that he denies the effectiveness of objective religion to bring salvation. However, on the other hand, he affirms that God is at work in religion. Presumably this means that objective religion can be used by God to bring people to salvation. God does this through the universal presence of his Spirit: 'Logically, if the breath of the gracious God is present, it follows that the Spirit is striving for life and wholeness in every sphere, including the religious.'[31]

So the Spirit of God is striving in some way to make even objective religion holy. This more positive evaluation affirms an effective link between objective and subjective religion. Subjective religion may raise the questions that create an objective religion God will use to draw all men and women to himself. Pinnock states that 'Religions as such do not mediate salvation.'[32] However, it is not clear what 'as such' means in this statement. Certainly, he affirms that 'God is drawing people to himself in a variety of ways, which can include the religious sphere.'[33] So though the explicit intention of religions may not be to lead people to salvation, in a Christian sense, nonetheless they may do so through the empowering presence of God.

Pinnock recognizes that there is much that is bad or evil about the world religions. The catalogue of evils and errors leads him to conclude: 'The idea that world religions ordinarily function as paths

---

[28] Ibid. 112.
[29] 'Inclusivist', 118.
[30] I.e. ibid. 99. To describe a religion as a 'vehicle of salvation' is to suggest that the religion as a historic institution provides the necessary means for men and women to find acceptance before God.
[31] Pinnock, 'Inclusivist', 102.
[32] Ibid. 116.
[33] Ibid.

to salvation is dangerous nonsense and wishful thinking.'[34] The pluralist seeks to argue that all the major religious traditions are legitimate means to a saving encounter with the divine reality. Pinnock is no pluralist. Indeed: 'Religions are not ordinarily stepping stones to Christ. More often, they are paths to hell.'[35] Through such forceful statements, Pinnock dismisses both pluralism and even the inclusivism of Roman Catholic theologian Karl Rahner. Pinnock is not reluctant to take a strong negative stance towards objective religion.

However, even these statements are ambiguous. In his presentation of the dark side of religion from Scripture, Pinnock points out that God's judgement is not only on paganism but also upon Israelite and Christian religion. The Israelites failed to keep the divine covenant, Jesus denounced many religious leaders of his day and the church herself may come under judgement. Though the world religions may be paths to hell, Pinnock also points out that 'One can go to hell as easily from church as from temple or mosque.'[36] The religious path to hell may be provided by any religion, including Christianity. We now find that Pinnock's denial that religions are vehicles of salvation is not as simple as it seems. Any objective religion, Christian or otherwise, may be a path to hell. Any subjective religion, whether found in a Christian or another, brings men and women into relationship with God.

Is there more to be affirmed about objective non-Christian religion? Pinnock is confident that there is. Religions may have access to aspects of spiritual reality that Christians know nothing about. They have 'positive contributions' and 'a wealth to share'.[37] Furthermore, religions have a role to play in helping people find God: 'we see religions reaching out to God, each in its own way'.[38] The positive value of religion lies in the fact that it is the means by which men and women ask ultimate questions and seek the reality of God. Because there is this sincere desire to seek God, the religions themselves may be used by God to draw men and women to himself. This is perhaps the nub of the ambiguity in Pinnock's position. He

---

[34] *Wideness*, 90.
[35] Ibid. 91.
[36] Ibid. 90.
[37] Ibid. 139.
[38] *Unbounded*, 33.

wants to deny the traditional inclusivist claim that religions may be vehicles of salvation. He is aware that such claims can lead quickly to a semi-Pelagian conclusion that salvation is through human endeavour. However, he also wants to affirm that God may choose to use religions to draw people to himself. Whether Pinnock is able to do this without raising the suspicions of developing a semi-Pelagian position is a question to which we must return.

Pinnock's inclusivism affirms the salvific purpose of objective religion, not in religions themselves, but in the purposes of God. God has sovereign intentions to make use of the world religions: 'It is safe to assume, even before reviewing the biblical evidence for it, that God will be working to bring those cultural entities we call religions into closer conformity with his purpose for the creation.'[39] This is a particularly positive statement of the purpose of objective religion. Given Pinnock's limited concept of divine sovereignty it is quite striking that such bold claims may be made for God's omnipotence in this matter. Even with his revised understanding of sovereignty, Pinnock declares that God may override human intentions and bring religions into conformity with his wider divine plan.[40]

According to Pinnock, the human searching for God expressed by objective religion is being met by his searching for humanity through the Spirit. It is the Holy Spirit who is at work leading religions to God: 'People look to religion for answers to deep questions. God is at work drawing them. Spirit, who is at work everywhere, is at work in the history of religions, and religions play a part in the history of grace, as the Spirit moves the world towards the kingdom.'[41] Pinnock draws up a range of biblical evidence for his claim. Central to this is his identification of a 'holy pagan tradition'.[42] Including the likes of Noah, Job, Jethro and Rahab, Pinnock identifies a class of people who are not part of the explicit Israelite community but who have faith in Yahweh. Again, he takes this to be explicable according to the distinction between objective and subjective religion. Their personal faith was in God, whatever

---

[39] *Wideness*, 116.

[40] As ably discussed by Patrick Richmond in this volume.

[41] *Flame of Love: A Theology of the Holy Spirit*, 203.

[42] *Wideness*, 81. 'Pagan' is rather an unfortunate term today but Pinnock adopts the expression from the work of Jean Daniélou (ibid. 109) and for the sake of consistency I will continue to use the term here.

failings their objective religion may have had. God was using that frail objective religion to lead them to himself.

This leads to the claim that Christ is, in some sense, the fulfilment of religion. Again, one must bear in mind the 'cautious' version of inclusivism with which Pinnock develops his theology. This allows him some ambiguity with regard to whether Christ is either the fulfilment of subjective or of objective religion. Regarding subjective religion, the gospel is fulfilment because 'It may not fulfil the religions as such, but it does fulfil the longings of the soul.'[43] If one purpose of religion is to ask ultimate questions then it may be true that the gospel is the ultimate answer to those questions and subjective religion finds its fulfilment in Christ. However, objective religion has its part to play here too: 'Even religions and their symbol systems are structures that give people dignity and hope. God is moving the world towards its fulfilment in Jesus Christ.'[44] The doctrine of sovereignty is relevant again as God somehow overrules human-made religions that are ordinarily 'paths to hell' so that they are caught up in God's transformation of human life into something pleasing to himself. The claim that God is 'moving the world' is difficult to assess. If by this, Pinnock means that all of human history is inexorably within God's plan and timing such that one day everyone will give an account to Christ then most Christians would agree with the claim. However, given Pinnock's doctrine of sovereignty it is unlikely he means this. It is more likely that Pinnock means God has a powerful influence upon all institutions in the world to lead those who belong to them into an encounter with Christ as Saviour.

Pinnock uses a principle of analogy to explain his understanding of fulfilment. Just as Christianity is the fulfilment of the Old Testament aspirations and prophecies of Israel, so too Christ is the fulfilment of pagan ambition:

> The history of Israel, for example, led to the coming of Jesus. Here God was at work apart from Jesus Christ but leading up to him. By analogy with Israel, we watch for anticipations in other faiths to be fulfilled in Christ. We do not affirm the possibility of God's revealing himself outside Christianity begrudgingly – we welcome it![45]

---

[43] Ibid. 102.
[44] Ibid. 103.
[45] *Flame*, 208.

The false assumption that leads this argument astray is the claim that God was at work in Israel 'apart' from Jesus Christ. Without doubt, a New Testament reading of the history of Israel is consistently Christocentric. The presence of Christ in all the Scriptures was an assumption of the apostles and has been held continuously throughout church history. The claims of Christ himself, 'These are the Scriptures that testify about me' (Jn. 5:39), and those of the apostles, 'Christ died for our sins according to the Scriptures' (1 Cor. 15:3), provide precedent for the reading of the Old Testament as an implicit revelation of Christ. God was not at work in Israel apart from Christ.

Pinnock argues that 'God' is more basic to Scripture than 'Christ'[46] and by doing so continues the same kind of distinction between faith and knowledge. According to Pinnock, the Bible is essentially God centred rather than Christ centred. This was also the controversial claim of the pluralist theologian, John Hick. He wanted to move Christians from being 'Christocentric' to being 'Theocentric' in his demand for a 'revolution' in theology. Hick urged 'a shift from the dogma that Christianity is at the centre to the realisation that it is *God* who is at the centre' of religious worship.[47] Doctrinal claims concerning the person of Christ are of only relative validity whereas the God beyond them is the true object of our worship. Hick sought to uncouple specific Christian knowledge from the more general category of faith in God and this allowed him to develop his pluralist theology.

While Pinnock remains a critic of Hick it is interesting to notice similarities in the structure of their arguments. Both rely upon a distinction between the specific, cognitive knowledge of Christians and a general, saving knowledge of God. However, the biblical claim is that God has been disclosed perfectly in Christ: 'The Son is the radiance of God's glory and the exact representation of his being' (Heb. 1:3, NIV). The distinction between God and Christ means little by Christian standards. Indeed, the God of the Old Testament is not left undefined but revealed as 'Yahweh', the Lord God (Ex. 3:16).[48] Hick's desire for an underdefined concept of God

---

[46] *Wideness*, 53.

[47] J. Hick, *God and the Universe of Faiths*, 131.

[48] See further Nathan MacDonald's essay in this volume.

stems from his assumption that the same reality must be at work in all the major religious traditions. By holding to this presupposition the concept of 'God' becomes vacuous. As Hick's work continued he would shift from speaking of God to speaking of 'ultimate Reality'.[49] This shift would also lead to the charge of agnosticism.[50] Pinnock also dangerously empties the notion of God of its determinative meaning in his treatment of Israel as analogous to pagan religions in its relationship to Christ.

The reason why Hick's argument has similarities to that of Pinnock is probably found in the fact that both are building on the work of Wilfred Cantwell Smith.[51] It is not that Pinnock is guilty by association with such theologians, but rather that his methodology shares certain features which leads him into similar problems. Pinnock and Hick seek to distinguish 'faith' from 'knowledge'.[52] By so doing, faith becomes an attitude of mind independent of any framework of belief. This definition makes it difficult to give any meaning to the distinction between true and false faith. The Christian definition of faith would certainly involve some specification of the object of that trust. Christian faith is faith *in* Christ. As Dewi Arwel Hughes comments on Smith's definition: 'it could be accepted only by a "Christian" who sees his or her belief about Jesus as peripheral to the essence of faith'.[53] Hughes points out that Smith not only distinguishes belief from faith but assumes that belief must

---

[49] Hick, *Interpretation*, 11.

[50] Forcefully argued by G. D'Costa, 'John Hick and Religious Pluralism: Yet Another Revolution' in H. Hewitt, *Problems in the Philosophy of Religion*, 3–18.

[51] We have already noted this with reference to Pinnock. Hick, in *God Has Many Names*, 5, along with his foreword to Smith, *Meaning*, refers to Smith's influence upon his own thought. In my assessment of these issues I am, of course, departing from the argument of my fellow contributor Chris Partridge who I would understand to be mistaken in some similar ways.

[52] Hick's doctoral thesis, prior to his adopting the pluralist view and prior to Smith's ground-breaking publication, is a conceptual account of how faith and knowledge are distinct categories. See J. Hick, *Faith and Knowledge*, first published 1957. I offer my own assessment of this in C. Sinkinson, *John Hick: An Introduction to his Theology*.

[53] D.A. Hughes, *Has God Many Names?*, 92.

presuppose faith. Faith then becomes a nebulous concept compatible with all kinds of contradictory doctrinal views.[54] As we continue to outline Pinnock's theology of religions we shall see that a certain vagueness in his account is not simply stylistic but the result of his non-cognitive understanding of faith.

To summarize Pinnock's view of the purpose of religion, he acknowledges that religion is ambiguous and a mixture of good and evil. The purpose of God is to use objective religion in order to lead men and women into a genuine faith relationship. This must mean that religions ultimately share a salvific purpose even if that were not their intention. Even if a religion was not deliberately created in order to lead men and women to Christ, this will be, to some extent, its function within the sovereign purposes of God. Given religious diversity, this leads us to ask how Pinnock suggests that we test the truth claims of religions. How do we disentangle truth from error, salvation from damnation?

Testing religion

We have already noted the role of the pragmatic test in Pinnock's *Case for Faith*. However, alongside the pragmatic test he also points to historical and logical tests that the truth-claims of religions may be subjected to.[55] In keeping with the Christian worldview he maintains that the central criterion for testing the validity of religious claims must be Christ himself.[56] What does this mean? Should religions conform to the express teaching of Jesus in matters both ethical and doctrinal? Should religions inspire behaviour that is similar to that of Jesus? Again, in seeking answers to these questions we meet with ambiguity.

Pinnock is clear that the doctrinal or explicit teaching of Jesus and the Scriptures on truth and error is not the central criterion. Apparently, 'the issue for God is not the content of theology but the

---

[54] This point regarding faith runs parallel to Alister McGrath's observation that Smith interprets the concept of truth in 'such an experimental and elastic manner that contradiction is virtually excluded as a matter of principle' (in Okholm and Phillips, *Four Views*, 161).

[55] Pinnock, *Unbounded*, 33–4.

[56] 'Inclusivist' 114; *Wideness*, 109.

reality of faith'.[57] The reality of faith is thus the subjective religion, not the expressed doctrinal convictions of a believer. This claim is oddly incongruous with Scripture. For example, Paul describes conversion this way: 'That if you confess with your mouth, "Jesus is Lord", and believe in your heart that God raised him from the dead, you will be saved. For it is with your heart that you believe and are justified, and it is with your mouth that you confess and are saved' (Rom. 10:9–10, NIV). The Jewish physiology was a little different from our own such that the seat of the intellect lay in the heart. Paul is not suggesting a heart response rather than an intellectual response because that distinction would not have made sense in this context. Commenting on this passage along with Acts 4:12, Pinnock denies that any negative claim is being made: 'They are celebrating the beauty of the gospel of Christ, not decrying earlier forms of the gracious divine working on which people had to depend before the gospel came.'[58] Regardless of Pinnock's extrapolation, the passage still affirms some sense of doctrinal, cognitive response to God. There is an intellectual belief followed by its verbal expression. Of course, it must be more than mere intellectual belief but it cannot be less than that. Indeed, if we examine Pinnock's 'holy pagan tradition' we find exactly this to be the case.

Melchizedek 'was a priest of God Most High' who had some knowledge that Abram was serving God's purposes in history (Gen. 14:18–20).[59] From the lips of Job we find the remarkable confession 'I know that my Redeemer lives, and that in the end he will stand upon the earth. And after my skin has been destroyed, yet in my flesh I will see God' (Job 19:25–6). It is hard to see the relevance of Abel and Noah given that the Genesis account assumes that at this point in history they would have had quite a high-level acquaintance with the creator God. Examples like Rahab and Ruth do little to help the case because they clearly join the covenant community of God. It is true that by using this evidence Pinnock is able to show that believers had different degrees of

---

[57] *Wideness*, 105.
[58] Response in Ockholm and Phillips, *Four Views*, 25.
[59] Pinnock discusses the meaning of this in 'Inclusivist', 109, where he describes El Elyôn as a pagan name for God. Yet 'God most High' is used regularly elsewhere to identify none other than Yahweh (i.e. Ps. 78:35); see further E. Jenni and C. Westermann (eds.), *Theological Lexicon of the Old Testament*, 2:107–12.

knowledge. However, what he is not able to show is any evidence that we have a right to use ethical criteria independently of cognitive criteria to substantiate the claim that non-Christians have saving faith. Pinnock's work raises the question whether one can have genuine faith without at least some minimal theology. Can one have a saving 'knowledge of God' without any intellectual knowledge of the God of Scripture? The 'holy pagan tradition' does not provide evidence of this.

Pinnock claims that Cornelius was an anonymous Christian of some kind before he met the apostle Peter. According to this interpretation, the role of the apostle was to bring the subjective faith of Cornelius to fulfilment. This point raises important questions. Did Peter commend Cornelius for already having an implicit faith relationship with God or was his commendation the realization that it is possible for Gentiles as well as Jews to become Christians as long as they come to God with a sincere desire to get right with him? What extra thing did Cornelius receive from the preaching of the gospel? According to Pinnock, only assurance and clarity of mind. As far as faith is concerned, he argues that Cornelius was already saved.[60] However, the point of the passage seems to be that God accepts both Jews and Gentiles into the church as they respond to the gospel. Luke makes very clear that Peter brought salvation to the household of Cornelius rather than simply more information or the gift of the Spirit. This is clear when Peter later explains that the angel had already said to Cornelius: 'Send to Joppa for Simon who is called Peter. He will bring you a message through which you and all your household will be saved' (Acts 11:14). The statement assumes that without a response to the gospel message Cornelius and his household remain unsaved. As John Stott describes Cornelius: 'his salvation came through his penitent, believing response to the gospel, not through his previous religion and righteousness'.[61]

On the assumption, which seems to be false, that Peter is affirming a faith already present, Pinnock draws out two criteria from the Cornelius incident. One is cognitive (pagans must fear God), and the other ethical (pagans must do what is right).[62] We may consider

---

[60] *Wideness*, 166.
[61] John Stott in D.L. Edwards, *Essentials: A Liberal-Evangelical Dialogue*, 323.
[62] *Wideness*, 96.

the cognitive criteria a little further. No evangelicals argue that all believers must share the same level of cognitive content in order to be saved. The issue is only what would count as minimal content for us to consider someone a true believer.

In the case of Cornelius he was in a class of people described in Scripture as 'God fearing'. This means that they had some knowledge of Yahweh, the Old Testament Scriptures and Jewish tradition, without themselves being Jews. Cornelius clearly had explicit knowledge of the Lord God. Pinnock generalizes this sense of knowledge to include any veneration of a divine creator. This includes Jews, Muslims and those who belong to African tribal religions.[63] However, the mere fact that Christians, Jews and Muslims affirm the worship of a creator is simply not enough to establish that they worship the same God. Indeed, as Carson points out, 'By this sort of criterion, Pinnock seems prepared to say that people believe in some *other* god only if their god is unlike the biblical God on every conceivable front.'[64] A single overlapping characteristic cannot establish the case. Mormons and Christians both speak of a creator God but in the former case this claim is qualified by limitations upon God's uniqueness and eternity that make it problematic to affirm that they both worship the same God. Pinnock's broad generalization of what is identified by 'God' allows him to include most religious people within the cognitive criterion. However, in accordance with this test Pinnock does identify religions that fail. In these terms, he describes Zen Buddhism as an example of failure to fear God because it is atheistic.

However, the ethical criterion passes more forms of religion than the slightly restrictive cognitive criterion. Pinnock describes much that is noble, good and commendable in the behaviour of the world religions. Indeed, the founders of great religions are to be examples for us of righteousness. Having faulted Zen Buddhism by the cognitive criterion, Pinnock affirms the broader Buddhist religion by the ethical criterion. Indeed, Gautama the Buddha spoke of a 'gracious and good power . . . which promotes redemption and salvation'.[65] Thus, even Buddhism is in touch with God after all. The teachings

---

[63] Ibid. 97.
[64] D.A. Carson, *The Gagging of God*, 295.
[65] *Wideness*, 100.

of the Buddha, which were at best agnostic,[66] still promote salvation.

How does one go about using these cognitive and ethical criteria? This calls for some form of apologetic encounter between religions. Pinnock commends some form of inter-religious dialogue as the proper form of apologetic engagement. Indeed, he argues that the example of the apostle Paul teaches us the centrality of dialogue to evangelism: 'Paul was prepared to begin the conversation with people to see where it would lead.'[67] Pinnock concedes that evangelicals have shied away from dialogue for fear of relativism. Many proponents of inter-religious dialogue have argued for a relativistic framework where no absolute truth claims can really be made.[68] Pinnock does not deny that there is an objective truth which should not be sacrificed on the altar of tolerance. However, he also leaves open certain questions regarding where dialogue will take us in the future. He continues his distinction between faith (a response to Jesus) and knowledge (orthodox theology) by pointing out that our purpose in dialogue is 'to see people become followers of Jesus, whether or not they become baptized members of our churches'.[69] Quite what it means to follow Jesus without being obedient to his commands to be baptized and join with his other followers is not clear. However, Pinnock is resolved to retain this distinction between faith and knowledge. Dialogue might lead to a transformation of Buddhism whereby Buddhists become followers of Jesus without becoming Christians or belonging to churches: 'What God wants to do with the religions in history is his business. History is open-ended as far as these institutions are concerned.'[70] Pinnock keeps the door wide open for the idea that other religions might become vehicles of salvation through the process of inter-religious encounter with Christianity.[71]

---

[66] H.M. Vroom, *Religions and the Truth*, 158–9.

[67] *Wideness*, 131.

[68] E.g. L. Swidler (ed.), *Death or Dialogue?*; D. Lochhead, *The Dialogical Imperative*.

[69] *Wideness*, 146–7.

[70] Ibid. 147.

[71] Given 2,000 years of religious history it is worth asking where historically one can find this happening? Perhaps Professor Don Cupitt, of Cambridge, describing himself as a Christian-Buddhist, could be seen as an example of this kind of development in practice.

The significance of dialogue in the New Testament is that it suggests that there is some kind of 'point of contact' between Christian and non-Christian thought. If by dialogue Pinnock simply meant engagement through points of contact then there would be little disagreement. He points out examples of this in Christian engagement with ancient Greek philosophy, so why should one not seek points of contact with Muslims or Buddhists? The classic evangelical claim is that the knowledge of God the creator is universally available although consistently suppressed by sinful hearts. Vestiges of this knowledge are to be expected among non-Christians. For example, Bruce Demarest is confident enough to claim that

> through universal consciousness of dependence upon a supreme being, the universal sense of the difference between right and wrong, the order, regularity and intelligibility of nature, and the continuous judgements on persons and nations in history, God is known in rudimentary fashion by all people in all times and places.[72]

There is no reason to deny some sense of a general revelation of God in creation. What is open to question is whether it can do any good without a response to God's special revelation in Christ. It is this distinction that Pinnock repudiates: 'We are told to believe that special revelation is gracious, but general revelation itself is not.'[73] All revelation is special and creates the possibility of salvation or it is not revelation at all. In making this claim Pinnock has also dispensed with the distinction between special and common grace. The classic evangelical claim is that God's grace is active globally but God's saving grace is expressed through the preaching of the gospel. Though Pinnock is critical of this distinction it is hardly without exegetical warrant.[74]

---

[72] B. Demarest, 'General and Special Revelation: Epistemological Foundations of Religious Pluralism' in A.D. Clarke and B.W. Winter (eds.), *One God One Lord in a World of Religious Pluralism*, 143.

[73] 'Inclusivist', 253

[74] The essay by Daniel Strange identifies helpful distinctions regarding grace and revelation. See also C. Gunton, 'The Trinity, Natural Theology and a Theology of Nature' in K.J. Vanhoozer (ed.), *The Trinity in a Pluralistic Age: Theological Essays on Culture and Religion.*

A useful evidential resource for Pinnock's claim is found in Don Richardon's volume *Eternity in Their Hearts*.[75] This is a collection of stories gathered from missionary experiences that do seem to suggest a global knowledge of the creator God. In some cases remarkable knowledge of God's character, the fall of humankind and the need for a redeemer have been known among people who have lived entirely in isolation from Christianity or Judaism. The work does not carry much critical appraisal of the claims it presents but the mere possibility of such knowledge can be explained theologically. Indeed, given even the limited claims Demarest makes for general revelation there is good reason to expect such knowledge to be abundant in the world.[76] For example, the Mbaka people of the Central African Republic have a religion with many Judaeo-Christian parallels including practices of baptism and animal sacrifice. Richardson declares that they have 'redemptive lore'. However, his claim is limited to the fact that this lore 'contributes to the redemption of a people solely by facilitating their understanding of what redemption means'.[77] Such lore does not actually provide the means of salvation. The gospel was necessary to bring redemption but knowledge of what redemption would require was already known among the Mbaka. Richardson's evidence fits well with the classic understanding of general revelation and common grace.

The prime motivation for Pinnock's work on the nature of saving faith and his affirmation of its presence among non-Christians stems from his distaste with the alternative. If salvation requires a personal, cognitive response to the person and work of Christ then must we consider condemned the many millions of men and women who have not had the opportunity to hear the message? To this question we must turn.

---

[75] D. Richardson, *Eternity in Their Hearts*.

[76] Demarest castigates Richardson for collapsing the general/special revelation distinction but I don't think this problem is necessarily evident in 'Eternity in Their Hearts', which makes no real claim for salvation apart from the preaching of the gospel (Demarest, 'General and Special Revelation', 146–7).

[77] Richardson, *Eternity*, 59.

Finding salvation

Evangelicals have not always maintained the restrictivist position regarding other religions. Loraine Boettner is often quoted as an example of a hardline restrictivist.[78] Building upon the Reformed doctrine of the absolute sovereignty of God, Boettner claims that God never intended the unevangelized to be saved. If he had intended their conversion then he would have provided gospel preachers. In an oft-maligned passage Boettner comments on the unevangelized: 'When God places people in such conditions we may be sure that He has no more intention that they be saved than He has that the soil of northern Siberia, which is frozen all year round, shall produce crops of wheat.'[79] However, even Boettner is not quite so restrictivist as this may sound. His strong doctrine of election allows him to reach the conclusion that all who die in infancy will be saved. This is not because such infants are guiltless with regard to original sin but because their premature death is evidence of their election.[80] Nonetheless, restrictivism is not popular among evangelicals today.

Many evangelicals have understood the problem and sought to explain the difficulty without overt recourse to the doctrine of election.[81] Pinnock describes himself as having been helped a great deal by Norman Anderson who wrote an extremely useful work on the relationship between Christianity and other religions.[82] Using the classic distinction between special and general revelation he was able to make favourable assessments of certain features in non-Christian religions without in any way suggesting that God was using religions to bring men and women to himself. However, Anderson conceded that it might be possible for a non-Christian to

---

[78] He is dealt with in J. Sanders, *No Other Name*, 50–51.

[79] L. Boettner, *The Reformed Doctrine of Predestination*, 120.

[80] See also B.B. Warfield, 'The Development of the Doctrine of Infant Salvation' in idem, *Studies in Theology*, 411–44, and R.A. Webb, *The Theology of Infant Salvation*.

[81] Helm, 'Are They Few'; John Stott in Edwards, *Essentials*, 320–29; C. Wright, *The Uniqueness of Jesus*, 50–51; Alister McGrath in Okholm and Phillips, *Four Views*, 151–80. Pinnock is very favourable in his response to McGrath's 'particularist' position but admits that it relies too much on a Reformed theology which he does not share.

[82] N. Anderson, *Christianity and World Religions*.

reach a point where they realized the futility of any kind of salvation by works and recognized their need for divine grace. If this were to happen it would be because 'the God of all mercy had worked in his heart by his Spirit, bringing him in some measure to realize his sin and need for forgiveness, and enabling him, in the twilight as it were, to throw himself on God's mercy'.[83] According to Anderson this would require some special work of God, through his Spirit, in bringing men and women to an understanding of their need for a redeemer. Perhaps this point in their lives would be expressed in language similar to that which we have referred to as found on the lips of Job. This position is a great deal more cautious and careful than that of Pinnock. While Anderson suggest a possibility at work among individuals, Pinnock argues that the structures of the world's religions are being used by God for his salvific purposes.

In contrast to Pinnock's position it would be more biblical to say that regarding those who belong to other religions, if there are those who are saved it is in spite of their religions and not through them. This provides the key distinction between exclusivism and inclusivism. The inclusivist seeks means through which a non-Christian might be saved not in spite of but through their religious affiliations. Here Pinnock's position really parts company with evangelical exclusivism. Pinnock describes the religions as responses to general revelation that are being drawn by the universal spirit of God toward himself. This is as close to calling religions 'vehicles of salvation' as Pinnock will get and it is very close indeed.

The pressure Pinnock feels is no doubt shared by most thoughtful Christians. There is a widespread cautious optimism among evangelicals regarding the problematic case of those who have never heard the gospel. In contrast, though Pinnock frequently deals with those who have never heard, they are not really his focus. For example, he closes an essay by posing this question: 'Is God's grace limited to the relatively few who, often through accidents of time and geography, happen to have responded to the gospel?'[84]

---

[83] N. Anderson, *Christianity*, 148–9.

[84] 'Inclusivist', 255. In passing one might note that the classic evangelical position does not make any such limitation on God's common grace, only on the saving grace of God. God's grace is globally available but his saving grace is mediated through the special work of his Spirit especially through the preaching of the gospel.

The interesting point about this question is that Pinnock is not asking whether the availability of God's grace is being restricted to those who have heard the gospel. He is asking whether saving grace is restricted to those who have responded to the gospel. This is very significant. Pinnock's focus isn't simply those who have never heard but those who have never responded. Therefore, all non-Christians have alternative routes to God's grace and not just the unevangelized or children dying in infancy. As we have seen, Pinnock's framework affirms that even atheists living in evangelized lands may have saving faith. It is not only those who have never heard whom God might reach in a special way but even those who hear and reject that message.

However, at this point we reach a crucial question. How do we discern the saving work of God among people? Because Pinnock resists a cognitive definition of 'faith' a cognitive criterion is not appropriate. We cannot simply ask what it is that people believe about God or salvation. Instead, Pinnock rests his case on ethical criteria. Faith is present where qualities of goodness, love and justice are present. Indeed, if one can only see moral change – there being no verbal expression – Pinnock concedes that this is enough.[85] He consistently uncouples the connection between faith and knowledge: 'God looks for faith in us more than for theological knowledge. We are saved by faith, not by what we know (Heb. 11:6).'[86]

According to Pinnock, God relates to persons in terms of 'a heart response and faith direction'.[87] While he underlines the determinative nature of God's grace in prompting this behaviour, such determination must be interpreted in the light of his own particular libertarian anthropology. Therefore, the issue is not that we have certain knowledge but that our lives are heading in the right direction. Is there goodness and are there Christlike qualities being realized in our lives? The only criterion we can use to assess the presence of grace is the character of human behaviour.

These problems may be clarified by making brief reference to Pinnock's idea that there will be a post-mortem encounter with Christ before the issue of judgement is settled. The moral decisions

---

[85] *Wideness*, 98.
[86] *Unbounded*, 142.
[87] *Wideness*, 112.

of this life will be confirmed at that time. Pinnock asks whether really wicked people, like Adolf Hitler, might be saved at that point: what injustice if they were, he ponders! His answer basically means that good people will be saved and bad people will be lost.

> Someone like Job, who loved God already in life on earth, would receive the Good News about Jesus gladly, because that is what he was longing for. Someone like Herod, on the other hand, who sought to kill the baby Jesus on earth, would only hate God all the more on the last day because he would see more grace in God to hate.[88]

God's intense and salvific love is the same for every man and woman who will stand before him, 'the variable is the condition of the human souls appearing in God's presence'.[89] If there is no discrimination in the way God's grace touches all lives then the only additional component that will make a difference in judgement is the quality of human behaviour. Pinnock's use of Job as an example is misleading here. He identifies Job as one who 'loved God already in life on earth' – because Job had cognitive knowledge of the God of the covenant and responded to him in love and repentance. It is exactly this cognitive knowledge that is absent from his notion of implicit faith. The kind of evidence that someone is longing for Christ is really no different from good ethical behaviour. Pinnock's comment that divine grace prompts such behaviour does little to assuage the fears that we have entered a Pelagian world of salvation by works.

Conclusion

Pinnock asks important questions regarding the fate of the unevangelized and the place of non-Christian religions within the purposes of God for human history. It is possible that there simply are no concrete answers that can be given and many evangelicals will prefer to remain agnostic regarding such issues. Pinnock is a bold theologian to write on this theme and his honesty and integrity is commendable. It is also welcome that Pinnock maintains the

---

[88] Ibid. 170.
[89] Ibid. 171

necessity of an atoning work on our behalf through Christ as the ground of salvation. However, I consider his theological framework to be seriously faulty. Terms such as 'faith', 'god' and 'salvation' are emptied of meaningful content. He has defined his terms in such a way that they can encompass any religion. In contrast, I would suggest that the terms have specific meaning within Scripture, which prevents such elastic application. The mere fact that Mormons, Christians and Hindus may all speak of faith, god and salvation does not mean that they are all talking about the same thing.

It is ironic that many contemporary, non-evangelical theologians have begun to move in entirely the opposite direction to Pinnock. The post-liberal theologians have emphasized the formative role of doctrine and belief. As George Lindbeck recognized: 'Luther did not invent his doctrine of justification by faith because he had a tower experience, but rather the tower experience was made possible by his discovering . . . the doctrine in the Bible.'[90] While post-liberalism raises problems of its own, such statements are a helpful corrective to the vague liberal notion that undefined experience gives rise to doctrinal claims.[91] Applying his thought to pluralism, Lindbeck concludes: 'Adherents of different religions do not diversely thematize the same experience; rather they have different experiences.'[92] The recognition that experience is already theory-laden has become a key theme in contemporary theology and philosophy. This should not be a new discovery for evangelical thought.[93] If we are to retain the meaningfulness of our terms then the 'God' of the Bible is not the 'God' of the *Bhagavadgita* and the 'faith' of Job is not the 'faith' of the Buddha. There are many good people who are Buddhists or Muslims but they, like Christians, stand in need of personal repentance and faith in a redeemer who can forgive. Whether this has happened or not can only be judged

---

[90] G.A. Lindbeck, *The Nature of Doctrine*, 39.

[91] Evangelical responses to the post-liberal arguments are found in T.R. Phillips and D.L. Okholm (eds.), *The Nature of Confession*. A very helpful assessment of Lindbeck is provided in A.E. McGrath, *The Genesis of Doctrine*, 14–34.

[92] G.A. Lindbeck, *Doctrine*, 40.

[93] Francis Schaeffer affirmed this in his approval of the work of Michael Polanyi. See F.A. Schaeffer, *Collected Writings*, 1:313–18.

by the cognitive criteria of Scripture. With such evidence unavailable there is simply nothing we can say about those who have never heard. However, regarding the world religions as institutions, a judgement is possible. Do they teach people their own sinfulness and need of redemption? Do they point their adherents to the need for a sacrificial substitute? Without such evidence one cannot see how God is moving the religions towards fulfilment in Christ. The 'faith' Pinnock defends, and affirms as present in the world religions, is little more than general, moral goodness.

9

A Hermeneutic of Hopefulness:
A Christian Personalist Response to
Clark Pinnock's Inclusivism
Christopher Partridge

Introduction

As one of the most important contemporary evangelical thinkers willing to face difficult questions and to engage critically and creatively with some key issues, theologies and philosophies, Clark Pinnock has done a great deal that is good for evangelical theology. As such his voice deserves a more sympathetic hearing than it has so far received by the evangelical community. This is nowhere more true than in his attempt to construct a theology of religions,[1] the development of which should be one of the most pressing concerns of contemporary Christian theology, not least evangelical theology. Informed by a broad grasp of Christian thought and a devout evangelical piety, his accessible work in this area provides a much needed corrective to the often uninformed responses of many evangelical Christians. While we may not agree with every aspect of his thesis, faced with the need for a cogent response to the issues raised by interfaith dialogue and religious plurality, we are indebted

---

[1] See the following: 'The Finality of Jesus Christ in the World Religions' in M.A. Noll and D.F. Wells (eds.), *Christian Faith and Practice in the Modern World*, 152–68; 'Toward an Evangelical Theology of Religions', 359–68; *A Wideness in God's Mercy: The Finality of Jesus Christ in a World of Religions*; 'An Inclusivist View' in D.L. Okholm and T.R. Phillips (eds.), *Four Views on Salvation in a Pluralistic World*, 95–123.

to Professor Pinnock for going some way to addressing these concerns from a biblical perspective.[2]

The following discussion is primarily concerned with Professor Pinnock's understanding of the methods God employs in order to communicate with and save the unevangelized in this life, particularly his understanding of general revelation, the Logos and the Holy Spirit.[3] Furthermore, with the intention of contributing to the construction of an evangelical inclusivism,[4] the essay both defends the principal thrust of Pinnock's work and, in dialogue with it, sets forth an explicitly personalist approach (many aspects of which, needless to say, will require more theological and philosophical justification than it is possible to offer here[5]).

For those unfamiliar with the term 'personalist', in brief, I am using it in this essay as shorthand for the type of theology that emphasizes the personal and relational nature of God, humanity and divine–human relations.[6] This is based on the conviction that this personalist view of reality is set forth throughout the biblical narrative and supremely in the person and work of Jesus Christ. More specifically:

---

[2] I was disappointed not to see the inclusion of an extract from Pinnock's work in the recent collection of readings edited by Richard Plantinga, *Christianity and Plurality: Classic and Contemporary Readings*.

[3] It does not therefore address his arguments for a post-mortem encounter as set out in *Wideness*, 168–72.

[4] While, for convenience, I will use the terms 'exclusivist', 'inclusivist' and 'pluralist' in this essay, I have long felt that, logically, all three paradigms are 'exclusivist' and that therefore the threefold typology is redundant. All three approaches set up norms, make exclusivist claims and establish criteria for deciding truth. This point has been made well by G. D'Costa in 'The Impossibility of a Pluralist View of Religions', 223–32.

[5] For a fuller discussion see C.H. Partridge, *H.H. Farmer's Theological Interpretation of Religion: Towards a Personalist Theology of Religions*.

[6] A list of the most important personalist thinkers, all of whom develop distinctive forms of personalism, would include, from a philosophical perspective, the British philosopher John Macmurray, the American philosophers B.P. Bowne and E.S. Brightman and the Jewish philosopher Martin Buber, who wrote the important and influential work *I and Thou*. In Christian theology, such a list would include the British theologians John Oman and H.H. Farmer, the German theologian Karl Heim and the Swiss theologian Emil Brunner.

1.   We were created to live in relationship with each other (hence the importance of loving relationships and communities for the development of healthy persons) and with God (hence the importance of Christ, divine-human reconciliation and the Christian community for healthy spirituality).

2.   To use Martin Buber's famous terminology, there is a difference between *I-thou* relationships and *I-it* relationships. For example, I have an *I-it* relationship with my computer, in that, because it is not a person with a will to respect or to seek the consent of, I can manipulate it in accordance with my will; it becomes an instrument of my will. I do not have such a relationship with my wife. However, should my wife or I ever descend to the level of treating the other dictatorially or manipulatively, our loving *I-thou* relationship would be seriously eroded and become more of an *I-it* relationship in which one of us is then treated less like a person and more like an object. The point is that, to the extent that a will is overridden and pressed into the service of another will, that relationship is depersonalized: persons become objects. Needless to say, the more relationships are of this *I-it* nature, the more unhealthy and destructive they are emotionally, psychologically, spiritually and, often, physically. On the other hand, the more relationships are of an *I-thou* nature, the ideal being relationships of love and trust, the more healthy they are.

3.   God is the source and ground of the personal world. Although, theoretically, he could be dictatorially coercive or manipulative in a way that violates personhood and treats humans like objects or will-less puppets, he will not act in this way. Rather, within the terms of the personal world, God is tirelessly and self-sacrificially reaching out in reconciling love to the persons he has created. He seeks reconciliation between humans, the establishment of loving communities and, above all, divine-human reconciliation.

4.   Not least because of the continuity and interconnectedness of the personal world, the effects of divine-human reconciliation cannot but overflow into a person's relationships with other persons in a multitude of positive and enriching ways. Similarly, of course, poor relationships, whether human-human or divine-human, will have a negative impact upon other areas of

one's relational life. A person cannot, for example, hate another person, or treat another person manipulatively without
it affecting one's relationship with God.[7]

5.   The church, the community of the reconciled, the body of
     Christ, is both the inevitable by-product of divine-human rec-
     onciliation and the ideal community within which to live the
     reconciled life. Although humans sinfully inhibit the effects of
     reconciliation, the divine pressure is always towards the estab-
     lishment of divine-human and human-human relationships
     which witness to the loving nature of God.

From a Christian personalist perspective, a perspective which is
fundamentally Christ-centred, whether one thinks of election,
atonement, Scripture, anthropology, the sacraments or indeed any
aspect of Christian belief and practice, it is correctly understood
when it is interpreted relationally.[8]

The foundation stones of Pinnock's inclusivism

Pinnock's theology of religions is relatively straightforward. Central
to his thesis are two fundamental, interconnected axioms. These are
the *universality* axiom and the *particularity* axiom: 'the first consists of
the boundless mercy of God which makes possible an optimism of
salvation; the second axiom consists of the finality of Jesus Christ as
the decisive manifestation and ground of God's grace toward sinners'.[9] As he argues, these are central to the message of the Bible.
'For God so loved the world [universality] that he gave his one and
only Son [particularity]' (Jn. 3:16, NIV).[10]

---

[7] The indissoluble connection between divine-human and human-human relations is evident throughout the Bible. Whether one thinks of
marital relations, parent-child relations, relations with enemies, it is made
very clear that 'whoever loves God must also love his brother' (1 Jn 4:21).
See e.g. Ex. 20:12; Lev. 19:18,34; Mt. 5:44–6; 7:12; 18:10; Jn. 13:34–5;
15:13; 1 Cor. 13:1–7; Gal. 5:22; Eph. 5:25; 1 Jn. 4:7–11; 5:2.
[8] For a more comprehensive overview of Christian personalism see
Partridge, *H.H. Farmer's*, ch. 1.
[9] *Wideness*, 49.
[10] For a short but worthwhile discussion of the biblical support for these
two axioms see J. Sanders, *No Other Name*, 25ff., 257ff.

Does God desire the salvation of all persons or has he created persons with whom he does not desire communion? Although there are Christians who, working with a doctrine of limited atonement, would want to argue that, while God might love everyone, he has only provided for the salvation of certain people,[11] I suspect that the majority of contemporary Christians, including evangelicals, would understand passages such as John 3:16 and 1 Timothy 2:3 in a way that indicates universality: 'God our Saviour . . . wants *all men* to be saved and to come to a knowledge of the truth' (NIV). Making the most of such passages, Pinnock develops an essentially Wesleyan thesis, central to which is the conviction that God's grace is universal and the atonement unlimited. God's redemptive work in Christ is intended for all.[12]

Pinnock, however, is not simply concerned to state the case for God's universal salvific will; he also wants to argue against the belief that only a few people will ultimately be saved. 'My intention is . . . specifically to refute the fewness doctrine and replace it with an optimism of salvation based in Scripture.'[13] In other words, he rejects the doctrine that only those who have explicitly heard the Christian message are in a position to be saved. If God truly loves all and

---

[11] L. Boettner's rigorous Calvinist logic leads him to declare that those geographically isolated from the gospel have been 'providentially placed in pagan darkness'. Moreover, he continues, 'when God *places people* in such conditions we may be sure that he has no more intention that they will be saved than he has that the soil of northern Siberia, which is frozen all the year round, shall produce crops of wheat' (L. Boettner, *The Reformed Doctrine of Predestination*, 120, quoted in J. Sanders, *No Other Name*, 50–51). For an interesting discussion of 'hyper-Calvinist' views of mission and other faiths see K. Cracknell, *Justice, Courtesy and Love: Theologians and Missionaries Encountering World Religions, 1846–1914*, 20ff.

[12] 'There can be no question that Paul means to say that the one died for all mankind . . . [Moreover] even the places where the word "many" is used must be interpreted in this wide and universal sense . . . Joachim Jeremias has shown that practically everywhere in the New Testament in the passages concerning the death of Christ for the many the meaning is that he died for all. Paul's proclamation that God was reconciling the world to himself and John's statement that the Lamb carries the sins of the world are therefore representative of New Testament theology as a whole' (W.A. Visser't Hooft, *No Other Name*, 99–100).

[13] *Wideness*, 17.

desires all to be saved, it is very difficult to argue cogently that he could both be this sort of God and limit the possibility of salvation to the very slim stream of human history which has heard the gospel, let alone the far smaller number of humans who have actually understood it in a meaningful way. While wanting to insist that Christ is 'the Way, the Truth and the Life', I am convinced that many conservative Christians would nevertheless feel the force of the following words of John Hick:

> We say as Christians that God is the God of universal love, that he is the creator and father of all mankind, that he wills the ultimate good and salvation of all men. But we also say, traditionally, that the only way to salvation is the Christian way. And yet we know, when we stop to think about it, that the large majority of the human race who have lived and died up to the present moment have lived either before Christ or outside the borders of Christendom. Can we then accept the conclusion that the God of love who seeks to save all mankind has nevertheless ordained that men must be saved in such a way that only a small minority can in fact receive this salvation?[14]

While Pinnock wants to address this apparent moral contradiction, he is unwilling to tread Hick's pluralist path which abandons the doctrine of Christ's finality and, arguably, leads only to agnosticism. Indeed, Pinnock even makes the rather dubious claim that it is 'important' to reject the fewness doctrine because otherwise one invites 'pluralist theologies to come into play'.[15] While one can agree that it is important for Christians to be aware of the consequences of their statements and avoid giving needless offence, it has to be said that the possible danger of leading a person to accept pluralist/relativist theologies (as was the case with Hick who started his career as an exclusivist[16] is, in the final analysis, no reason at all, let alone an important reason, to reject the fewness doctrine. Doctrines should not be determined by their general acceptability or popularity.[17]

---

[14] Hick, *God and the Universe of Faiths*, 122.

[15] *Wideness*, 17.

[16] See Hick, *God Has Many Names*, 2ff.

[17] Pinnock's concern that Hick was driven to pluralism because of 'unacceptable' Christian doctrines seems a little inconsistent with his rejection

The only sound theological reason for rejecting the belief that only a tiny number of people will ultimately be saved is that the Bible itself encourages an optimism of salvation.

Pinnock's rejection of pessimism regarding God's intentions is rooted in his doctrine of God who 'is patient . . . not wanting *anyone* to perish, but *everyone* to come to repentance' (2 Pet. 3:9, NIV; emphasis mine). He thus argues that contemporary evangelical theologians need to begin by revising a theology founded on 'a cruel and arbitrary deity' and establishing an optimism of salvation which insists that 'God is committed to a full racial salvation. The God we love and trust is not One to be satisfied until there is a healing of the nations and an innumerable host of redeemed people around his throne (Rev. 7:9; 21:24–26; 22:2–6).'[18] If we accept that, as H.R. Mackintosh once commented, 'God loves us even more than he loves himself',[19] then, again, it is difficult not to feel the force of at least this point of Pinnock's thesis.

The belief that 'God judges the heathen in relation to the light they have, not according to the light that did not reach them',[20] also relies heavily on a particular understanding of faith. With reference to Hebrews 11, he argues that faith in God, regardless of the extent of theological understanding, is salvifically efficacious. For example (and it is not difficult to find other biblical examples), concerning non-Israelites such as Naaman (2 Kgs. 5:15–18) and characters living prior to the call of Abram such as Abel, Enoch and Noah, it is clear that 'these men, being neither Jews nor Christians, pleased God because they sought him with the faith response which pleases him'.[21] Enoch 'was commended as one who pleased God. And without faith it is impossible to please God . . .' (Heb. 11:5–6, NIV). The Bible 'recognises faith, neither Jewish nor Christian, which is nonetheless noble, uplifting, and sound'.[22] Abel,

---

[17] (*continued*)   of those theologians who simply bow to current trends and cultural pressure. See e.g. 'Toward', 362.

[18] Ibid. 19–20.

[19] Quoted in T.F. Torrance, 'The Atonement. The Singularity of Christ and the Finality of the Cross: The Atonement and the Moral Order' in N.M. de S. Cameron (ed.), *Universalism and the Doctrine of Hell*, 235.

[20] Pinnock, 'Toward', 367. Pinnock unfortunately uses here an outdated and offensive generalization, 'the heathen'.

[21] *Wideness*, 22.

[22] See ibid. 92.

Enoch, Noah, Job, Abimelech, Jethro, Rahab, Ruth, Naaman, the Queen of Sheba, Melchizedek, Cornelius and other 'pagan saints' were, he argues, 'believing men and women who enjoyed a right relationship with God and lived saintly lives, under the terms of the wider covenant God made with Noah'.[23] For example, whatever the identity of the mysterious Canaanite priest-king of Salem, Melchizedek ('king of righteousness'), he seems to provide some support for 'a hermeneutic of hopefulness'.[24] Not only does Abraham accept a blessing and give tithes to this priest of El Elyôn (Gen. 14:17–20) – El also being, significantly, the Canaanite high God – but he is revered elsewhere in the Bible (Ps. 110:4; Heb. 5:6,10; 6:20; 7:1–3). Hence Pinnock has a point when he claims that 'the compiler of Genesis wants to tell us that, though Abram had a special calling from the Lord, he is not to think (and we are not to think) that there are no other believers among the nations and no positive contributions to be appreciated from non-Israelite religions and culture'.[25] He thus chastises evangelicals for not taking the 'pagan saint' phenomenon seriously enough and adjusting their pessimistic theologies accordingly:

> For some reason evangelicals have tended to conceal God's generosity in the Bible. We feel a little uncomfortable with the fact that Daniel expected King Nebuchadnezzar to know who the God of heaven was and respect him, and the fact that pagan sailors on Jonah's boat feared God and sacrificed to him. In order to protect, as we suppose, the uniqueness of God we have suppressed this positive witness to universal revelation.[26]

---

[23] See ibid. For a helpful discussion of the significance of the covenant with Noah see G. Fackre, *The Doctrine of Revelation: A Narrative Interpretation*, 61ff.

[24] 'I intend to make the case for salvation optimism, and for a hermeneutic of hopefulness that may assist us in negotiating a necessary paradigm shift away from our current pessimism . . . I want evangelicals to move away from the attitude of pessimism based upon bad news to the attitude of hopefulness based on Good News, from restrictivism to hopefulness, from exclusivism to generosity. If we could but recover the scope of God's love, our lives and not just our theology of religions could be transformed' (Pinnock, *Wideness*, 20).

[25] Ibid. 26.

[26] 'Finality', 160.

According to the Bible, people can believe in God, earnestly seek him and be saved without explicit knowledge of Christ and without being a member of the covenant community of Israel. Does this not, therefore, give us hope that God might deal likewise with those who, for example, live after the advent of Christ, but are in the same position simply because they were born in a geographical location which made access to the gospel impossible? On the basis of 'the faith principle' (the principle that salvation depends on fulfilling the conditions of Heb. 11:6), Pinnock argues that Christians can be hopeful. There are 'true believers in the wider world who trust God and walk faithfully before him . . . From the earliest chapters of the Bible we learn a fundamental (if neglected) truth, that salvation history is coextensive with world history and its goal is the healing of all the nations.'[27]

Turning to the second of Pinnock's axioms, *particularity*, there is no doubt in Pinnock's mind as to the truth and significance of John 14:6.[28] Pinnock firmly and forthrightly emphasizes the uniqueness and finality of Jesus Christ for human salvation. He defends a high Christology,[29] he attacks relativism,[30] and he insists that 'God is reconciling the world to himself, not through religious experience, not through natural revelation, not through prophets alone, not through all the religions of the world, but exclusively through Jesus Christ.'[31]

Having made these claims, he argues that 'a biblically based Christology does not entail a narrowness of outlook towards other people. The church's confession about Jesus is compatible with an open spirit, with an optimism of salvation, and with a wider hope. Sensitivity to religious pluralism does not require radical revision of our doctrine of Christ.'[32] His point is simply that, while salvation is

---

[27] *Wideness*, 22–3.

[28] See ibid. 79.

[29] 'the Chalcedonian definition is a permanent fixture and an accurate (so far as it goes) description of Christ's true identity . . . Christians ought to confess that Jesus was and is the unique vehicle and means of God's saving love in the world, and its definitive Saviour . . . There is a kind of exclusivity here that simply cannot be given up' ('Finality', 155). See also *Wideness*, 52ff.; 'Toward', 362f.

[30] See *Wideness*, 69ff.; 'Toward', 363.

[31] *Wideness*, 49.

[32] Ibid. 74.

always through Christ, it is not necessary for a person to have explicit knowledge of Christ to be included in that salvation. However, as we will see below, while Pinnock comes very close to the statements of Vatican II and, by implication, to the theology of Karl Rahner, he is unhappy with the latter's notions of 'anonymous Christianity' and non-Christian faiths as 'lawful religions'. Such understandings, he argues, erode the important emphasis on the need for conversion. This nervousness about following too closely in Rahner's footsteps is significant in that it again reiterates his unswerving evangelical insistence on the uniqueness and finality of Christ.[33]

General revelation

Too often general revelation is discussed with an attitude of unease and an unwillingness to credit it with positive value. Pinnock is thus correct to insist that evangelicals need to 'buck a strong tradition that refuses to grant any gracious element in general revelation'.[34]

Before turning specifically to Pinnock's thought on the subject, I will begin by briefly looking at a couple of theologians who arguably stand in the above 'strong tradition' which needs to be bucked. We begin with some comments from G.C. Berkouwer, who makes the important point that general revelation needs to be understood within the context of special revelation:

> Special revelation confronts us with a new, historical working of God in Word and deed revelation, the revelation of God's mercy, which did not arise in the human heart, but in the Father-heart of God . . . In it men see the free and historical working of God, to which he is neither obligated nor bound, and which opens to lost mankind the only way to the knowledge of God and salvation . . . Anyone who fails to do justice to this exclusive way radically misjudges the earnestness and profundity of special revelation . . . Whoever desires to point out and

---

[33] He speaks of 'strong desire to affirm in no uncertain terms the uniqueness and finality of Jesus Christ and to regard as heretical any attempt to reduce or water down this conviction' ('Finality', 153).

[34] 'Finality', 160.

follow another way than *this* revelation, fails to hear *this* revelation and gropes in the dark. However, this may never lead us to denying the revelational character of God's universal working in created reality. Knowledge and revelation are *not* identical. And from the fact of human blindness we may not conclude the absence of God's revelation.[35]

Perhaps the most important point to note for our purposes is the distinction he makes between the ontic and the noetic, between the fact of general revelation and the knowledge which ends up in human heads: 'Knowledge and revelation are *not* identical.' He argues that while there is a universal revelation, human sin leads to a distorted reception of that revelation. Likewise, John Calvin understands the religions of the world to testify to the fact that humans are naturally endowed with an awareness of the creator (*sensus divinitatis*). Unfortunately, argues Calvin, because the human spirit is a 'factory of idols', it is 'in vain that so many burning lamps shine for us in the workmanship of the universe to show forth the glory of its Author. Although they bathe us wholly in their radiance, yet they can of themselves no way lead us into the right path.'[36] There is revelation, but the spiritual blindness caused by sin mitigates the human perception of its content. Hence, on an apparently more pessimistic note than Calvin, Berkouwer makes the following point: 'God's works are always great, profound and wonderful, and they shed forth the light of his eternal power and divinity. Man who is out of communion with God faces this revelation *blindly*.'[37]

Having said that, as with most Christian theologians, Berkouwer insists that revelation is never inconsequential. The objective fact of revelation means, among other things, that (1) humans are culpable and 'without excuse'; (2) humans are spiritually restless and, to varying degrees, feel the need for 'religion' and transcendence; (3) humans are left with an uneasy conscience and a sense of guilt from which relief is sought; and (4) humans are imbued with a sense of truth, goodness, justice and an aversion to evil – 'there is still a *working* of the law written in human hearts which neither know God nor

---

[35] G.C. Berkouwer, *General Revelation*, 313–4.
[36] J. Calvin, *Institutes of the Christian Religion*, J.T. McNeill (ed.), tr by F.L. Battles, 68.
[37] Berkouwer, *General Revelation*, 312–3 (my emphasis).

serve him'.[38] In short, general revelation makes us accountable to God, alerts us to our sinful state, and provides us with enough moral sense to live together and relate to each other and the world around us, albeit falteringly, in the way God intends. The problem is that, because of sin, revelation is turned into idolatry, and in turn a manifestation of false religion.

While there is truth in this line of argument, the path to pessimism is blocked. The theology is flawed. On the one hand, it is argued that the *sensus divinitatis* and the perception of truth is a direct result of general revelation, and, on the other hand, we are told that it provides 'no true knowledge' of God and thus the ontic and the noetic are separated.[39] The problem is that the ontic and the noetic are clearly *not* separated. The fact that general revelation has provided at least some understanding of God and his relations with humanity and produced a restless human soul, indicates that while we may not be dealing with the knowledge imparted by special revelation, we are dealing with knowledge; there has been some noetic impact. As a direct result of general revelation, humans have some innate knowledge about who God is and what he wills which, although corrupted, is true.

Pinnock does not make this mistake. Indeed, instead of a nervousness about the noetic impact of general revelation, he celebrates it. Furthermore, for Pinnock, general revelation is not simply the basis for human culpability. He draws attention to the fact that this blinkered argument leads the theologian of religions to a very unhappy conclusion indeed: 'I am offended by the notion that the God who loves sinners and desires to save them tantalizes them with truth about himself that can only result in their greater condemnation.'[40] I suspect that many people will instinctively empathize with Pinnock's revulsion. Too often intellectually impressive armchair systematic theologies are produced with little regard to their less than impressive implications. Bearing in mind the missionary God revealed in Jesus Christ, the loving, crucified God of the New Testament, surely his general revelation to humanity takes into

---

[38] Ibid. 202. For a brief but worthwhile discussion of both Berkouwer and Demarest, see Fackre, *Revelation*, 50–57.
[39] Calvin also insists that 'All fall away from true knowledge of him.'
[40] 'Finality', 160.

account the nature of those for whom it is intended. Is it not the purpose of general revelation and the work of providence in common grace to lead people to seek God? 'Is there not one author of both general and special revelation?'[41]

Leaning heavily on passages such as Acts 10:34–5 ('God does not show favouritism but accepts men from every nation who fear him and do what is right', NIV) and Acts 14:17 ('he has not left himself without testimony . . .' NIV), Pinnock argues that

> people possess truth from God in the context of their own religion and culture . . . In Paul's speech upon the Aeropagus we hear how God has providentially ordered history 'that they [people in general] should seek God, in the hope that they might feel after him and find him. Yet he is not far from each one of us' (Acts 17:27).[42]

Quite simply, it is argued that, just as sin is ubiquitous, so is God's love and witness. Hence, without denying the existence of darkness and blindness within other faiths, Pinnock affirms that non-Christian faiths 'reflect to some degree general revelation and prevenient grace . . . Because of cosmic or general revelation, anyone can find God anywhere at anytime, because he has made himself and his revelation accessible to them. This is the reason we find a degree of truth and goodness in other religions.'[43]

Now, while I would concur with much of the above, it is, I believe, important to go beyond understanding general revelation as merely the communication of knowledge to understanding it in terms of a personal encounter.[44] Although it would be untrue to

---

[41] *Wideness*, 104. He quotes Dale Moody: 'What kind of a God is he who gives man enough knowledge to damn him but not enough to save him?'

[42] 'Finality', 158.

[43] *Wideness*, 104.

[44] Interestingly, Donald Bloesch wants to abandon the term 'general revelation' because it implies a divine–human personal encounter: 'If revelation is essentially personal encounter, general revelation would seem to contradict this essential dimension of revelation.' In my opinion, general revelation is exactly the right term precisely because it so obviously *does not* contradict the essential dimension of personal encounter. I find Bloesch's suggestion that this activity of God should be understood as 'an exhibition' which *exposes* humanity to divine mercy and wrath, but does

claim that this personalistic approach to general revelation is wholly absent in Pinnock's discussions, it is neglected. This is unfortunate, because it is theologically important that, to quote Johan Bavinck, 'Time and again humankind is confronted with the certainty that God exists and *actually encounters* him. But each time he resists these impressions and escapes them. Yet God still concerns himself *fully and personally* with human beings. It is not easy to explain how God does it, but it happens.'[45] Again, Jannie du Preez notes that, for Bavinck, 'general revelation in the biblical sense is of a very *personal* nature; it is a self-manifestation of God in his everlasting concern for people collectively as well as individually'.[46] Likewise, it is my contention that God *personally* approaches and encounters all persons, including, of course, those in other faiths. However, this encounter is instantly distorted by sin. That is to say, at the root of an individual's faith experience there is a genuine response to the loving personal outreach of God (the nature of which will be discussed more fully below), which is then, to some degree, distorted and repressed by sin.

Faith and tradition

Following on from the above, I want to affirm the distinction between, on the one hand, philosophical reflection and institutional religious expression, and, on the other hand, the personal faith responses of individuals. In other words, what I have in mind is the distinction between 'faith and cumulative tradition' (Wilfred Cantwell Smith), or 'living and empirical religion' (H.H. Farmer). While it would be naïve to think that one could separate faith and empirical religion much as one might separate reagents in a

---

[44] *(continued)* not *disclose* divine light and truth, obscure and unconvincing. See D.G. Bloesch, *A Theology of Word and Spirit: Authority and Method in Theology*, 164f. Emil Brunner posits a similarly unconvincing argument (see Partridge, *H.H. Farmer's*, 108–15).

[45] J.H. Bavinck, 'Human Religion in God's Eyes: A Study of Romans 1:18–32', 50. Cf. also C.E.B. Cranfield, *A Critical and Exegetical Commentary on the Epistle to the Romans*, 1:113–16.

[46] J. du Preez, 'Johan Herman Bavinck on the Relation Between Divine Revelation and the Religions', 111.

laboratory, there is some value in conceptually distinguishing them (whether one uses the above terms or not). I say this because I am convinced that to understand the phenomenon of religion properly one needs to understand personal faith. Yet there is a problem, for faith is, to quote Smith, 'something too profound, too personal, and too divine for public exposition . . . faith lies beyond that sector of [the] religious life that can be imparted to an outsider for his inspection'.[47] Faith, as I am using the term here (though Farmer's term 'living religion' is perhaps preferable), is the personal apprehension of the approach of God, an individual's personal encounter understood within the context of a particular culture or tradition. Hence, although it lacks the necessary *Christian* personalist emphases, the following distinction is helpful:

> By 'faith' I mean personal faith . . . inner religious experience or involvement of a particular person; *the impingement on him of the transcendent*, putative or real. By 'cumulative tradition' I mean the entire mass of overt objective data that constitute the historical deposit, as it were, of the past religious life of the community in question: temples, scriptures, theological systems, dance patterns, legal and other social institutions, conventions, moral codes, myths and so on; anything that can be and is transmitted from one person, one generation, to another, and that an historian can observe.[48]

Therefore, to know something of the culture or religious tradition is not to know the individual personal faith-responses evoked within it. While this distinction requires more unpacking and justification than it is possible to provide in this essay, the point is simply that some recognition of it is important when seeking to understand the religious lives of other people.

Bearing in mind this distinction and the above thesis concerning general revelation as the personal approach of God to the human soul, it is interesting to note that regardless of what official or orthodox theologies state and cumulative traditions proclaim, when the personal faith of individual believers is explored, one often finds

---

[47] W.C. Smith, *The Meaning and End of Religion: A Revolutionary Approach to the Great Religious Traditions*, 170.
[48] Ibid. 156–7 (my emphasis).

conceptions of personal deities. Hence, it is not without significance that, as Farmer observed many years ago,

> in so far as Buddhism and Hinduism have become religions of the masses, the impersonalistic metaphysic has receded into the background and the object of religious devotion has become pronouncedly personal. The impersonal Absolute had to be conceived as presenting itself in personal form before it could decisively lay hold of the religious impulse. The Buddha has been deified, the Bodhisattvas and the Amida Buddha are personal beings. In Hinduism the neutral, all-embracing Brahma is believed to have manifested itself in the Trimurti, that is, the three divine personalities of Brahma, Vishnu, and Shiva, and these have become, along with other deities, the real objects of a religious devotion which in the Bhakti cults is of a warmly personal kind.[49]

The point is that, at the level of faith (which often eventually finds empirical expression), evidence of the pressure of a personal God on the human soul can be seen throughout religious history. However, taking seriously the corrupting effects of sin, which in turn lead to

---

[49] H.H. Farmer, *The World and God: A Study of Prayer, Providence and Miracle in Christian Experience*, 30. Cf. also N. MacNicol, 'Is There a General Revelation? A Study in Indian Religion', 241–57; and K. Ward, *Holding Fast to God: A Reply to Don Cupitt*: 'The "pure Land" school and to a lesser extent, most Mahayana schools of Buddhism . . . regard the Buddha as a personal saviour and hope for personal immortality. In such schools, the average believer probably reveres the gods, regards the Buddha as his saviour, and tries to build up merit for future lives' (152). Hans Küng makes a similar point: 'Experts in Buddhism can point out that Buddhism as practised *in reality* does know "God", indeed a number of gods taken over from popular religion (Indian religion or some others): those personified natural forces or divinised kings and saints who are called on for protection and help . . . The Buddha Gautama himself regarded the gods (*devas*) as real but provisional, since they too were subject to birth and rebirth . . . [Moreover] Nirvana, Shunyata and Dharmakaya . . . are all terms which the great majority of Buddhists do not understand in a nihilistic way but as a positive reality, and which can be regarded by Christians as parallel terms for the Absolute. They fulfil analogous functions to the concept of God' (H. Küng and K.-J. Kuschel [eds.], *A Global Ethic: The Declaration of the World's Parliament of Religions*, 61–3).

the overbearing influence of culture, social relations, environment and ego, we are not surprised that, although some of the traces of the divine-human encounter remain, sometimes even the idea of a personal God is wholly repressed (as, for example, in some forms of Buddhism). Nevertheless, even in such philosophically atheistic religions, at the level of personal faith the effects of the divine-human encounter are often nurtured and a warm devotional life emerges, at the heart of which is some sense of personal relationship with the divine. Of course, in what Ninian Smart has called 'transpolytheistic' and 'transtheistic' belief systems, devotion to personal deities may be frowned upon and dismissed as inferior forms of the religious life.[50] My point is simply that the very existence of this apparent deep need for personal deities and for personal divine-human fellowship is significant, in that it is some indication of the divine-human encounter.

The Logos and the Holy Spirit

It is important to remember that the Logos, which was made flesh in Jesus of Nazareth, is present in the entire world and in the whole of human history. Though Jesus Christ is Lord, we confess at the same time that the Logos is not confined to one segment of human history or one piece of world geography. The second Person of the Trinity was incarnate in Jesus, but is not totally limited to Palestine. In a real sense, when missionaries take testimony about Jesus to the world, they take the Gospel to places where the Logos has already been active. They will discover noble insights and actions which are the result of God working among the peoples.[51]

This insistence on the wider work of 'God the Logos' is the key to Pinnock's balancing of the two axioms. 'Sent by God, the eternal Son and Logos upholds all things by his power and enlightens everyone coming into the world. The Logos is at work in the whole world like a schoolmaster bringing people to Christ.'[52] Pinnock

---

[50] See N. Smart, *Dimensions of the Sacred: An Anatomy of the World's Beliefs*, 34ff.
[51] *Wideness*, 77.
[52] Ibid. 103.

then goes on to state that those 'who respond belong to the larger people of God. The Logos connects Jesus of Nazareth to the whole world and guards the Incarnation from becoming a limiting principle.'[53]

This thesis, of course, is not particularly novel. A similar understanding of the Logos doctrine can be found in writings of the early Christian apologists (although not as frequently as one is often led to believe). Justin Martyr's 'First Apology' is perhaps the most obvious text.[54] In what amounts to a semi-philosophical understanding of general revelation, Justin argues that the Logos is the 'Reason' in which all humanity participates. While Jesus is the Logos incarnate, there are seeds of Reason (*logos spermatikos*) scattered throughout the world. T.F. Torrance notes that 'Logos, in Justin's thought is not merely "word" or "speech" but the divine Mind or reason expressing itself and acting upon us as Word.' Moreover, he continues, 'through the divine Word the Holy Spirit enters into the course of time and creates a patterned series of events, that are providentially directed, leading up to the incarnation of the Word in Jesus Christ'.[55] Hence, in his 'First Apology' Justin is able to affirm that a pneumatologically guided path to the incarnation can be traced through the ancient philosophers in whom the germinal logos is clearly evident. As Geoffrey Lampe observes, Justin adapts

> the Stoic theory of the immanent rationality by virtue of which the world is an ordered cosmos, and in harmony with which all wise and virtuous men must seek to live, so as to support his contention, not merely that Christianity is the proper fulfilment of the insights and aspirations of revealed (Hebraic) and natural (Greek philosophical) religion, but that all 'those who have lived with "the Logos" are Christians even though they may have been considered to be "atheists", such as Socrates among the Greeks and Abraham and Elijah among "barbarians".[56]

---

[53] Ibid. 104.

[54] The 'First Apology' has been reprinted in E. Plantinga (ed.), *Christianity and Plurality: Classic and Contemporary Readings*, 31–61.

[55] T.F. Torrance, *Divine Meaning: Studies in Patristic Hermeneutics*, 95.

[56] G.W.H. Lampe, 'Christian Theology in the Patristic Period' in H. Cunliffe-Jones, *A History of Christian Doctrine*, 31.

That is to say, present in all persons, the Logos enables a reception of God's self-communication and thus some limited knowledge of him. Non-Christians can thus live 'in accordance with the Logos' (*kata logon*). 'Those who responded rightly to the potentialities for communion with God which had thus been built into their rational nature could be reckoned among Christians, so that "whatever among all men has been well said belongs to us Christians".'[57] Similar statements can also be found in the writings of other apologists. Indeed, the apologists were even prepared to argue that non-Judaeo-Christian prophecy could be a divinely inspired source of truth. For example, as Michael Nazir-Ali has pointed out, various Greek sibyls were 'specifically regarded as having prophesied the coming of Christ'.[58]

Having said that, some critics of the contemporary use of Logos theology have argued that

> Justin was not simply approving of Greek culture and philosophy in general terms. Rather, he was making the very important discrimination that those philosophers whom he suggested had lived *kata logon* were those who had attacked the idolatry of their own contemporary paganism, such as Socrates. That is, it was not the Greek religion itself that was a manifestation of the *logos*, but on the contrary it was those who saw its inadequacy and rejected its polytheism and its demons who showed evidence of the work of the *logos*.[59]

While there is truth in this, it need not contradict a cautious inclusivism. For example, we have seen that while Pinnock is happy with aspects of Rahner's work, he is keen to distance himself from the notion of 'lawful religion' for, it would seem, just this reason. To claim that the Logos is 'at work in the whole world like a schoolmaster bringing people to Christ', as Pinnock does, need not necessarily imply that religions *per se* are manifestations of the Logos. Like Justin, Pinnock is very clear that religion can be 'false and vile'.[60] The faith experiences of individuals must not be confused with

---

[57] Ibid.
[58] M. Nazir-Ali, *Citizens and Exiles: Christian Faith in a Plural World*, 11.
[59] C. Wright, *The Uniqueness of Jesus*, 129–30.
[60] See his discussion of 'false religion' in *Wideness*, 86–92.

empirical religion. From a personalist perspective, bearing in mind that, generally speaking, God deals with individual persons rather than religions *en bloc*, it is not difficult to see how the Logos might encounter and work transformingly within an individual seeker while judging the religion to which he or she belongs. The point is that the Logos thesis does not necessarily imply that the religion itself is a manifestation of the Logos.

As to Pinnock's pneumatology, while he does not spend time unpacking the relationship between the Logos and the Holy Spirit, his understanding of the Spirit as the ubiquitous presence of God is related and important. Indeed, he declares that his inclusivism is 'a pneumatology of universality'.[61]

> God the Spirit also proceeds from the father and is present in the whole world. God's breath flows in the world at large, not just within the confines of Christian movements . . . The Spirit is the overflow of God's love. We see his activity in human culture and even in the religions of humanity. The doctrine of the Trinity means that God, far from being difficult to locate in the world, can be encountered everywhere in it.[62]

Not only does this emphasis on the Spirit allow a fuller Trinitarian understanding of God's activity, but, as with the Logos doctrine, it allows a more optimistic theology of religions, a theology which holds together the particular and the universal. John Taylor put it beautifully many years ago:

> The Holy Spirit is *universally* present through the whole fabric of the world, and yet *uniquely* present in Christ and, by extension, in the fellowship of his disciples. But even that unique presence is not enclosed, either in Christ or in his church, but exists between Christ and the other, between Christians and those who meet them. The centre is always a circumference, yet it proves to be the circumference of *that* centre and not another. This interplay of the unique and the universal is clearly seen in the witness which the Holy Spirit bears to Jesus Christ. In the first instance, it is the power of the Spirit in the person of

---

[61] 'Inclusivist', 143
[62] *Wideness*, 104.

Jesus – the works that this man does and the authority with which he speaks – which testify most convincingly to his identity. This is extended in the witness to Christ which the Spirit enables the church to give by its life and testimony. But that same Spirit also speaks in the hearts of all men, for God has nowhere left himself without a witness that always, to a greater or lesser degree, points to Christ.[63]

This brings me to a possible weakness in Pinnock's theology, namely a failure to emphasize the strong bond that exists between Christ and the Spirit. Running through the whole of the New Testament is a conviction made explicit in passages such as John 20:22–3 and Romans 8:9 that the Spirit stands in the closest possible relation to Christ, so that the Spirit's presence is equivalent to that of Christ. However, as is evident in Pinnock's unhappiness with the ancient and admittedly problematic *filioque* clause,[64] he seems to play down the fact that, in Michael Green's words:

> It is the task of the Paraclete to universalise the presence of Jesus. In the days of his flesh Jesus was limited by space and time. His physical departure made possible the coming of the Spirit as Paraclete and there would be no barriers of space and time to prevent disciples being in intimate contact with him. Indeed they would find the relationship even closer than companionship with Jesus in the days of his flesh. [Jesus' followers] had known Jesus as Paraclete . . . during his ministry. He had dwelt *with* them, but the one whom he promises as another Paraclete will dwell *in* them (John 14:17). There it is in a nutshell. The Spirit universalises the presence of Jesus in the hearts of disciples.[65]

Clearly this has important implications for an inclusivist theology of religions. The immanent presence of God working in the depths of a person's being is the Spirit who 'universalises the presence of Jesus'. My point is simply that it is important for a Christian theology of religions to keep Jesus to the fore and to emphasize the indissoluble bond that exists between any reconciling activity and his person and work. Hence, as Tom Smail insists,

---

[63] J.V. Taylor, *The Go-Between God: The Holy Spirit and the Christian Mission*, 180–81.

[64] *Wideness*, 78.

[65] M. Green, *I Believe in the Holy Spirit*, 42–3.

The Western emphasis on the strong relation between the Spirit and the Son is part of the Gospel as given and is needed as a bulwark against Christless mysticism, religious pluralism and charismatic excess which can easily intrude when we try to enter into life in the Spirit as something apart from life in the Son.[66]

Again, I am not saying that the Spirit-Son relationship is not acknowledged in Pinnock's theology of religions, only that it is underdeveloped and far more should be made of it in order to address, at least in part, the important Trinitarian concerns made pointedly in the following comment by Kevin Vanhoozer: 'The underlying question that must be asked of these Trinitarian theologies of religions concerns the manner in which, and the extent to which, the Spirit is the Spirit of Jesus Christ.'[67]

Lawful religion, repentance and salvation

The points I want to make regarding repentance and salvation can best be made in response to Rahner's thesis on 'lawful religion':

Until the moment when the Gospel really enters into the historical situation of an individual, a non-Christian religion . . . does not merely contain elements of a natural knowledge of God, elements, moreover, mixed up with human depravity which is the result of original sin and later aberrations. It contains also supernatural elements arising out of the grace which is given to men as a gratuitous gift on account of Christ. For this reason a non-Christian religion can be recognized as a *lawful* religion (although only in different degrees) without thereby denying the error and depravity contained in it.[68]

---

[66] T. Smail, *The Giving Gift: The Holy Spirit in Person*, 132. See also G. Badcock, 'Karl Rahner, the Trinity, and Religious Pluralism' in K.J. Vanhoozer (ed.), *The Trinity in a Pluralistic Age: Theological Essays on Culture and Religion*, 153.

[67] K.J. Vanhoozer, 'Does the Trinity Belong in a Theology of Religions: On Angling in the Rubicon and the "Identity" of God' in Vanhoozer, *Trinity*, 62.

[68] K. Rahner, 'Christianity and the Non-Christian Religions', in *Theological Investigations*, 5:115–34.

This thesis needs to be understood in the light of Rahner's exposition of the 'supernatural existential', a term he uses as shorthand for his teaching that all persons are created into a relationship with God.

> [A person's] natural desire for the supernatural as a link between nature and grace is conceivable and necessary if by 'desire' is understood an 'openness' to the supernatural . . . God creates human beings . . . in such a way that they *can* receive [the] love which is God, and that they can and must at the same time accept it for what it is: the ever-astounding wonder, the unexpected, unexacted gift.[69]

That is to say, God in his grace has created all persons with an 'orientation towards mystery', a natural openness to himself. And corresponding to this openness there is the offer of divine self-communication. Maurice Wiles makes the important point that 'it is emphatically a matter of *offer*; men and women are free to ignore it or reject it, as well as accept it. This respect for human freedom characterizes all God's dealings with the world.'[70] In accepting one's openness, a person receives the goal of salvation: reconciliation with God in Christ. Moreover, Rahner then goes on to argue that the grace of God actually operates to qualify non-Christian religions as channels of salvation, or mediators of grace. Hence his claim that non-Christian religion is '*lawful* religion'.[71] Persons are not saved *in spite of* non-Christian religious structures but *through* them. Because, we are social creatures he insists that salvation must be mediated through the social groupings and institutions to which we belong.[72] This means that the sacraments, symbolisms, rituals

---

[69] K. Rahner, 'The Supernatural Existential' in G.B. Kelly (ed.), *Karl Rahner: Theologian of the Graced Search for Meaning*, 111.

[70] M. Wiles, *Christian Theology and Inter-religious Dialogue*, 56.

[71] 'A lawful religion means here an institutional religion whose "use" by man at a certain period can be regarded on the whole as a positive means of gaining the right relationship to God and thus for the attaining of salvation, a means which is therefore positively included in God's plan of salvation' (Rahner, 'Christianity', 66–7).

[72] Without these religions 'there is no way of saying at all where God and his history of salvation and revelation can be found in the world' (Rahner, *Theological Investigations*, 17:41f., quoted in D.F. Wright, 'The Watershed

and worldviews of other religions can be 'graced'. 'We . . . must rid ourselves of the prejudice that we can face a non-Christian religion with the dilemma that it must either come from God in everything it contains and thus correspond with God's will and positive providence, or be simply a purely human construction.'[73] The mixed elements of Israelite religion, as judged in the light of the New Testament, is, he claims, sufficient to dissolve that dilemma.[74] Having said that, it should be pointed out that non-Christian religion is only *lawful* up to the time when the Christian religion becomes 'a real historical factor in an individual history and culture'.[75]

Rahner then continues with his famous claim that, if this argument is sound, then

> Christianity does not simply confront the member of an extra-Christian religion as a mere non-Christian but as someone who can and must be regarded in this or that respect as an *anonymous Christian*. It would be wrong to regard the pagan as someone who has not yet been touched in any way by God's grace and truth.[76]

In short, Christians are distinct from non-Christians because they are able to name the reality anonymously present in the non-Christian's faith. And since salvation cannot be divorced from Christ, the saved person of another faith must be termed an 'anonymous Christian'.

Although there is much in Rahner's overall argument that I would want to affirm, including (with qualifications) the notion of the anonymous Christian, it cannot simply be accepted as it stands. In particular, it seems to me that Pinnock is right to feel

---

[72] *(continued)* of Vatican II: Catholic Attitudes Towards Other Religions' in A.D. Clarke, and B.W. Winter [eds.], *One God, One Lord in a World of Religious Pluralism*, 164).

[73] Rahner, 'Christianity', 69.

[74] Cf. ibid. 72ff.

[75] Ibid. 58. 'wherever in practice Christianity reaches man in the real urgency and rigour of his actual existence, Christianity – once understood – presents itself as the only still valid religion for this man, a necessary means for his salvation and not merely an obligation with the necessity of a precept' (59).

[76] Ibid. 75 (my emphasis).

uncomfortable with the theory of 'lawful religion', which he argues is 'naïve speculation. It is a nice idea in principle, but oblivious to the realities staring us in the face.'[77] Having said that, although arguably Rahner fails to account sufficiently for the plain phenomenological discontinuity between Christianity and other faiths, it is perhaps unfair to claim that he is 'oblivious to the realities staring us in the face'. He specifically states that, when he refers to a religion as 'lawful', he is not denying its 'error and depravity'.[78] Indeed, he insists that there are gradations in non-Christian religion, even to the extent that some may not be 'lawful religion'.

Nevertheless, there are problems with the thesis. While I would agree that 'every human being is really and truly exposed to the influence of divine, supernatural grace',[79] I do not accept that this constitutes an existential openness of being in the sense that Rahner argues. That is to say, while alive to the 'error and depravity' in other faiths, Rahner's 'openness' betrays a far too weak doctrine of sin – which in turn leads to a muted understanding of missiological urgency. Hence, while Pinnock is right to identify this area as problematic, the problem actually lies with Rahner's doctrine of sin, not with his grasp of the nature of human religion. His understanding of sin as a person's indifference to their graced openness to God fails to recognize that it constitutes a real problem for humanity. Hence, the transition from nature to grace is understood more in terms of an evolution from non-reflective faith to reflective faith, rather than a radical repentance.

This brings us to a key element in the personalist theology of religions I am proposing, namely *repentance*. While this could be more explicitly unpacked in Pinnock's theology, it is implicitly there as part of his 'faith principle'. Believing that religions are often 'paths to hell . . . idols of our creation and deceptions of the Evil One',[80] the faith principle implicitly requires repentance at some level; hence his argument that Rahner's thesis on lawful religion erodes the need for conversion. In the model I am suggesting, repentance, in the sense of a turning of the whole person towards God, is fundamental.

---

[77] *Wideness*, 91.
[78] Rahner, 'Christianity', 61.
[79] Ibid. 63.
[80] *Wideness*, 91.

If a person finds salvation in another faith, it is the result of, at some point, a considered, conscious decision. A person feels the pressure of, to use Farmer's terminology, God's demand and succour – however that may be conveyed – and responds in 'faith' to *that* pressure. I stress this because, although there are elements in non-Christian religions which are 'noble, uplifiting and sound',[81] and, when taken in isolation and judged according to Christian standards, are to be commended, in the final analysis, religions are 'organised totalities or they are nothing. As organised totalities they are radically different from, radically discontinuous with, Christianity.'[82]

This highlights the important truth that persons are, as indeed Rahner affirms they are, bound up within a whole web of worldviews and relationships from which they cannot simply be extricated. For Rahner, however, such structures can be 'lawful' mediators of grace. My disagreement with this is simply that, although certain aspects of religious structures and worldviews can be mediators of grace, the extent to which they are is very limited – indeed, on the whole, they are an impediment. That is to say, as a result of the social structures within which persons function, in responding to revelation they respond sinfully. This is so when persons in any context, whether Christian or non-Christian, are led to think and act sinfully as a result of conditioning and social pressure (not to mention their own egocentricity). In short, because non-Christian (and even some Christian) empirical religion is not only the result of human sin and alienation from God, but socially perpetuates that alienation, any notion of 'lawful' religion must be treated with great caution. I do not deny that God may, for example, use Islamic ethical monotheism, the Jewish understanding of community, the Buddhist concept of non-violence, the Hindu *bhakti* notions of divine love and grace, or the Confucian respect for the family to communicate and reveal truth about himself and the world of persons. However, because these are part of, and determined by, a whole network of other far less helpful and false beliefs, things are not as straightforward as Rahner seems to suggest. Put simply, *both* because of the massive sin-perpetuating influence of social and religious structures upon persons-in-relation (which in turn serve to

---

[81] Ibid. 92.
[82] H.H. Farmer, 'The One Foundation', 206.

confirm their own distorted thoughts and actions) *and* because of the nature of personhood and reconciliation *per se*, a radical repentance is required. Hence any Christian theology of religions, including Pinnock's, needs to be clear about this.

There are, of course, questions of process still remaining concerning salvation outside some cognisance of the person and work of Christ. While agnosticism is appropriate here, some biblical pointers allow a cautious joining up of a number of the dots.[83] We have seen that, for Pinnock,

> the faith principle is the basis of universal accessibility. According to the Bible, people are saved by faith, not by the content of their theology. Since God has not left anyone without a witness, people are judged on the basis of the light they have received and how they have responded to that light. Faith in God is what saves, not possessing certain minimum information.[84]

While there is much truth in this, it seems to me that his thesis, particularly his rather nebulous understanding of faith, would benefit from development along personalist lines. Although, as I have indicated, relational themes are there in Pinnock's theology of religions (it would be difficult for a Christian theology to avoid them), they do need to be more fully and systematically integrated. In particular, the following general points might be considered:

1. As I have argued, Pinnock needs to be as clear as Bavinck that general revelation is 'of a very *personal* nature; it is a self-manifestation of God in his everlasting concern for people collectively as well as individually'.[85] More particularly, when we speak of general revelation, we speak of a divine-human personal encounter.

2. The history of religions is the history of sinfully distorted human responses to the approach of God. Because of sin, there is a culturally determined distorted perception of revelation.

---

[83] Although some of these biblical texts have already been referred to, for a brief overview of other passages supporting inclusivism see J. Sanders, *No Other Name*, 217ff.

[84] *Wideness*, 157–8.

[85] Du Preez, 'Johan', 111.

This accounts in part for the plurality of religions. Because, as Farmer argued, 'sin organises itself into social systems, which, [are] entrenched in the habits and traditions of a whole class of people',[86] a person's religious response will not only be distorted, but it will be moulded by those habits and traditions. Environment, family, friends, interests and culture all play a dominant role in a person's interpretation of God and reality.[87] In other words, as is generally recognized, all that has gone into moulding a person will necessarily influence, if not dictate, their understanding of reality. Hence, although an interpretation may not be wholly false, it will, to a significant degree, have the stamp of the interpreter upon it. It thus follows that, since there are many interpreters, influenced by many cultural and environmental factors, there will be many interpretations of the divine–human encounter. Indeed, I would agree with John Hick that 'the different encounters with the divine which lie at the basis of the great religious traditions . . . [are] encounters from different historical and cultural standpoints with the same infinite divine reality and as such they lead to differently focused awarenesses of that reality'.[88] He continues:

> These encounters have taken place within different human cultures by people of different ways of thought and feeling, with different histories and different frameworks of philosophical thought, and have developed into different systems of theology embodied in different religious structures and organisations.

---

[86] H.H. Farmer, *Things Not Seen: Studies in the Christian Interpretation of Life*, 157.

[87] Klaus Klostermaier makes an interesting point which demonstrates that even very mundane factors can help to shape a person's understanding of God. 'Theology at 120°F in the shade seems . . . different from theology at 70°F. Theology accompanied by tough chapatis and smoky tea seems very different from theology with roast chicken and a glass of good wine. Now who is really different, *theos* or the theologian? The theologian at 70°F in a good position presumes God to be happy and contented, well-fed and rested, without needs of any kind. The theologian at 120°F tries to imagine a God who is hungry and thirsty, who suffers and is sad, who sheds perspiration and knows despair' (*Hindu and Christian in Vrindaban*, 40).

[88] Hick, *Universe*, 141.

These resulting large-scale religio–cultural phenomena are what we call the religions of the world.[89]

That said, Hick's comments require qualification. While from a personalist perspective Hick's thought is, to say the least, weak, his doctrine of sin is conspicuous by its absence. A sound doctrine of sin leads us to the conclusion that there are, in varying degrees, inadequate and false interpretations of ultimate reality, not merely different ones.

3.   While God clearly does communicate with some persons directly, as arguably was the case with, for example, Abraham, Samuel and Paul on the road to Damascus, and while this form of communication must be included in any theology of God's mission to the unevangelized, I want to suggest that a way in which God might encounter persons in a particularly focused and intense way is through the ethical and humanitarian claims of others. Because of the nature of the personal world, in lovingly and practically responding to the claims of other humans, persons in other faiths are obediently responding to the claims of God: 'the living awareness of God as personal is not apart from the social environment – the infinite personal is given through the finite personal'.[90] Before applying this to the theology of religions, three brief points need to be made: (a) In accordance with God's respect for persons, when he brings an individual's will into harmony with his own, he does so, not by the exercise of overbearing force and coercion, but always by, as Farmer argued, 'eliciting from man his own inner perception of its righteousness and his own spontaneous surrender to it in obedience and trust'.[91] (b) Our experienced awareness of God is not inferential, but rather intuitive, in that there is an immediate apprehension of another personal purpose or will standing over against our own. To quote Farmer's writings again: 'The religious man is aware of a certain peculiar type of resistance being set up within the sphere of his values and preferences: the resistance, namely, of absolute, sacred, unconditional values – values which are apprehended as calling for

---

[89] Ibid. 143.
[90] Farmer, *The World*, 200.
[91] Ibid. 70.

obedience at literally any cost.'[92] In other words, persons are aware of an absolute 'claim' upon them. (c) God's claim for obedience and trust can meet persons 'in the claim of their fellows for their *love*'.[93] In other words, the claim of God and the claims of other persons for love, justice, etc. are apprehended together. 'The claim of my neighbour is always part of God's claim on me: God's claim on me meets me always in and through the claim of my neighbour.'[94]

What is the significance of this for a theology of religions? My suggestion is simply that *one* of the ways God challenges persons and brings them to moments of crisis which demand repentance and a change of life in accordance with his will is through the claims of other persons upon them. Of course, what I am suggesting is far more than salvation by being nice to people – Christ and the Spirit are intimately involved in this interpersonal activity graciously enabling understanding.

4. As to how the Spirit might thus operate in a person, Vernon White, while not constructing a theology of religions, makes a couple of points which seem to me to be helpful. Firstly, we should not understand righteousness simply to be a matter of divine declaration which bypasses human involvement, since 'such an event would, arguably, replace one person by another, rather than redeem the existing person; it would also render this whole creative enterprise redundant since we might just as well have been made thus in the first place'.[95] Rather, we must actually *become* righteous. Secondly, we become righteous when 'the Spirit communicates the divine personhood of the Logos to our natures'.[96] In a way that respects the person, the Spirit can relate Christ's atoning achievement to all people. As to the 'causal joint' between Christ's Spirit and our spirits, White thinks of it in terms of what amounts to interpersonal influence. Hence the fact that

---

[92] Ibid. 23.

[93] H.H. Farmer, *God and Men*, 96 (my emphasis).

[94] Ibid. 53.

[95] V. White, *Atonement and Incarnation: An Essay in Universalism and Particularity*, 54.

[96] Ibid. 49.

in human relations 'the *experience* of the one may draw the other through into the same maturity, whether it is the business of learning to swim or learning to pray'.[97] Yet, as White argues, such a relationship (if it is healthy and non-manipulative) cannot be considered as a violation of a person's personal integrity. The changed person will want to say 'not I but the grace of another . . . yet still I'. Of course, when the influential pole of this relationship is the Spirit of Christ, operating in the depths of our beings, the potential for influence is obviously greatly magnified.[98] My suggestion is that, if an unevangelized person has a salvific 'faith', it is the result of this divine activity.

To return to the particular suggestion that God might work through human relationships, my point is that, in living a life of love and commitment towards others, in obedience to what a person perceives to be more ultimate demands, that person's will is, with the enabling of the Spirit, graciously being brought by God into line with his own. This is not by coercion and manipulation, but 'by eliciting a person's own spontaneous surrender to it in obedience and trust'. In short, in certain interpersonal situations, a person will apprehend 'the dimension of the eternal', the claims of others will assume a spiritual and moral depth to such an extent that they are perceived as being binding and absolute. In obedience to these demands a person meets, perhaps salvifically, with God.

5.   Because of sin, the obedient response will always be perceived as a serious business. It will require repentance, a turning away from self-centredness. It will almost certainly require opposition to aspects of a person's culture or religion. For example, notions of 'untouchability', certain attitudes towards women, and the exploitation of the poor, all of which may be ingrained in a culture, should begin to be questioned. Hence, such humanly unevangelized people will increasingly live lives of godly devotion and reconciliation, seeking justice and the upbuilding of community.[99] In particular, there will be evidence of 'love, joy, peace, patience, kindness, goodness,

---

[97] Ibid.
[98] Ibid. 55–6.
[99] See MacNicol, 'Is There?', 257.

faithfulness, gentleness and self-control' (Gal. 5:22–3, NIV). Correspondingly, within the constraints of the particular context and worldview, there will also be dissatisfaction with, and possibly opposition to, 'sexual immorality, impurity and debauchery; idolatry and witchcraft; hatred, discord, jealousy, fits of rage, selfish ambition, dissentions, factions and envy; drunkenness, orgies, and the like' (Gal. 5:19–21, NIV).

Prevenient grace

Many of the building blocks for an evangelical inclusivism can be found in the theology of John Wesley. Just as Pinnock has made use of some of these substantial blocks in his theological construction work, so elements of my own thesis can be strengthened by Wesleyan theology.

Of particular note is Wesley's doctrine of 'preventing' or 'prevenient' grace. For Wesley, no human being was excluded from the love of God and none would be lost because Christ had not died for them. If a person is not finally reconciled to God in Christ, the fault lies with the person, not with God; humans have a responsibility to respond to grace. Insisting upon a strong doctrine of original sin (and thus opposing Pelagianism), he argued that it is prevenient grace which empowers persons to accept or to refuse faith. Prevenient grace is thus important for those of us who are unhappy with limited atonement because, as Colin Williams has pointed out, it with this doctrine that Wesley 'broke the chain of logical necessity by which the Calvinist doctrine of predestination seems to flow from the doctrine of original sin'.[100]

As to the promising aspects of the doctrine itself, in brief:

1.   as a result of the incarnation, humanity *per se* has been graciously enlightened. Wesley even claimed that God had 'in some measure re-inscribed the law on the heart of his dark, sinful creature'. As Herbert McGonigle comments, 'This re-inscribed law, the work of prevenient grace, enables fallen man to respond to further grace and in this way the working of

---

[100] C.M. Williams, *John Wesley's Theology Today*, 44.

God that leads to salvation proceeds in the soul unless hindered by disobedience and rebellion.'[101] As biblical support for this universal enlightenment, Wesley was fond of quoting John 1:9: 'The true light that gives light to *every man* was coming into the world.'

2. In particular, Wesley was convinced that the Holy Spirit is at work within every person. Indeed, he understood conscience to be a manifestation of prevenient grace. Therefore, any moral sense and desire for God should not, strictly speaking, be understood as *natural* ability; it actually flows from the person and work of Christ and is inwardly applied by the Holy Spirit. Conscience he points out, is correctly described by his contemporaries as '*natural* conscience' because 'it is found in all men'. However,

> properly speaking, it is not natural, but a supernatural gift of God, above all his natural endowments. No; it is not nature, but the Son of God, that is the 'true light, which enlighteneth every man that cometh into the world'. So that we may say to every human creature, 'He', not nature, 'hath showed thee, O man, what is good'. And it is his Spirit who giveth thee an inward check, who causeth thee to feel uneasy, when thou walkest in any instance contrary to the light which he hath given thee.[102]

This, of course, means that no person is in a purely natural/sinful state in that all have been changed by the work of Christ and the action of the Spirit.

While there is a need for the Spirit-Son relationship to be more fully developed, much of what I have argued above can be understood in terms of prevenient grace. Indeed, while clearly a man of his age in many respects, Wesley was prepared to accept that the logic of his thought led in an inclusivist direction. As Williams notes, 'it is [Wesley's] belief that Christ works even in those who do not hear the gospel in this life'.[103] For example, he insists that the following

---

[101] H. McGonigle, *John Wesley's Doctrine of Prevenient Grace*, 21.

[102] J. Wesley, 'On Conscience' in *The Works of John Wesley* 7:187f., quoted in H. Lindstrom, *Wesley and Sanctification: A Study in the Doctrine of Salvation*, 48.

[103] Williams, *John Wesley's*, 45.

Quaker doctrine is orthodox Christian belief: 'The benefit of the death of Christ is not only extended to such as have distinct knowledge of His death and sufferings, but even unto those who are inevitably excluded from this knowledge.'[104] Again, 'he believes that those who do not hear the gospel are judged according to their response to this grace by which Christ works within them in a hidden way'.[105] Wesley declares:

> Inasmuch as to them little is given, of them little will be required . . . No more therefore will be expected of them, than the living up to the light they had. But many of them . . . *we have great reason to hope*, although they lived among the Heathens, yet were quite of another spirit; being taught of God by his inward voice all the essentials of true religion.[106]

The idea of 'being taught of God by his inward voice all the essentials of true religion' is a lovely way of expressing an aspect of God's personal engagement with the unevangelized. Wesley was clearly operating with a hermeneutic of hopefulness.

Concluding comments: religious studies and the essence of religion

While I feel that Pinnock is a little guilty of this himself, I do welcome his criticism of 'scholars who try to settle theories without consulting the actual situation'.[107] Rarely does one find evangelicals making this point. As one whose own research interests over the last decade have gradually moved from systematic theology to religious studies, I am convinced that the interface between the two disciplines is where much future Christian theology needs to be done. As I have argued elsewhere, not only is it important for Christian theologians to address religious plurality, but, when they do so, it is

---

[104] J. Wesley, *The Letters of John Wesley*, 2:118.
[105] Williams, *John Wesley's*, 45.
[106] J. Wesley, 'On Faith' in *The Works of John Wesley*, 7:197, quoted in J. Sanders, *No Other Name*, 250 (my emphasis).
[107] Pinnock, 'Inclusivist', 106–7

important that they turn to religious studies.[108] Although I recognize that there are only so many hours in a day, and getting to grips with current Christian thought is enough work for one lifetime, nevertheless, ideally, a theological interpretation of religions should be provided by one who has sought to understand a faith empathetically from the 'inside', to see as the believer sees, to feel as the believer feels. Just as Christians would expect others to spend time seeking to understand the Christian faith from the inside in order to avoid caricatures and misunderstanding, so they should do no less when seeking to understand non-Christian religions and when formulating theologies concerning those religions: 'in everything, do to others what you would have them do to you . . .' (Mt. 7:12, NIV). Moreover, it is the Christian's duty to make sure that his or her theology is based on the most accurate understanding possible. Unfortunately, it is not difficult to find Christian theologies, theories and descriptions of religion based on inadequate research, misinformation and offensive caricature. For the sake of the gospel and the construction of reliable, comprehensive Christian theologies, Christians need to work at securing an accurate and informed understanding of the world in which they live.

Concerning the question of an essence of religion, clearly the thesis set forth in this essay is similar to Pinnock's. However, it explicitly identifies the underlying continuity as a personal divine-human encounter, a consequence of the gracious and loving outreach of God. In the previous essay Chris Sinkinson quite correctly drew attention to criticisms of essentialist definitions of religion, particularly the argument that religions are different in so many respects that it is difficult to see what a common essence might look like. However, while there is not space to respond fully, in my view the present thesis is resistant to such critiques. In brief, while wherever possible seeking to be true to the facts of religion, I am not attempting to provide a definition which might be empirically verified in all respects. That is to say, this is a *Christian theological interpretation of religion* which, while committed to religious studies, and while not seeking to deny the differences between religions, and while taking seriously the empirically obvious lack of ethical uniformity and

---

[108] C.H. Partridge, 'The Academic Study of Religions: Contemporary Issues and Approaches'.

doctrinal consensus, also works with a Christian doctrine of sin. As such it takes the distorting effects of sin seriously, which, as we have seen, can account for a great deal of plurality, including atheism. In short, an external discontinuity does not undermine the thesis that there is an internal continuity in the form of a divine-human encounter which may, in some persons, be wholly repressed. The distinction between subjective and objective religion, or faith and cumulative tradition is again important to bear in mind.

Although I suspect that he himself would be the first to admit that his theology of religions does require development (whose theology does not?), Pinnock is to be applauded for resolutely pressing on with the development of a hermeneutic of hopefulness and thereby taking us a good way down the path to a cogent and intelligent evangelical inclusivism.

10

Presence, Prevenience, or Providence? Deciphering the Conundrum of Pinnock's Pneumatological Inclusivism[1]

Daniel Strange

For 'presence' is no easy simple notion!

Henri Blocher[2]

Introduction

On encountering the work of Clark H. Pinnock, one is often struck by the almost 'impressionistic' feel of his theology. Here is a theologian who likes to paint with broad brushstrokes and who over the years has covered the entire canvas that is systematic theology. His palette, far from being monochromic (a description which I think he might level at many evangelicals who resource themselves entirely from their own community) is an eclectic kaleidoscope of colours as he draws inspiration from the full spectrum of the Christian tradition – Protestant, Catholic and Eastern Orthodox. It is not difficult to see why Pinnock's theology has courted much attention from the evangelical community (both positive and negative), for its distinctive adventurousness.

---

[1] The material for this essay originates from various sections of my PhD thesis, under the supervision of Dr Gavin D'Costa, entitled 'The Possibility of Salvation Among the Unevangelised: An Analysis of Inclusivism in Recent Evangelical Theology'.

[2] H. Blocher, 'Immanence and Transcendence in Trinitarian Theology' in K.J. Vanhoozer (ed.), *The Trinity in a Pluralistic Age: Theological Essays on Culture and Religion*, 110.

However, while there may be some attractiveness in this style of theology, there are also some serious methodological and hermeneutical drawbacks. Firstly, Pinnock has not concentrated his work in one area of systematics, with the result that no one area has received comprehensive treatment, and as a result is often left without detailed explanation. The consequence of this is at times a worrying ambiguity and underdevelopment in theological argumentation. Secondly, because he 'picks and mixes' ideas from differing Christian traditions, transposing them into his own theological framework, in terms of cohesion and comprehensibility it is difficult to tell whether what has taken place is a legitimate evangelical adaptation of a particular teaching, or a wholesale transportation of an idea, together with the particular theological and philosophical baggage or trimmings that come with it.

In this essay I want to concentrate on one area of Pinnock's theology which for me clearly highlights these problems: his pneumatological understanding of God's relationship to the world in terms of the divine presence, and its impact on Pinnock's construal of divine grace. In order to do this, I am not going to focus specifically on Pinnock's doctrine of God (although I will have recourse to refer to it), but rather explore this issue through Pinnock's inclusivist position concerning the unevangelized: that is his insistence that those who have never heard the gospel can be saved. I believe that Pinnock's inclusivism is an excellent gateway for exploring many aspects of his theology as here many different strands of his thinking are woven together. The essay will be divided into two parts. In the first part I will attempt to interpret some important themes in Pinnock's inclusivism, referring to the 'touchstones' of Charles Wesley, the Second Vatican Council and Karl Rahner or, I should say more accurately, *particular interpretations* of Wesley, Vatican II and Rahner. In the second part I will suggest that if my interpretation is correct, then Pinnock's position compromises some fundamental tenets of the evangelical faith.

An interpretation of Pinnock's inclusivism

The axioms of universality and particularity

Pinnock believes that all theology must speak of universality and inclusion as opposed to views which are narrow and restrictive.

Subsumed under Pinnock's inclusivism are two related but separate areas: his 'theology of religions' and his belief that the unevangelized can be ontologically saved by Christ while being epistemologically unaware of him. It is on this second area that I wish to focus in this essay. A common thread that can be seen in all of Pinnock's work concerning other religions and the unevangelized is his desire to uphold two fundamental axioms which he believes to be non-negotiable for any responsible Christian understanding of religious pluralism. The first can be called the 'universality axiom' and consists of firstly, a belief in God's love for all humanity; secondly, his universal salvific will; and thirdly, an optimistic hopefulness in the numbers that will eventually be saved. The second axiom can be called the 'particularity axiom' and stresses the finality of Jesus Christ, retains the language of a 'high Christology', and emphasizes that any and everyone saved is saved through the person and work of Christ.[3] Pinnock comments on the relationship between these two axioms:

> The two axioms are inseparable, and both are primary in their own way. The universality axiom is theologically first but grounded in the other; the particularity axiom is epistemologically and redemptively first but intelligible because of the other. They belong together and enjoy an interchangeability in terms of the order.[4]

Having attempted to establish both biblically and theologically the two foundational axioms of universality and particularity,[5] Pinnock takes an important logical step, for he claims that given the truth of the above axioms, salvation must be universally accessible.[6] Now we

---

[3] Pinnock establishes these two axioms in 'Toward an Evangelical Theology of Religions'; *A Wideness in God's Mercy: The Finality of Jesus Christ in a World of Religions*, chs. 1 and 2; and *Flame of Love: A Theology of the Holy Spirit*, ch. 6. Karl Rahner also lays the foundation for his 'theology of religions' by affirming both the *solus Christus* and the universal salvific will of God. See his 'Christianity and the Non-Christian Religions' in idem (ed.), *Theological Investigations*, 5:115–34.

[4] 'Toward', 360.

[5] See *Wideness*, 17–81.

[6] On defining universal accessibility, Pinnock concurs with the evangelical apologist Stuart Hackett: 'If every human being in all times and ages

come to a theological conundrum, for Pinnock admits that despite God's universal provision of salvation, the majority of the human race has never heard of Christ through no fault of their own, because they have not had access to the preaching of the gospel through human messengers, and so have been unable explicitly to accept or reject the love of God. Given that Pinnock believes in the principle of universal accessibility and that many will eventually be saved (*Heilsoptimismus*), he concludes that many will be saved from among the unevangelized, realizing too that many of the unevangelized are not spiritually neutral but inhabit different religious worldviews other than Christianity. How is their salvation possible if they have never heard of Christ? He admits, 'the idea of universal accessibility, though not a novel theory, needs to be proven. It is far from self evident, at least biblically speaking. How can it best be defended?'[7]

I have entitled Pinnock's defence 'pneumatological inclusivism' because of the great emphasis on the work of the Spirit, the third person of the Trinity, who makes grace and salvation universally accessible even to those who have never come into contact with the gospel of Christ. Although the initial exploration into the work of the Spirit can be seen in *Wideness* (1992),[8] it is only fully developed in 'An Inclusivist View' (1995) and *Flame of Love* (1996). I wish to build Pinnock's picture of the Spirit's mission in three parts.

1. Spirit and Creation.

Pinnock wants to remind us that the omnipresent Spirit was and is involved in creation as well as redemption, indeed, 'there could not

---

[6] (*continued*) has been objectively provided for through the unique redemption in Jesus, and if this provision is in fact intended by God for every such human being, then it must be possible for every human individual to become personally eligible to receive that provision – regardless of his historical, cultural, or personal circumstances and situation, and quite apart from any particular historical information or even historically formulated theological conceptualisation – since a universally intended redemptive provision is not genuinely universal unless it is also and for that reason universally accessible' (*The Reconstruction of the Christian Revelation Claim*, 244).

[7] Pinnock, *Wideness*, 157. Karl Rahner also believed in the principle of universal accessibility, see *Theological Investigations*, 5:128.

[8] *Wideness*, 78.

be redemptive actions unless first there had been creative actions . . . The Spirit who brings salvation first brooded over the deep to bring order out of chaos.'[9] There is a unity to the work of God in creation and redemption and not a dualism: 'It is not as if creation before the Fall was graceless. Spirit is moving the entire process toward participation in the love of God, and the whole creation is caught up in it.'[10] In Pinnock's social understanding of the Trinity, all of creation is an overflowing and outpouring of God's intrapersonal love that has always existed between the three persons. Creation, then, is a fruit of God's love, 'being love, God ever seeks to share being and communicate presence with it. As a bond of love, as one who fosters fellowship, the Spirit opens up the relationship between God and the world.'[11] God created the world for his own pleasure and wants a relationship with it. This involves risk, as part of being in a significant relationship is that love cannot be coerced but must be freely given. God is looking for the echo of Trinitarian life in his creation – this is what brings him delight.[12] The Spirit's role is to mediate God's presence in creation, making it possible for the creature to participate in God, 'as the Spirit mediates the relationship between Father and Son, he also mediates the relationship between creatures and God. The goal is that we may enjoy the responsive relationship the Son enjoys with the Father . . . bringing creation to its goal is the main task of the Spirit.'[13]

Pinnock believes that an important implication of the omnipresence of the Spirit is that 'God is present to us in creation, and the world is a natural sacrament.'[14] This presence involves a struggle as the Spirit has to break down the human rejection of God which is often seen in the world. However, 'when sin abounds, the Spirit's grace does much more abound'.[15] The Spirit cannot be restricted by ecclesiastical boundaries, and because of the Spirit, God is close to every person and can relate to every person through creation. Psalm 139:7, 'Where can I go from your Spirit? Where can I flee from

---

[9] *Flame*, 50.
[10] Ibid. 52.
[11] *Flame*, 56.
[12] Ibid. 57.
[13] Ibid. 60.
[14] Ibid. 62.
[15] Ibid.

your presence?' (NIV), sums up this idea, as does Paul in Acts 17:27, 'God did this so that men would seek him and perhaps reach out for him and find him, though he is not far from each one of us' (NIV). Pinnock states:

> The cosmic breadth of Spirit activities can help us conceptualise the universality of God's grace. The Creator's love for the world, central to the Christian message, is implemented by the Spirit . . . There is no general revelation or natural knowledge of God that is not at the same time gracious revelation and a potentially saving knowledge. All revealing and reaching out are rooted in God's grace and are aimed at bringing sinners home.[16]

A primary truth for Pinnock is that grace is present wherever the Spirit is, for the Spirit is the love of God in the world. Therefore, instead of the historic Christian axiom *extra ecclesiam nulla salus* (outside the church there is no salvation), Pinnock wishes to hold to the axiom *extra gratia nulla salus* (outside grace there is no salvation).[17]

There are two observations I wish to make concerning Pinnock's understanding of presence. Firstly, there is what might be called a 'uniformity of presence and revelation'. Pinnock does not indicate any different ways in which God is present to his creation: 'The Spirit is present in all human experience and beyond it. There is no special sacred realm, no sacred–secular split – practically anything in the created order can be sacramental of God's presence,'[18] nor does he distinguish (in terms of salvific content) between general and special revelation. Secondly, there is the relationship between the Spirit and the doctrines of providence and divine immanence. On providence Pinnock writes: '*Providence* refers to God's sustaining and governing all things, and therefore indirectly to Spirit's moving in continuing creation.'[19] Pinnock's references to divine immanence are important in understanding the trajectory of his theological paradigm which he calls the 'trinitarian openness of

---

[16] Ibid. 187.
[17] Ibid. 194. The characteristics and concrete mediation of this grace will be described shortly.
[18] *Flame*, 62.
[19] Ibid. 53.

God'. Pinnock's paradigm of Trinitarian openness seeks to restore a
balance in theology by reaffirming the immanence of God.
Expounding this further he writes:

> By divine immanence I mean that God is everywhere present in all that
> exists. The world and God are not radically separated realities – God is
> present within every created being. As Paul said, quoting a Greek poet,
> 'In him we live and move and have our being' (Acts 17:28). Today we
> understand the world as an interconnected ecosystem, a dynamic and
> developing whole, which has made this idea of God's immanence
> even more meaningful. It has become easier for us to imagine God the
> Spirit everywhere working as creativity in the whole cosmic situation .
> . . Social trinitarian metaphysics (a relational ontology) gives us a God
> who is ontologically other but at the same time is ceaselessly relating
> and responsive.[20]

2. The Spirit and prevenient grace.
Having noted the universal presence of the Spirit, Pinnock now begins to describe further the particular characteristics of the Spirit:

> The Spirit embodies the Prevenient grace of God and puts into effect
> that universal drawing presence of Jesus Christ. The world is the arena
> of God's presence, and the Spirit knocks on every human heart, pre-
> paring people for the coming of Christ; the Spirit is ever working to
> realise the saving thrust of God's promise to the world. From the Spirit
> flows that universal gracing that seeks to lead people into fuller light
> and love.[21]

It is vital to discern Pinnock's use and understanding of 'prevenient
grace'. In evangelicalism, the term has been primarily associated
with Wesleyan theology,[22] and initially it will be useful to review

---

[20] 'Systematic Theology' in idem et al. (eds.), *The Openness of God: A
Biblical Challenge to the Traditional Understanding of God*, 111f.
[21] 'An Inclusivist View' in D.L. Okholm and T.R. Phillips (eds.), *Four
Views on Salvation in a Pluralistic World*, 104.
[22] See J. Wesley, *The Works of John Wesley*, 5:141; 6:508–12; 7:373–4, 382;
9:103; 10:229–32; 12:157; 14:356. Pinnock refers to two main works on
Wesley: R.L. Maddox, *Responsible Grace: John Wesley's Practical Theology*,
83–93; H.R. Dunning, *Grace, Faith and Holiness: A Wesleyan Systematic
Theology*, 158, 338, 431–6.

John Wesley's understanding of the term before coming to Pinnock's use of it.

Prevenient grace in Wesleyan theology
Wesley's anthropology retains the doctrine of 'total depravity' in line with Calvinist theology. This is the belief not that human beings are as sinful as they can possibly be, but that in their corrupted nature inherited from Adam, every faculty of their being is affected by sin and they are unable to make any move towards God by themselves. Human beings are 'free' according to their nature but in their nature they always choose to reject God: they are slaves to sin. Within western theology, Reformed Protestants have drawn logical conclusions that such a doctrine leads ultimately to the doctrines of unconditional election and limited atonement.[23] Roman Catholicism on the other hand has generally denied that human beings are totally depraved, and teaches that they are free (albeit through an act of grace in creation) to turn to God in their natural state. Wesley was not satisfied with either of these options. Maddox writes that Wesley felt that the Protestant position limited the scope of grace, whereas the Catholic position underestimated the depth of the Fall:

> Thus his orienting concern drove Wesley to search for a way to affirm that *all* possibility of our restored spiritual health – including the earliest inclination and ability to respond to God's saving action – is dependent upon a renewing work of God's grace, *without* rendering our participation in this process automatic. In this search he turned to an emphasis on 'prevenience;' i.e. that God's grace always pre-vents (comes before) and makes possible human response.[24]

The idea is that one of the universal benefits of Christ's death is that inherited guilt and total depravity are cancelled.[25] Prevenient grace

---

[23] This is because the gift of faith is given only to those who are elected and for whom Christ died.

[24] Maddox, *Responsible*, 83.

[25] Texts cited for this are Tit. 2:11; Jn. 1:9; 12:32. In the contemporary analyses consulted concerning Wesley's understanding of prevenient grace, there is no detailed treatment as to the root of this grace. Where does it originate? It is almost assumed that it originates in the death of Christ because of its soteriological function. If this is true then one must

restores to our nature the ability to respond positively to God's offer
of salvation. This restoration is the ability to discern some rudimen-
tary truths about God as well as the ability to discern between good
and evil, that is, a conscience. As well as this we are able to respond
freely to God: our liberty has been restored. This liberty is the
power to accept or reject God's overtures to us: grace is therefore
resistible. Here Maddox points to a crucial distinction in Wesley,
for prevenient grace is not only the partial restoration of faculties in
humankind, but is also God's initial overture to individuals. If people keep rejecting God's overtures, then they may harden their
hearts, 'the restored potential of our faculties to perceive and respond would theoretically remain upheld, but would be fruitless
because unaddressed'.[26] Such a person would need future overtures
to be 'awoken'.

Continuing his analysis, Maddox notes that there is much variation in Wesleyan scholarship as to the exact status of prevenient
grace. He refers to Thomas Langford's fourfold typology.[27] At one
end of the spectrum is the idea that the benefits of prevenient grace
are part of the nature of humanity: 'this position verges on dismiss-
ing total depravity and attributing prevenient grace to creation
rather than merciful restoration; i.e. humans are accountable
determinators of their destiny simply by the virtue of being human'.[28] The opposite to this reading is the idea that prevenient grace
awakens ourselves to our inability and drives us to despair. We realize we can do nothing and can raise no resistance to God's saving
grace.[29] Maddox comments that Langford believes a truer reading to
lie between these extremes, here the difference being one of emphasis: 'some scholars stress the possibility of human participation in
salvation that prevenient grace restores . . . Other scholars shy away
from any language of human initiative. They argue that the

---

[25] (*continued*)   ask how (if at all) it operated before the time of Christ. Presumably one answer given is that the benefits of the cross must be seen
eternally as God is outside time.

[26] Ibid. 88.

[27] Ibid. See T. Langford, 'John Wesley's Doctrine of Justification by
Faith', *Bulletin of the United Church of Canada Committee on Archives and
History*, 55–8.

[28] Maddox, *Responsible*, 89.

[29] Ibid.

provisions of prevenient grace are simply preparatory to God's further initiative in salvation.'[30]

Maddox notes one more characteristic of prevenient grace that needs mentioning as it is extremely pertinent for understanding Pinnock. Wesley often equates God's grace with God's love, 'since love is inherently a relationship between two persons, this identification suggests that Wesley's conception of grace . . . is fundamentally relational in nature'.[31] The question now is whether Wesley understands prevenient grace to be 'created' or 'uncreated'. Maddox states that western theology has generally seen grace as 'created', that is, 'a divinely-originated *product* bestowed on humanity',[32] and then debated over whether it is the imputation of an alien righteousness (a conservative Protestant position), or the infusion of an actual character in us (Roman Catholicism). However Eastern theologians have understood grace to be uncreated: it is not a product or possession given to humanity but 'the Divine energies *per se* present within us' through the Holy Spirit.[33] Both Maddox and Langford interpret Wesley's notion to be on the uncreated side: 'prevenient grace should not be considered *from* God, but the gift *of* God's activity in our lives, sensitizing and inviting us'.[34] They therefore state that Wesley's consonance is with the Eastern Orthodox position.

Prevenient grace in Pinnock's theology

Coming to Pinnock's understanding of prevenient grace, one notices that his position has gradually developed over the last twenty years and in this case must be seen in tandem with the development of his theological anthropology. In his essay 'Responsible Freedom and the Flow of Biblical History' (1975),[35] he refers to sin as being 'inherited' not in a biological or legal sense but historically: we are born into a sinful world and are affected by our surroundings. The

---

[30] Ibid.
[31] Ibid. 85f.
[32] Ibid.
[33] Ibid.
[34] Ibid. 89.
[35] Clark Pinnock, 'Responsible Freedom and the Flow of Biblical History' in idem (ed.), *Grace Unlimited*.

misuse of our freedom is the basis of our responsibility before God. The Fall did not take away our ability to choose, rather 'it initiated a historical process in which man uses his freedom in morally perverted ways. It did not nullify the fact of man's freedom; it only altered the moral direction of it.'[36]

In 'From Augustine to Arminius' (1989), this is given more detail.[37] On theological anthropology, he states that he had two paths to follow: either opt for a doctrine of prevenient grace or question the category of total depravity. Believing that the Bible had no developed doctrine of prevenient grace, Pinnock concentrated on the second path: 'what became decisive for me was the simple fact that Scripture appeals to people as those who are able and responsible to answer to God (however we explain it) and not as those incapable of doing so, as Calvinian logic would suggest'.[38] In *Theological Crossfire* (1990), Pinnock continues to deny total depravity but at the same time begins to explore the possibility of a Wesleyan notion of prevenient grace: 'Wesley began to move in a better direction . . . he taught that the natural propensity to sin can be conquered by God's grace, which is at hand.'[39]

By the time of writing *Wideness* (1992), Pinnock's position on prevenient grace seems clearer for it contains the most unambiguous espousal of the doctrine. Referring to Romans 3:11, Pinnock states:

> Paul is saying that sinners left entirely on their own without the prevenient grace of God do not naturally seek God . . . Apart from divine grace sinners do not have the inclination to seek God, but under the influence of prevenient grace they may choose to do so . . . the grace of God mitigates the effects of sinful human life and preserves the creature from self-destruction.[40]

---

[36] Ibid. 104f.

[37] Although Pinnock deals with the issue of freedom, he seems not to have dealt explicitly with this issue of prevenient grace after 1975 until his next work on Arminianism, 'From Augustine to Arminius: A Pilgrimage in Theology' in idem (ed.), *The Grace of God and the Will of Man: A Case For Arminianism*', in 1989.

[38] 'Augustine', 22.

[39] C.H. Pinnock and D. Brown, *Theological Crossfire: An Evangelical/Liberal Dialogue*, 127f.

[40] *Wideness*, 103.

I think that what Pinnock is attempting to do here is to deny total depravity (contra Wesley) because this would impinge on libertarian freedom and absolve us of responsibility before God, *and at the same time* adopt a notion of prevenient grace in the second sense that Wesley used it, that is referring to God's overtures to the human being.

Pinnock gives further explanation of this in his latest works and yet again the key to understanding his position is his reference to the person and work of the Spirit. With reference to whether prevenient grace is created or uncreated, Pinnock does not explicitly mention the distinction or which side he favours. However a few statements he makes suggests (albeit quite cryptically) that he comes down on the uncreated side. For example, in 'An Inclusivist View' (1995) he writes, 'The Spirit *embodies* the prevenient grace of God and puts into effect that universal drawing action of Jesus Christ.'[41] *Flame of Love* (1996) continues this idea: 'Spirit challenges everyone to relate to God by means of his self-disclosure ... God is revealed in the beauty and order of the natural world and *is* the prevenient grace that benefits every person,'[42] and 'Spirit prepares the way for Christ by gracing humanity everywhere. Spirit supplies the prevenient grace that benefits every person.'[43]

But is this prevenient grace solely an external overture that can be accepted or rejected by humanity in its natural state? Although Pinnock mainly sees prevenient grace as an offer to the human, he still does refer to an internal working of this grace: 'Spirit prepares the sinner to be disposed for relationship, but the outcome is not assured. People may resist God's overtures ... grace works within us, but we may stifle the invitation and shut ourselves off.'[44] For Pinnock part of being made in the *imago Dei*, means that we can always respond to or resist the Spirit's overtures; this is part of what it means to be human, and has not been destroyed by the Fall: 'There is an ember of the image still in us, and the Spirit blows upon it. People have capacity for the faith God looks for. The Spirit woos us but does not impose on us ... Salvation requires both the operation of grace and the human will.'[45]

---

[41] 'Inclusivist', 104 (my emphasis).
[42] *Flame*, 61 (my emphasis).
[43] Ibid. 63.
[44] Ibid. 158f.
[45] Ibid. 160.

How are we to understand these statements? Clearly in holding together both prevenient grace and a denial of total depravity, there is an ambiguity in a statement like 'God invites us to turn because we *can* turn.'[46] Does this mean that we can turn to God in our natural state without prevenient grace? Or does it mean that we need God's prevenient grace to be able to turn to God? Is our ability to respond to God grounded in creation (being made in the image of God) or grounded in restoration (the work of prevenient grace after the Fall)? Pinnock definitely believes that prevenient grace co-operates with the human will: 'Apart from grace there cannot be faith, but faith is authentically a human response and act of cooperation. Faith does not make grace unnecessary, and grace does not make faith automatic.'[47]

Within the context of Wesleyan theology, Pinnock seems closest to Langford's first interpretation that says that the benefits of prevenient grace are part of what it means to be human. What all humans witness throughout their lives are the overtures of the Spirit – that is prevenient grace. What is interesting here, is that Langford refers to this position being implied in Umphrey Lee's claim that for Wesley, the 'natural man' is a logical abstraction.[48] For me, language like this suggests that discussing Pinnock's concept of prevenient grace in the context of Wesley's soteriology may in fact be the wrong context in which to understand Pinnock, and may be the cause of confusion over what exactly he is saying.

This feeling is heightened as Pinnock contrasts his version of prevenient grace with the Calvinist doctrine of God's 'common' grace which is also a universal grace.[49] The distinction to be made here, is that although common grace is universal and indiscriminate, it is not saving grace and special grace is needed to remove the penalty and guilt of sin. Special grace is irresistible and discriminate; it comes only to the elect.[50] For Pinnock such a distinction between

---

[46] Ibid.

[47] Ibid. 161.

[48] Maddox, *Responsible*, 89, n. 173. Langford is commenting on Umphrey Lee, *John Wesley and Modern Religion*, 124–5, 315.

[49] See Berkhof's definition of 'common grace' in *Systematic Theology*, 436.

[50] For a useful summary of common grace see W. Grudem, *Systematic Theology: An Introduction to Biblical Doctrine*, 657–67.

common grace and special grace is dualistic, as for him it implies two Spirits at work in the world.[51] For him where there is the Spirit, there is grace, for the Spirit embodies grace. All grace is an overflow of God's Trinitarian love.

So there can be no distinction between common and special grace because Pinnock's definition of grace is not so much God's unmerited and undeserved favour (although it includes this), but rather it is God's providential presence in all humanity that has the potential to lead to salvation. Again it should be added that just as I noted a 'uniformity' in Pinnock's theology with regard to God's presence and revelation, so the same can be said about Pinnock's conception of grace: all grace is saving grace, wherever God is present so saving grace is present. By Pinnock positing one type of universal potentially saving grace, the context for discussion appears to have moved out of the doctrine of soteriology which in evangelical theology has been the traditional location in which to discuss grace, and moved into the doctrine of creation.

Putting together the above insight on the location of grace, I want to suggest that a more suitable context in which to understand Langford's first interpretation, and therefore Pinnock's view of prevenient grace which I have aligned to it, is a particular understanding of the traditional nature-grace debate as evident in much contemporary theology. If one adds to this what I have said about the Spirit's immanence in creation, then I think one can begin to see more clearly the theological context and genesis of Pinnock's position. At this juncture, I enter into the third and final part of my description of the Spirit's mission according to Pinnock.

3. *The Spirit and the 'supernatural existential'.*

Kevin Vanhoozer talks about prevenient grace but not in the Wesleyan sense. Referring to those like Pinnock who hold an 'open view' of God, he writes:

> For these theologians, there is only one kind of grace, one kind of call, and one kind of way in which God is related to the world. God exerts a constant attractive force on the soul – a kind of divine gravity. This universal call comes through a variety of media: the creation itself,

---

[51] See *Wideness*, 103; *Flame*, 200.

conscience, as well as proclamation about Christ. Grace is therefore 'prevenient': that which 'comes before' a person's ability to repent and believe.[52]

This returns us to Pinnock's notion of divine immanence through the cosmic presence of the Spirit. Compare Pinnock's version of prevenient grace with another insight of Vanhoozer:

> Tillich, Schleiermacher and many other modern theologians agree that God is the one to whom we are always/already related . . . God is not a being alongside other beings, but an energy that is constantly being experienced to sustain us on our way, whether or not we are conscious of the fact: 'all divine grace is always prevenient.' [Schleiermacher, *The Christian Faith* (Edinburgh, 1928), p. 485, n. 2] For much modern theology, then, prevenient grace has become a matter of *ontology*.[53]

Rather than seeing nature and grace as distinct and separate concepts, Pinnock appears to be advocating the infusion of the two with saving grace being present within the natural realm from creation. As he writes: 'We refuse to allow the disjunction between nature and grace . . . on the supposition that, if the triune God is present, grace must be present too.'[54]

Noting this insight on nature and grace, and in order to understand Pinnock's notion of prevenient grace further, I want to place Pinnock's argument on the Spirit's immanence and embodiment of grace within the context of the Roman Catholic understanding of nature and grace and more specifically within the context of Vatican II and Karl Rahner's notion of the 'supernatural existential', his own solution to the nature-grace debate and what Duffy calls 'the single most significant Catholic contribution to an understanding of the nature-grace dialectic in the twentieth century'.[55] This move into the realm of Catholic theology is prompted by Pinnock

---

[52] Vanhoozer, *Trinity*, 223.
[53] Ibid. 224f.
[54] Pinnock, 'Inclusivist', 98.
[55] S.J. Duffy, *The Graced Horizon: Nature and Grace in Modern Catholic Thought*, 206.

himself: 'I make no apology as an evangelical in admitting an enormous debt of gratitude to the Council for its guidance on this topic.'[56]

Noting the classical Thomist distinction between *gratia creata sive communis* (the gracious providence of the creator of all beings), and *gratia increata sive supernaturalis* (salvific Christological grace and the participation in the properties of the triune God), Miikka Ruokanen notes that through development, the standard dogmatic position on the possibility of salvation *extra Ecclesiam* by Vatican II was that by natural grace

> all rational beings . . . are able to recognise the existence of their Creator through analogy with nature, and to understand basic moral truths on the basis of natural moral law engraved on their consciences. God may offer a special kind of grace for achieving eternal blessedness to such a man of 'good will' who reveres God, seeks his truths, and is obedient to his voice heard on conscience.[57]

Given what I have already noted about the immanence of the Spirit in creation, I think there is a strong affinity between Pinnock's version of prevenient grace and the '*nouvelle théologie*'[58] which attempted to merge the distinction between *gratia creata sive communis* and *gratia increata sive supernaturalis*. Ruokanen writes:

> All human beings, created in God's image, are, by virtue of creation and incarnation, already partakers in supernatural divine light of revelation, and in the superadditional grace of the Triune God; innate *gratia creata sive communis* is supernatural christological and pneumatological grace as such. In the modern concept of grace, the independent theology as focused on nature as well as the concept of natural moral law are weakened in favor of the theologies of redemption and sanctification.[59]

---

[56] 'Inclusivist', 97.

[57] M. Ruokanen, *The Catholic Doctrine of Non-Christian Religions According to the Second Vatican Council*, 13.

[58] Ibid. 25.

[59] Ibid. In this category Ruokanen includes Henri de Lubac, Jean Daniélou, Karl Rahner, Heinz Robert Schlette and Hans Küng.

In *Flame of Love* Pinnock claims that Karl Rahner's 'supernatural existential' defends the doctrine of prevenient grace and the universality of the Spirit's operations albeit in existential neo-Thomistic language.[60] Rahner too seeks to mediate universality and particularity and the 'supernatural existential' opens up the possibility to accept or reject God's grace. Departing from the classical distinction between nature and grace, Rahner does not view grace as an external 'add on' to human nature, but rather sees nature as being infused with grace, so blurring the traditional distinctions between the two concepts: 'This "supernatural existential," considered as God's act of self-bestowal which he offers to men, is universally grafted into the very roots of human existence.'[61] This grace is uncreated. As Badcock notes, 'What is communicated, as Rahner puts it, is not information about God, or some non-divine creaturely reality that mediates grace, but rather grace as the gift of God himself: "God in his own proper reality makes himself the innermost constitutive element of man."'[62] Both Duffy and Ruokanen echo this point:

> Thus the supernatural existential that marks historical humanity's situation is seen to be God's ever-present offer of God's own Self. So it is that grace, transcendental revelation, and supernatural existential express one and the same reality. The supernatural existential refers to the abiding divine immanence in which God offers to humanity Godself and the possibility of the free response of faith.[63]

> From the ontological point of view, God is the 'innermost substance' (*entelekheia*) of the world. Because of the essential presence of God in being, the human world has become habitually saturated with the grace of God. Consequently, ontologically every man exists under the influence of divine supernatural grace.[64]

---

[60] See *Flame*, 199.

[61] K. Rahner, 'Church, Churches and Religions' in *Theological Investigations*, 10:36.

[62] G. Badcock, 'Karl Rahner, the Trinity, and Religious Pluralism' in Vanhoozer, *Trinity* 145.

[63] Duffy, *Graced Horizon*, 210.

[64] Ruokanen, *Catholic Doctrine*, 32.

Human existence then is 'supernatural' as there is a transcendental revelation infused into our nature. Therefore like Lee's claim, the 'natural man' is a logical abstraction because he cannot be separated from the graced man. As Demarest notes:

> Grace, in fact, interpenetrates nature and divinizes it; i.e, supernaturally imparts to it divine life and power. Man thus finds grace where he finds himself – in the everyday life of his finite spirit. Man as transcendental consciousness, discovers that he is energised by the *élan* of grace, as the inescapable condition of his existence. On this showing, the existence even of the unbeliever is constantly being shaped by the supernatural grace that inexorably is being offered to them. Even secular experience in a profound sense is an experience of grace.[65]

This divine self-communication can be accepted and said to be 'salvific'.

> When a person in theoretical or practical knowledge or in subjective activity confronts the abyss of his existence . . . and when this person has the courage to look into himself and to find in these depths his ultimate truth, there he can also have the experience that this abyss accepts him as his true and forgiving security.[66]

This is a transcending of the ego and a grasping for God, even though it may be unreflexive and unthematic: it is a real act of faith prompted and made possible by grace. It is a universal possibility and takes place wherever we are living.

In understanding prevenient grace in this way, Pinnock can now demonstrate clearly the principle of universal accessibility:

> God wants a relationship with sinners, and if we accept the category of prevenient grace, we acknowledge that God offers himself to creatures. Spirit speaks to everyone in the depths of their being, urging them not to close themselves off to God but to open themselves up. Because of Spirit, everyone has the possibility of encountering him – *even those who have not heard of Christ may establish a relationship with God through prevenient grace.*[67]

---

[65] Bruce Demarest, *General Revelation: Historical Views and Contemporary Issues*, 190.

[66] K. Rahner, *Foundations of the Christian Faith*, 132.

[67] *Flame*, 199 (my emphasis).

A practical application of this is that the Spirit can offer prevenient grace to an unevangelized person who has been brought up in a culture which espouses false beliefs, that is, beliefs which are contradictory to the truths of the Christian revelation. In 'An Inclusivist View' and *Flame of Love*, Pinnock appears to separate the propositional from the ethical, 'While it is true that incorrect beliefs do not lead people to faith that is not the whole story about religion . . . The act of faith is more than cognitive. Authentic faith and holy action may flow from persons inhabiting an uncompromising religious and doctrinal culture.'[68] Pinnock links the idea he is developing with the Catholic concept of the 'baptism of desire' an idea first propounded in the Middle Ages,[69] given formal ecclesiastical expression by Pius XII in 1949,[70] and picked up again at Vatican II.[71] Here, acts of love and charity demonstrated a desire for Christ which would be sufficient to be saved. Pinnock uses this idea, putting it into the language of the Spirit: 'One can avoid the one-sided Christic view by referring to the Holy Spirit who renders effective the mission of Christ and makes God's reign present everywhere.'[72] God who is omnipresent through the Spirit knows how to recognize inclinations toward him even where the gospel is not known:

> Such a desire for God does not give people everything they will ultimately need – it is a weak initiation and lacks the nurturing context of church. But it allows a decision to turn from self-centredness and to give oneself to God and neighbour. It involves a kind of rising to life and dying to self. It is . . . a work of grace. It involves being gifted and enriched by God.[73]

This is not salvation by works, but rather that good works may signal a positive response to the promptings of the Spirit and prevenient grace. These are the fruit of the Spirit as outlined in Galatians 5:22–3. Such a response may be non-cognitive and

---

[68] 'Inclusivist', 118.
[69] See 'Baptism of Desire' in K. Rahner (ed.), *Sacramentum Mundi: An Encyclopedia of Theology*, 144–6.
[70] Ibid.
[71] See e.g. *The Documents of Vatican II, Lumen Gentium* no. 16.
[72] *Flame*, 206
[73] Ibid.

implicit and may even accompany, at an explicit propositional level, false beliefs or a mixture of true and false beliefs. One should look past the propositional to the direction of a person's heart:

> They called Socrates an atheist because he did not believe in the unworthy gods of Athens, but we assume that he had more faith than the general populace of that city. Did Jesus not tell us that giving the thirsty a drink of cold water is an act of participation in the selfless love of God revealed in the gospel and makes one his sheep (Matt. 25:31–40)? *Created in God's image, a person can decide to accept the mystery of one's being, which is the goal of his or her life.*[74]

Though Jesus is not known to the unevangelized, the Spirit is present and may be experienced implicitly through acts of love. For Pinnock, this seems to be another way of saying yes to Jesus, be it subconscious and unthematized. Here, I would like to suggest that on this concept of 'ethical faith', Pinnock appears closer to Rahner's 'supernatural existential' than to the statements of Vatican II, particularly if Pinnock has relied on Ruokanen's analysis of the Council. For, although Ruokanen notes that 'Rahner's concept of anonymous Christians is a logical continuation of the principle expressed by Pius XII of the "implicit desire" of a non-Christian to conform to God's will',[75] he still interprets the statements of the Council through the traditional nature-grace distinction. Pinnock himself, however, sees far less of a distinction between a natural grace and supernatural grace. For him all grace is saving grace because it is the same omnipresent and immanent Spirit who embodies grace. Compare Pinnock's statement about 'accepting the mystery of one's being' with Rahner's idea that 'in order to have a relationship with God, man does not need first to find some "object" in which to trust or to believe. To know God is inseparable from being aware of one's own existence.'[76] Rahner writes:

> Our whole spiritual life is lived in the realm of the salvific will of God, of his prevenient grace, of his call as it becomes efficacious: all of which

---

[74] 'Inclusivist', 119 (my emphasis).
[75] Ruokanen, *Catholic Doctrine*, 31.
[76] Ibid.

is an element within the region of our consciousness, though one which remains anonymous as long as it is not interpreted from without by the message of faith. Even when he does not 'know' it and does not believe it, that is, even when he cannot make it an individual object of knowledge by merely inward reflection, man always lives consciously in the presence of the triune God of eternal life . . . The preaching is the express wakening of what is already present in the depths of man's being, not by nature, but by grace. But it is a grace which always surrounds man, even the sinner and unbeliever, as the inescapable setting of his existence.[77]

In his own analysis of Rahner, Bruce Demarest rightly says that in Rahner's theology the 'traditional concept of revelation as an intrusion *ab extra*, which conveys truths in the form of propositions, must be abandoned'[78] in favour of a transcendental revelation (the 'supernatural existential' which replaces general revelation), and a predicamental historical revelation (the conceptual thematization or objectification of the transcendental revelation which replaces special revelation).

In the final chapter of *Flame of Love*, Pinnock deals briefly with the doctrine of revelation. Noting that God reveals himself through creation and history as well as Israel and Christ, and rejecting both liberal theology which defines revelation in terms of human experience, and traditional evangelical theology which is too cognitive in its view of revelation, Pinnock propounds his own definition of revelation:

Revelation is neither contentless experience (liberalism) nor timeless propositions (conservatism). It is the dynamic self-disclosure of God, who makes his goodness known in the history of salvation, in a process of disclosure culminating in Jesus Christ. Revelation is not primarily existential impact or infallible truths but divine self-revelation that both impacts and instructs. The mode of revelation is self-disclosure and interpersonal communication.[79]

---

[77] Rahner, 'Nature and Grace' in *Theological Investigations*, 4:180f.
[78] Demarest, *General Revelation*, 190.
[79] Pinnock, *Flame*, 226.

The whole *raison d'être* of the ethical faith principle is the separation of the cognitive and the ethical, the idea being that a positive acceptance of prevenient grace can take place even though at a cognitive level God may have been rejected. Again, compare this idea to Rahner:

> The grace of Christ is at work in a man who never expressly asked for it, but who already desired it in the unspeaking, nameless longings of his heart. Here is a man in whom the unspeaking sighings of the Spirit has invoked and petitioned for that silent but all pervading mystery of existence which we Christians know as the Father of our Lord Jesus Christ.[80]

Can Pinnock's understanding of prevenient grace be compared to Rahner's 'supernatural existential'? Clearly there are significant differences, in that Rahner's framework for his theological anthropology is transcendental Thomism. However, both Pinnock and Rahner wish to affirm God's universal salvific will; the universal accessibility of saving grace (grace being the self-communication of God himself); the notion that creation is in some way graced and can be sacramental of God's presence; and the idea that if one opens oneself up to the 'divine mystery', one can have a relationship with God. Pinnock appears to be striving for a Protestant version of Rahner's 'supernatural existential' using the language of the Spirit: 'Because he is at the heart of things, it is possible to encounter God in, with and beneath life's experiences. By the Spirit, power of creation, God is closer to us than we are to ourselves.'[81] While one must take account of their different theological backgrounds, one cannot but notice the similarities between Rahner's concept of 'anonymous faith' and Pinnock's 'ethical faith principle'.

A critique of Pinnock's inclusivism

From the above description of Pinnock's inclusivism, I wish to focus my critique in three areas which have traditionally been important for evangelical theologians.

---

[80] Karl Rahner, *The Church After the Council* (New York: Seabury, 1966), 62, quoted from Demarest, *General Revelation*, 191.
[81] *Flame*, 61.

Understanding divine immanence and divine presence

For Pinnock the idea of the 'two hands of God'[82] answers the question of access to grace:

> Access to grace is less of a problem for theology when we consider it from the perspective of the Spirit, because whereas Jesus bespeaks particularity, Spirit bespeaks universality. The incarnation occurred in a thin slice of Palestine, but its implications touch the farthest star.[83]

Here I want to make a number of points. Firstly, I think Pinnock is wrong to associate a universality to the Spirit and a particularity to the Son, and then attempt a mediation. Based on the two fundamental truths that firstly, the *opera ad extra* are the work of the triune God, and that secondly, the three persons are related *perichoretically*, it seems more appropriate to say that both Spirit and Son are associated with universality and particularity depending on how one defines these terms. If this construal is correct, then creation itself must show evidence of the activity of Son and Spirit as well as re-creation. This has been traditionally affirmed by seeing creation as from the Father, through the Son and by the Holy Spirit. Pinnock bases his inclusivism on the omnipresence of the Spirit and the universality of revelation in this creative act. Where there is the Spirit, there is prevenient grace, where there is prevenient grace there is the opportunity to turn to God explicitly or implicitly.

The problem with this argument is that it confuses and conflates the universal work of the Word and Spirit in creation and the particular work of the Word and Spirit in re-creation. This is not, as Pinnock claims, a neo-Marcionite tendency to see two Gods, one in creation and one in re-creation, but merely recognizes that the one Word and Spirit have different spheres of activity in creation and re-creation. The relationship between Word and Spirit is that they work together, objective revelation is the means through which the Spirit subjectively works, the Spirit illuminates and testifies to God's revelation.

---

[82] Ibid. 58. Pinnock borrows this phrase from Irenaeus. See Irenaeus's *Against Heresies* 5.6.1.
[83] Ibid. 188.

Secondly, in the axiom *opera ad extra indivisa servato discrimine et ordine personarum* it is indeed appropriate to associate the Spirit with God's immanence. The cosmic Spirit of God is omnipresent in the whole of creation 'as the executive of the Godhead . . . the divine principle of activity everywhere'.[84] Therefore it is possible to agree with Pinnock concerning the universal presence of the Spirit. However, the idea of 'divine presence' is complex and nuanced. I want to suggest that Pinnock's argument concerning the divine gracious presence is too simplistic and that this simplicity leads to a number of erroneous conclusions concerning a universal salvific presence.

Firstly, there is the nature of the divine presence. Although Pinnock affirms that God created the world *ex nihilo*[85] and is very careful to distinguish an ontological difference between God and the world,[86] he is not afraid to speak in language that without further explanation could well be interpreted as gravitating towards the boundaries of the 'panentheistic':

> God is not a being who dwells at a distance from the world, nor is God a tyrant exercising all-controlling power. Of course God is not the world and the world is not God, *yet God is in the world and the world is in him*. Because he is at the heart of things, it is possible to encounter God in, with and beneath life's experiences.[87]

Although this is not the place to go into a detailed critique of transcendence and immanence in Pinnock's 'trinitarian openness', I do want to note that evangelical orthodoxy has been very careful to balance equally both God's otherness from creation and his involvement in creation. In his *Institutio Theologicae Elencticae* (1679–85), the Reformed scholastic Francis Turretin makes a

---

[84] B.B. Warfield, 'The Spirit of God in the Old Testament' in idem, *Biblical Doctrines*, 105. For more on the Spirit's omnipresent immanence see S. Ferguson, *The Holy Spirit*, 15–23; Badcock, 'Rahner'; Edwin Palmer, *The Person and Ministry of the Holy Spirit*, 19–29; D.F. Wells, *God the Evangelist*, 16–18.

[85] Ibid. 109.

[86] E.g. in 'Systematic Theology' in idem et al. (eds.), *The Openness of God: A Biblical Challenge to the Traditional Understanding of God*, 112.

[87] *Flame*, 61 (my emphasis).

number of distinctions concerning God's immensity and omnipresence. He notes that God can be said to be present in three modes: by
power, by knowledge and by essence.[88] Commenting on this third
mode he defines God's presence not circumscriptively (as in bodily
presence), nor definitively (as in finite spirits), but repletively – it
completely fills all space.[89] He writes:

> Therefore God is said to be repletively everywhere on account of the
> immensity of his essence, that this should be understood in a most dif-
> ferent manner from the mode of being in place of bodies (i.e., beyond
> the occupation of space, and the multiplication, extension, division of
> itself, or its mingling with other things, but independently and indivis-
> ible). For wherever he is, he is wholly; wholly in all things, yet wholly
> beyond all; included in no place and excluded from none; and not so
> much in a place (because finite cannot comprehend infinite) as in him-
> self . . . This only is to be held as certain [that God's immensity and om-
> nipresence consists] in the simple and to us incomprehensible infinity
> of divine essence, which is so intimately present with all things that is
> both everywhere in the world and yet is not included in the world.[90]

Blocher notes that immanence implies transcendence and vice
versa: 'The pervasive and indwelling presence, *praesentia* with the
Latin connotations of power and command, involves no confusion
with created being: it *expresses* the other side of transcendence. Both
immanence and transcendence tell of the divine *more*, and *beyond*,
the true *akbar*.'[91] Blocher's Trinitarian formulation appropriates
transcendence to the Father, immanence to the Spirit, with 'the
Son, the second Person in trinitarian order, prevent[ing] us from
understanding transcendence and immanence in dialectical fashion'.[92] While I am not suggesting that Pinnock discards the notion

---

[88] F. Turretin, *Institutes of Elenctic Theology*, 1:197.
[89] Ibid.
[90] Ibid. 198.
[91] Blocher, 'Immanence', 111. Interestingly, Blocher notes that 'if etymology were the key to meaning, "panentheism" would be acceptable
(Acts 17:28); but, since the word was coined by Krause, it is used to soften
resistance to pantheism, to decorate a milder and more timid form of
pantheism' (118).
[92] Ibid. 123.

of divine transcendence and despite his protestations to that effect, without further explanation by him, it is difficult not to conclude in a statement like 'God is in the world and the world is in him'[93] that Pinnock may be guilty of firstly, disrupting the very careful balance between God's transcendence and immanence (in favour of immanence), and secondly, not delineating clearly enough the boundary between creator and created.[94] Certainly, I believe Pinnock needs to clarify his position further on this matter.

Secondly, and more pertinently to our discussion, I noted in my description of Pinnock's view of presence that there was a certain uniformity of God's presence in that all presence is potentially a saving presence. As Pinnock says, 'there is no special sacred realm, no sacred-secular split – practically anything in the created order can be sacramental of God's presence'.[95] However, orthodox evangelical theology has believed it to be important to distinguish a variety of different ways God is present in creation:

> Though God is distinct from the world and may not be identified with it, He is yet present in every part of his creation, not only *per potentiam* but also *per essentiam*. This does not mean, however, that He is equally present and present in the same sense in all his creatures. The nature of His indwelling is in harmony with that of his creatures. He does not dwell on earth as He does in heaven, in animals as He does in man, in the inorganic as He does in the organic creation, in the wicked as He does in the pious, nor in the Church as He does in Christ. There is an endless variety in the manner in which He is immanent in His creatures, and in the measure in which they reveal God to those who have eyes to see.[96]

It is crucial to distinguish between God's universal presence in sustaining and preserving all things, his presence to bless, and his

---

[93] *Flame*, 61.

[94] Blocher, 'Immanence', notes that this boundary is not always easy to draw: 'He [the Spirit] is so intimately united with created being that many passages remain ambiguous: do they speak of man's created breath or of God's own life-giving breath? We may never identify the two, but how close they are!' (122).

[95] *Flame*, 62.

[96] Berkhof, *Systematic*, 61.

presence to punish. When we make these distinctions we can say with Turretin: 'God is far off from the wicked (as to the special presence of his favour and grace), but is always present with them by his general presence of essence. Where God is, there is indeed his grace originally and subjectively, but not always effectively because its exercise is perfectly free.'[97] On this more nuanced understanding of presence, we do not have to conclude with Pinnock that God's presence is necessarily a 'redemptive' presence. I think that in his desire to prove universal accessibility, Pinnock has blurred and confused the general and universal operations of the Spirit in creation, the specific and particular operations of the Spirit in salvation, and mistaken saving presence with divine providence.

Thirdly, while I want to distinguish clearly between God's sustaining presence and God's redemptive presence, it is still possible to speak of God's universal *gracious* presence providing we make one final distinction. Here we come to the role of the Spirit as dispenser of divine grace. Pinnock is not necessarily wrong to link grace with creation and not just re-creation, providing he defines this grace as universal common grace and not particular saving grace. The manifestation of common grace is *essentially* different from salvific grace. While saving grace is seen as being supernatural and flowing from the cross:

> Common grace, on the other hand, is natural . . . it does not remove sin or set men free, but merely restrains the outward manifestations of sin and promotes outward morality and decency, good order in society and civic righteousness, the development of science and art and so on. It works only in the natural, and not the spiritual sphere.[98]

In the doctrine of common grace, God does not let the effects of the Fall go unchecked but restrains humanity by common grace. Common grace enables human beings to see God's revelation in creation and in this sense this revelation is itself a common grace as it gives human beings a rationality and makes understanding possible.[99]

---

[97] Turretin, *Institutes*, 200.

[98] Berkhof, *Systematic*, 439.

[99] For Demarest, *General Revelation*, it is the combination of general revelation and common grace which explains the presence of other religions:

However, general revelation is epistemologically inadequate because it can only speak of God as creator and not of God as re-creator. The act of re-creation has to deal with the penalty of sin as well as establishing a new creation. Here we see a new activity of Word and Spirit, the particular act of re-creation.

The Spirit and Christ

Pinnock links the universal love of God with the cosmic work of the Spirit in creation. The implication of this is that God is sacramentally present in all of creation because of the Spirit's omnipresence. Pinnock wishes us to see that there is no discontinuity between creation and incarnation:

> Spirit prepares the way for Christ by gracing humanity everywhere. In such global activities Spirit supplies the prevenient grace that draws sinners to God and puts them on the path toward reconciliation. What one encounters in Jesus is the fulfillment of previous invitations of the Spirit. God's love is the ever-present ground and goal of created things. We know this from Jesus Christ, but this truth has always been so, always a possibility. One does not properly defend the uniqueness of Jesus Christ by denying the Spirit's preparatory work that preceded his coming. Let us try to see continuity, not contradiction, in the relation of creation and redemption.[100]

In his attempt to mediate both the axioms of universality and particularity, Pinnock contextualizes Christology within pneumatology,

---

[99] (*continued*) 'On the basis of God's universal general revelation and common enabling grace, undisputed truths about God, man, and sin lie embedded to varying degrees in the non–Christian religions. In addition to elements of truth, the great religions of the world frequently display a sensitivity to the spiritual dimension of life, a persistence in devotion, a readiness to sacrifice, and sundry virtues both personal (gentleness, serenity of temper) and social (concern for the poor, nonviolence). But in spite of these positive features, natural man, operating in the context of natural religion and lacking special revelation, possesses a fundamentally false understanding of spiritual truth' (259). I believe that this link between common grace, general revelation and the presence of other religions is an area which demands further investigation by evangelicals.
[100] Ibid. 63.

not seeing the Spirit as 'tied' or subordinate to Christ as his substitute or instrument, but as being universally and salvifically present even where Christ is not known: 'Let us see what results from viewing Christ as an aspect of the Spirit's mission, instead of (as is more usual) viewing Spirit as a function of Christ's. It lies within the freedom of theology to experiment with ideas'[101] and,

> God sends both Son and Spirit . . . The relationship is dialectical. The Son is sent in the power of the Spirit, and the Spirit is poured out by the risen Lord . . . It is not right to be Christocentric if being Christocentric means subordination of the Spirit to the Son. The two are partners in the work of redemption.[102]

It is the Spirit who facilitates the Christ event: 'something happened through the total journey of Jesus that literally changed the world and opened the door wide to union with God'.[103] But what is this 'something' and why was it necessary? Pinnock suggests that the incarnation was the clearest and most decisive presentation of God in history, but that Jesus was, in fact, the 'fulfillment of a process'[104] which had been started by the Spirit. From the perspective of the Spirit, there is a continuity in what the Spirit has always been doing in creation, and what we see in the incarnation: 'Salvation can be a universal possibility if we recognise the universal, loving activities of the Spirit. God has always wanted friendship and reconciliation with sinners. *What Jesus made explicit and implemented has always been true.*'[105]

Statements like this generate a number of crucial questions concerning the precise nature of Pinnock's doctrine of the person and work of Christ, knowing that Pinnock rejects the traditional evangelical model of 'penal substitution'.[106] If God's love is grounded in

---

[101] Ibid. 80.

[102] Ibid. 82. Pinnock believes that an aid to this 'freeing' of the Spirit is the dropping of the *filioque* (and the Son) clause from the Creed. See *Flame*, 196f.

[103] Ibid. 93.

[104] Ibid. 195.

[105] Ibid. 105 (my emphasis).

[106] For some examples of Pinnock criticising the 'penal substitution model' see Clark H. Pinnock & Robert C. Brow, *Unbounded Love*, 147–9.

creation and the presence of the Spirit, then what exactly is the purpose of the incarnation and the atonement? If the cross is not the source of God's saving grace, then why is it needed? Does it effect salvation or does it merely reveal (albeit normatively) something already presupposed? Is it representative or constitutive? Is it, as Richard points out, not intrinsic to the structure of God's global grace but complementary?[107] Pinnock may wish to cover all possibilities by saying that divine grace is present everywhere, 'since God has created the whole world, since Jesus Christ died for all, and since the Spirit gives life to creation',[108] but it seems theologically crucial to know the relationships between these three truths and whether one is primary. Pinnock is unclear and ambiguous in answering these questions. About Pinnock's argument specifically regarding the salvation of the unevangelized, I would like to offer my thoughts on where I think Pinnock must go in his argumentation.

Firstly, there is the question concerning the theological grounds for a universally accessible grace. It would seem difficult to base a universal grace on the work of Christ because Pinnock insists that creation itself is gracious and a natural sacrament. Christ was the fulfilment of a process in the history of the Spirit. Everyone who has ever lived has been able to respond to the Spirit's prevenient grace, including all those who lived before Christ. One wonders then, what are the benefits of Christ to the unevangelized if grace is universally present outside the incarnation and has always been universally present. For Pinnock, Christ died for everyone, but this does not imply universalism, for salvation is conditional on the human response: 'a new situation now exists: we only have to accept what has been done and allow the Spirit to conform our lives to Christ'.[109] But does this new situation exist for the unevangelized? Pinnock's soteriology which puts emphasis on the human response needs to show how the unevangelized are saved *by Christ*. It is true that the unevangelized may implicitly decide to respond to prevenient grace by turning from self-centredness and giving themselves to God and neighbour, and this may well involve a dying to self and rising to

---

[107] R.P. Richard, *The Population of Heaven: A Biblical Response to the Inclusivist Position on who will be Saved*, 51.
[108] 'Inclusivist', 98.
[109] Ibid. 96.

life. Indeed, Christ may well be the normative and unique revelation of this self-sacrifice and the unevangelized person may be implicitly mirroring, and so participating in, Christ's representative journey. But the question remains how the salvation of the unevangelized believer is related directly to the work of Christ and not merely to the work of the Spirit in creation, of which Christ is but the ultimate expression.

The above analysis leads me tentatively to the conclusion that although Pinnock confesses a high constitutive Christology, it would appear in reality that the unevangelized can be saved outside Christ (but of course not outside God's grace) because Christ's work of re-creation and God's grace in creation are identical. At an epistemological level, the incarnation is unique, final and exclusive, but ontologically it only represents (albeit normatively) what the Spirit has been doing always from creation. Pinnock confesses a constitutive Christology and an objective redemption but his position on the unevangelized appears to question whether in fact he can coherently hold on to both doctrines. Rather than being Christocentric in his inclusivism, which I believe he would claim to be, Pinnock's position is pneumatocentric and as a result the particularity of Christ is compromised.

Such an analysis may help one understand more clearly the ramifications and significance of the definition of inclusivism given earlier, that Christ is ontologically necessary for salvation but not epistemologically necessary. Pinnock's desire to universalize the particular has meant a separation of the epistemological from the ontological. What I want to suggest is, that for Pinnock, this separation is *only* theologically possible because in reality not only is Christ not epistemologically necessary for the salvation of the unevangelized, but that there is a great deal of ambiguity as to how the unevangelized are *ontologically* saved by God's grace in Christ. Certainly they are saved by accepting God's grace through the Holy Spirit in creation. But ontologically what does this grace have to do with Christ? Without further explanation on Pinnock's part, there is a massive lacuna in the relationship between the work of Christ and the salvation of the unevangelized in Pinnock's inclusivism.

In summary, the point I have been trying to establish is that for Pinnock saving grace is universal because it is pneumatological and present in creation. The implication of this is that this grace is in some way separated from the Christ event. However, it is precisely this salvific pneumatocentricity over Christocentricity which I wish to dispute, because as Badcock states (interestingly referring to Rahner):

> There is a strong sense in New Testament pneumatology, however, and indeed in the Christian theological tradition in general, that the gift of the Spirit is something that flows from the Christ-event, and that it is of decisive importance precisely because it is an eschatological event, something that ruptures the previous continuities of natural human existence . . . The fact that the Spirit appears . . . to be given fundamentally at creation, appears to conflict with the links of Scripture and tradition that are made both between Pentecost and Calvary and between the Messianic age and the life to come.[110]

The doctrine of sin

The above statement by Badcock highlights my final area of concern. Pinnock's universality axiom concentrates on the universality of God's saving love and his universal gracious presence by the Spirit in creation, the ultimate demonstration of this being the incarnation. I have argued that because the unevangelized can freely accept or reject the Spirit's overtures of prevenient grace, and because the source of this grace and the ability to respond to it are located in creation and not in re-creation, there are major questions concerning the necessity and purpose of the atonement. In contrast to this, orthodox evangelical theology has argued that one cannot understand the atonement without understanding its necessity, and the Bible constantly refers to the universal depth of human sin as making Christ's penal substitution absolutely necessary in God's provision of salvation:

> Adam's sin plunged the entire human race into sin and condemnation. So humanity outside Christ is described as dead in sin, without God and without hope (Eph. 2:1,11–12), destined for judgement (Heb. 9:27) and eternal condemnation (Mt. 25:31–46; Rom. 5:12–21).

---

[110] G. Badcock, 'Karl Rahner, the Trinity, and Religious Pluralism' in Vanhoozer, *Trinity*, 153.

Underlying this grim reality is the basic truth that God's justice requires the punishment of sin and the sinner.[111]

This theme cannot be ignored or minimized. We are 'objects of wrath' (Eph. 2:3), 'dead in transgressions and sin' (Col. 2:3), slaves to sin who wilfully conform to the sinful nature.[112] Wright summarizes the Calvinist doctrine of humanity's sinful condition in five statements:

1. Since the Fall of Adam and Eve, all are born spiritually dead in their sin nature, and therefore require regeneration to a life they do not naturally possess . . .
2. Being fallen, the natural heart and mind is sinfully corrupt and unenlightened . . .
3. Because the whole of nature is involved in the Fall and its results, sinners are slaves to sin.
4. No one escapes the unrighteous tendencies of the sinful Adamic nature . . .
5. Left to themselves, those dead in trespasses and sins have no spiritual ability to reform themselves, or to repent, or to savingly believe . . .[113]

The doctrines of original sin and total depravity articulate the reality of the human condition.[114] Sin is universal and crippling. This is the 'bondage of the will', a moral inability to do good. Pinnock's inclusivism tends to underemphasize the 'guilty' nature of all humanity, both evangelized and unevangelized, with the result that divine salvific grace is replaced with divine salvific obligation. However, I believe that biblical anthropology presents the effects of the Fall as being so severe that the only universal thing we merit is judgement, wrath and condemnation, *not* love. The fact that God saves anyone is amazing!

---

[111] R. Letham, *The Work of Christ*, 125.

[112] Jn. 8:34; Rom. 6:17–20; 2 Pet. 2:19.

[113] R.K. McGregor Wright, *No Place for Sovereignty: What's Wrong with Freewill Theism*, 112–16.

[114] See Grudem, *Systematic Theology*, 490–514; G.R. Lewis and B. Demarest, *Integrative Theology*, 2:190–224; J. Murray, *The Imputation of Adam's Sin*.

It is appropriate at this point to note the relationship between the work of the Spirit and the universality and extent of sin. Pinnock's stress on the cosmic activity of the Spirit is the main feature of his 'pneumatological' inclusivism and while my critique has not denied this cosmic feature, it has criticized Pinnock for not distinguishing between general and special operations of the Spirit and between salvific and non-salvific operations of the Spirit. The whole tenor of Pinnock's argument is optimistic and positive: the Spirit embodies grace: 'the cosmic breadth of Spirit activities can help us conceptualise the universality of God's grace. The Creator's love for the world, central to the Christian message, is implemented by the Spirit.'[115] However, Pinnock's positive emphasis on the relationship between the Spirit and world, is perhaps too optimistic. Note Ferguson's comment:

> When we consider this emphasis on the cosmic and universal ministry of the Spirit in light of the explicit statements of the New Testament, we immediately encounter a surprising datum. The New Testament places the Spirit and the world in an antithetical, not a conciliatory, relationship. The world cannot see or know the Spirit (Jn. 14:17); the Spirit convicts the world (Jn. 16:8–11); the spirit of the world and the Spirit of God stand over against each other (1 Cor. 2:12–14; 1 Jn. 4:3).[116]

There are many aspects to the Spirit's work, dispensing grace being only one facet. While judging and convicting the world of guilt in regard to sin may be one of the more negative aspects of the Spirit's universal work, in order to gain a true biblical perspective on the world, this work must not be underemphasized or forgotten. The same Spirit that issues grace also brings judgement to a sinful humanity.

Finally and in the context of this discussion on sin, I want to note two implications for the nature and content of faith. In the ongoing internal evangelical debate between Arminians and Calvinists, Arminian soteriology is often accused by Calvinist theology of diluting *sola gratia* because saving faith originating from the free will of

---

[115] *Flame*, 187.
[116] S. Ferguson, *The Holy Spirit*, 246.

the individual becomes the 'hinge on which the atonement depends',[117] and the ground of justification: 'The Arminian teaching
on justification is in effect, if not intention, legalistic, turning faith
from a means of receiving from God into a work that merits before
God.'[118] Evangelical Arminians like Wesley attempted to respond to
this by adopting a doctrine of universal prevenient grace which is an
effect of the atonement and which mitigates the effect of Adam's
sin, making a free response to God possible.[119]

However, Pinnock's version of prevenient grace is more in line
with Karl Rahner's supernatural existential than Wesley's doctrine,
because Pinnock denies a total depravity claiming that *from creation*
human beings made in the *imago Dei* have always been able to say
yes or no to the Spirit's overtures: 'freedom is essential to the image
of God in us . . . salvation requires the operation of both grace and
the human will'.[120] This underestimation of the ontological and
noetic effects of the Fall, and the merging of nature and grace
post-Fall, goes directly against the majority of 'evangelical' teaching, Arminian and Calvinist. On this point, again Badcock's
comments on Rahner can be equally applied to Pinnock. Is it

> possible to maintain that God is close to all, so close that his presence is
> almost indistinguishable from the self, in view of the biblical teaching
> that all alike are objects of divine wrath? The fact that in Rahner the
> God of wrath has entirely given place to the God of love may be theo-
> logically welcome from a certain perspective, but can it be justified in
> biblical terms? Rahner himself does not provide such a justification,
> and it must be questioned whether one could ever be provided from
> strict exegesis of either the Old or the New Testaments. At the very
> least, one must say that while there are biblical themes relating to the

---

[117] Letham, *Work*, 231.

[118] J.I. Packer, 'Arminianisms' in R. Godfrey and T. Boyd (eds.), *Through Christ's Word: A Festschrift for P E Hughes*, 134.

[119] The main arguments against this view are (1) the lack of explicit biblical evidence supporting such an operation of grace; and (2) that the efficacy of grace is weakened as it can be accepted or rejected. See T.R. Schreiner, 'Does Scripture Teach Prevenient Grace in the Wesleyan Sense?' in T.R. Schreiner and B.A. Ware (eds.), *The Grace of God, The Bondage of the Will: Historical and Theological Perspectives on Calvinism*, 365–83.

[120] *Flame*, 160.

imago dei, for example, that lend support to his position, there are plenty of others that do not.[121]

Pinnock seems to be even more susceptible than traditional Arminianism to the accusation of semi-Pelagianism especially when one considers the ethical 'faith principle' where good works are a positive response to the Spirit's overtures.

Secondly, there is my response to Pinnock's question of existential viability – the 'fact' that many of the unevangelized perform acts of love and mercy and are 'holy' people, thus showing signs of the Spirit. For Pinnock this is a sign of a response to grace, an implicit acceptance of the mystery of one's being. I have already offered one explanation of 'good' acts in our discussion of common grace. Here it was said that the Spirit restrains sin in a non-salvific way and this is the cause of much 'good' we see both individually and culturally. However, in the context of our discussion of sin, we should raise the question as to whether acts that Pinnock calls 'good' are in fact 'good'. Here one must ask what the biblical definition of sin is. Although from one perspective sin can be defined as the failure to keep the law of God, Romans 1:21–5 hints that the root of sin is not the performance of evil but primarily a failure to glorify God as God. It is an idolatry which exchanges the glory of God for lesser created things. With this in mind, Schreiner writes:

> Such a conception of sin helps us to understand how people can perform actions that externally conform with righteousness yet remain slaves of sin. These actions are not motivated by a desire to honor and glorify God as God. They are not done out of an attitude of faith, which brings glory to God (Rom. 4:20). Faith brings glory to God because he is seen to be the all powerful one who supplies our every need, and thus deserving of praise and honour . . . The necessity of faith is underscored by Romans 14:23, where Paul notes that 'everything that does not come from faith is sin.' Slavery to sin does not mean that people always engage in reprehensible behaviour. It means that the unregenerate never desire to bring glory to God, but are passionately committed to upholding their own glory and honour.[122]

---

[121] Badcock, 'Rahner', 152f.
[122] Schreiner, 'Scripture', 367f.

The question for Pinnock to answer is how God can be the object of glorification (or perhaps more specifically how can God glorify himself in his Son Jesus Christ through the witness of the Spirit), when propositionally he is misunderstood or even not believed in. Surely, the marks of true faith must include both propositional and ethical elements – both are inextricably linked and cannot be separated.

Conclusion

Clark Pinnock still wishes to call himself an evangelical theologian and offers his inclusivism as a viable position for evangelicals to take regarding the salvation of the unevangelized. To date and in terms of sheer quantity of writing and exposure, and despite what I said at the beginning of this essay, Pinnock's defence of inclusivism, remains the most comprehensive within 'evangelical' theology, and it cannot be denied that the questions he raises concerning the unevangelized and 'other religions' are serious, relevant and demand a response. However, concerning his own response to these questions, I believe there to be a number of problems which must question the 'evangelicalness' of his formulation.

Firstly, on the level of historical sources, my own interpretation of Pinnock has shown that there appear to be good grounds for locating the roots of his inclusivism, not in evangelical theology but in contemporary Roman Catholic theology. Hence in terms of the nature of divine presence, the nature-grace debate, and the doctrine of revelation, Pinnock seems far closer to Vatican II and Karl Rahner than to John Wesley. While not wanting here to enter into a discussion about the nature and definition of 'evangelical', on his inclusivism alone, I think Pinnock's inclusivism (certainly in its later form) fits more comfortably into a non-evangelical context.

Secondly, and more importantly, there is the theological analysis of his position. With regard to upholding both axioms of universality and particularity, I believe Pinnock has failed because the ultimate result of his argument is a subtle universalization of the particular. So while Pinnock still thinks he maintains the finality, particularity and primacy of Christ in soteriology, the real consequence of his thinking is that the incarnation and atonement have been reinterpreted to conform with the universality axiom. This move poses questions concerning the normativity of the incarnation, the necessity and purpose of the atonement, and, more specifically, the relationship between the work of Christ and the salvation of the unevangelized. In other words, concerning the salvation of the unevangelized, the notion of *solus Christus* in Pinnock's theology appears to have undergone a significant redefinition and one is left asking the meaning of this fundamental evangelical tenet. That Pinnock does not adequately deal with these areas leads one to two possible conclusions concerning his argument.

Firstly, it could be said that all the above points illustrate one of the main weaknesses of Pinnock's theology in general, which is a lack of precision, and potential superficiality in argumentation. As I mentioned at the beginning of this essay, there are advantages to his style of theology, but there are disadvantages when one presses for details on key issues. Pinnock would probably concede this point admitting that a lot more work needs to be done in specific areas. If this is the case, then one awaits to see the results before making a judgement.

A more fundamental criticism concerns the issue of theological coherence. Pinnock does not hide the motives behind his inclusivism. For him, the universality axiom cannot be compromised. However, at the same time, he still wishes to hold to evangelical orthodoxy in his Christology, realizing the dangers of pluralism to Christological formulation. The resulting synthesis, though, when seen from the perspective of his inclusivism and the salvation of the unevangelized, is theologically ambiguous and without further clarification significantly redefines the orthodox interpretation of *sola Christus*, *sola gratia* and *sola fide*.

Perhaps even more serious is that, as a doctrine within his systematic theology, Pinnock's inclusivism is not disjointed or detached, but 'fits' well into his theological vision called 'trinitarian openness' and is indeed resourced by this wider framework (for example, the stress on divine immanence, the rejection of 'penal substitution'). As a result, in questioning his inclusivism, one would appear to be also questioning this overarching framework.

If the analysis I have presented in this essay is an accurate one, and if the quality of coherence is an important part of his theology (which I believe it is), I would like to contend that without further explanation and detail, Pinnock would have a choice to make: either reaffirm the particularity of the person and work of Christ with the consequence that his own version of pneumatological universality may have to be revised and qualified (as would elements of his 'trinitarian openness'), or continue to affirm his construal of universality at the expense of particularity. I believe that whichever way he goes on this issue will determine the evangelical or non-evangelical nature of his inclusivism – and perhaps ultimately his theology in general.

11

Clark Pinnock's Response to Part 3

In Part 3 the book turns to the topic of religious pluralism. It could have considered some other theme, such as my views about the inspiration of Scripture, but the decision was taken to discuss the wider hope or inclusivist model which I have set forth to help with religious pluralism. I appreciated Partridge's essay especially for two reasons aside from its excellence, a feature the other essays share. First, I have received a good deal of criticism up to this point in the book but here I find an evangelical sympathetic not only to inclusivism but to openness theism also, which he calls personalism. The others may think my ideas are unevangelical but Christopher at least does not. Of course, my joy is tempered by Strange's essay which is sympathetic to neither proposal! Second, Partridge makes this Part a dialogue among the contributors in a way which did not happen in Parts 1 and 2. He not only likes the inclusivist model but strengthens it and makes my job responding easier.

What is the link between the openness model of God discussed in Parts 1 and 2 and inclusivism discussed in Part 3? The openness model presents a gracious God who seeks loving relationships with all human beings but raises a problem too: How is salvation through Jesus Christ universally accessible? The urgency of this problem is illustrated in this letter which I received from an Asian-American pastor:

> As you articulated in your book, a growing number of people today especially Asian Americans with no ties to Christianity, are deeply troubled with the predominant teaching that all of their unsaved loved ones – dead or alive – are automatically going to go to hell. Why

should we be excited about going to heaven, if everyone we love is going to hell? What kind of good news is this? Being able to assure them that Jesus will make the right call at least gives them some measure of hope. For them, without this kind of hope, becoming a believer seems to demand not only the loss of unsaved loved ones but the loss of our own humanity.

Our Christian hope is filled with glorious themes: parousia, resurrection, kingdom, new creation, etc. We look forward with joy and a hope inspired by the Holy Spirit to the time when life will truly begin. But our hope is shadowed by a nagging concern about the fate of the unevangelized. The outlook is hopeful for those who have participated in God's covenants with Israel and the church, but not for the innumerable others whose lives have been lived outside these spheres. Tradition has often (though not always) taken the hardline position that outsiders to the covenants cannot be saved which means that a large proportion of humanity cannot be saved because (through no fault of their own) they have not been part of these arrangements. This can be enormously vexing. First-generation Christians like my pastor friend agonize over the question in relation to the destiny of their ancestors, and non-Christians ever since Porphyry continue to scoff.

According to inclusivism, God provides opportunities in this life for people to know him and his Spirit wherever they live. Of course there are other suggested options too which seek to ease the problem: God may get the message to those seeking God before they die; God may calculate what the response of unevangelized persons would have been had they heard the gospel; God may provide an opportunity to be saved at death or after death. I prefer the option, usually called inclusivism, which reflects the thinking of the early Fathers, of select individuals over the centuries, and which recently has become the official position of the Roman Catholic Church. According to this view, religions that have arisen prior to, or independently of, biblical revelation may be salvifically oriented to Christ in ways manifest to the eyes of God. By fastening onto 'the seeds of the Word', persons ignorant of God's full revelation in Christ may be associated with Christ in a measure sufficient for them to attain eternal life. The appeal of the model is that it manages to retain the centrality of Christ as the sole source of salvation, while at the same time not requiring one to believe that God consigns to perdition the majority of the race who are not Christians through no fault of their own.

In my work, I appeal to a number of scriptural themes which orient theology in this more hopeful direction and speak of a universal, divine, saving economy. I refer to God's cosmic covenant with humankind, the universal economy represented by categories like God's wisdom, spirit and word, the significance of pagan saints, Jesus' attitude toward believers outside Israel, and the openness of early Christians to God's work among the heathen before evangelization. I strive for a theological perspective that would, while holding fast to faith in Jesus Christ as traditionally understood, be able to recognize the grace of God at work beyond the church. Aware of the prevalent negative assessment of these matters among evangelicals, I had hoped to reorient us if I could to a more positive evaluation of the workings of grace outside the church.

In interpreting the Bible, no one comes from nowhere and everyone comes from somewhere. Therefore, allow me to identify three hermeneutical presuppositions in my work around this topic.

First, I recognize that the biblical writers feature as their main theme what God is doing through Abraham and his seed and that the testimony to the wider work of God, though it exists, is not the primary focus of Scripture. Thus I am exploring the sub-plot of God's dealings with the nations, prior to Abraham, and alongside the history of Israel and the church. Scripture concentrates on the ingathering of the nations through salvation history which begins with the call of Abram.

However, there is also (I think) a sub-plot which deals with what God is doing in the wider world. What God is doing in salvation history in the narrow sense does not entail the notion that this is the only set of divine initiatives that he has going on anywhere. Though one is struck by the Abrahamic covenant and its subsequent developments, it does not exhaust what the Bible has to say about salvation. This means that the material I appeal to is less ample than I could wish and that (therefore) the use that I make of it can be questioned. Critics might think that the evidences which I cite in support of the wider work of God are too imprecise and/or flimsy to make the points that I have in mind. In reply, I would say that I do not wish to exaggerate the evidence that I find but that I also do not

want to see data swept under the rug. For example, I should not exaggerate the significance of God's covenant with Noah or the
speech on the Areopagus but neither should anyone else underrate
such matters.

Second, as MacDonald insisted, the Bible is a complex book, on
this as on other subjects, and I do not assume only a single line of testimony on this or other questions. Neither my position nor any
other can be established by proof-texting which assumes a flat uniformity of biblical teaching, because of the dialectical quality in the
material. I see a complexity in Scripture with tensions and compli-
mentary elements. Take, for example, Paul's attitude in Romans
chapter 1 compared with his approach in Acts chapter 17. On the
one hand, in Romans, we see discontinuity with stress on the radical newness of Christ in contrast to pagan darkness – on the other
hand, in Acts, we see continuity between the gospel and the Greek
world waiting for the unknown God to be revealed, prepared by
their own poet-theologians. Are there not two tendencies here, of
continuity and discontinuity, which create a dialectical tension, not
to be suppressed? Or (to take another example) is there not the
Word made flesh but also the Word present from the beginning?
There is the active presence of the Logos not yet incarnate in the
world and the event of incarnation, which is the culmination of
God's revelation.

Recognizing the dialectical nature of the Bible forces us to go
deeper and to search for directions in texts not just statements. We
must ask: Where are we being led? We need to be open to the
dialogical nature of the biblical witness, be open to its overall drift,
and be sensitive to the struggle for truth in the Bible itself. The Bible
is a complex book and reading it can be like listening to a conversation. Not to see this can lead to a depreciation of the complex canonical   witness   which   often   presents   testimony   and
counter-testimony and requires us to 'tack' between them. If we
disregard   the   testimony   to   continuity,   we   may   end   up   in
restrictivism – if we disregard the testimony to discontinuity, we
may end up in religious pluralism. (Note: I only found fault with
MacDonald's 'tension' because it was a contradiction. I do in fact
accept tensions!)

Third, I am also influenced (as is plain by now) in my reading of
the Bible by an Arminian type of orientation which leads me to

favour a hermeneutic of hopefulness and to view God as a serious and inclusive lover. God loves his enemies and is kind to the ungrateful and wicked (Mt. 5:45; Lk. 6:35). Jesus proclaims God's acceptance to the riff-raff – to outcasts, sinners, renegades, prostitutes. He did not wait for them to make themselves respectable, but preached good news to them. God's love toward the race is radical, his generosity overflowing. I believe God wants everyone to be saved and come to a knowledge of the truth (1 Tim. 2:4), that Jesus was lifted up to draw everyone to himself (Jn. 12:32), and that God is not willing that any should perish (2 Pet. 3:9). God's grace abounds more than sin (Rom. 5:20) and God sent his Son as last Adam, signalling the desire to turn things around on a large scale.

It is inconceivable to me to imagine that God, who seeks out one lost sheep, would leave millions without hope of salvation. In short, I read the Bible in relation to what God has revealed in Jesus, which means (for example) that I read the early chapters of Genesis hopefully and notice clues of divine generosity sometimes passed over by others. I also read the Old Testament with liberty as Scripture which has reached its goal in Jesus Christ. From this point of view, it is hard for me to believe that God only first thought of saving humanity when Abram came along or that he would be content with saving only Abram's seed. Like the interpreters of the New Testament themselves, I do not treat the Old Testament as a text which contains unchangeable truths to which the readers and the readers' community make no contribution as to meaning. These texts have meaning as they are read and used by the people of God. We have a measure of interpretive freedom and ought to read all Scripture as a witness to the gospel of Jesus.

Both Sinkinson and Strange raise a point, which deserves response, about the place of moral virtue in recognizing the wider grace of God. It sounds to them as if I think non-Christians may be saved by being good people. What I actually mean is what the epistle of James teaches, that faith without works is dead and that genuine faith is made visible by works (2:14–26). Jesus too was looking for more than faith in people – he was looking for kingdom orientation. He looked for the cup of cold water and the outstretched hand (Mt. 25:31–46). The issue for Jesus was not so much whether people called him 'Lord' verbally, as it was doing the will of the Father (Mt. 7:21). He says, 'Here are my mother and my brothers!

Whoever does the will of God is my brother and sister and mother'
(Mk. 3:34–5). Jesus had an eye not only for those with the right lin-
eage and correct profession but for co-builders of the kingdom of
God.

The criterion of judgement is the self-giving love of God made
known in Jesus. The judgement is therefore not so much a matter of
doctrine as it is about how people respond to God's mercy. What is
important is participation in Christ's loving way of life which mani-
fests itself in the service of others. What is all-important are kingdom acts and the kind of faith which is revealed in works. As with
the father's two sons, it was not so much what they professed they
would do at first, but what they did in the end. Jesus asked, 'Which
son do you think pleased God?' As John the Baptist said, 'Being a
descendant of Abraham is neither here nor there; what counts is
your life, is it green and blooming? Because if it's dead wood, it goes
into the fire' (Mt. 3:9, *The Message*).

There is salvation for those who, without knowing God as revealed in the gospel, showed justice to the oppressed and acted in
accordance with God's purposes. Not everyone can have a personal
relationship with Jesus Christ because many have not been reached
by the proclamation. In their case what counts is whether their con-
duct agrees with the will of God as Jesus explained it. *Agapē* is the
sign of the operative presence of the mystery of salvation in a person. Jesus says that people can meet him in the poor, the sick, and
the dying and find the door to eternal life. Not just the name of Jesus
but the spirit of Jesus, the spirit of love, matters on the day of judgement. We evangelicals too with all our theological correctness will
be measured by the same standard.

The message of Jesus is the norm by which God judges those
who never meet Jesus personally. As the parable of the sheep and the
goats shows, those who have never known Jesus but who have done
works of love that are in accord with his message may participate in
the salvation of God's kingdom and be justified by God, while those
who are nominal Christians will be excluded from salvation. The
significance of Jesus Christ at the last judgement lies in his being the
criterion of God's relationship to us and the means by which God
judges all people, not just Christians. All of us will be examined
from the standpoint of our explicit or implicit relation to the teaching of Jesus, especially the love and mercy that found expression in

his mission. Even those who have not become confessing members of the church can have a share in the new life manifested in Jesus Christ, if their hearts are open to the nearness of God's kingdom that Jesus proclaimed. Jesus could take such a 'liberal' stance because he believed that God's kingdom was larger than Israel and church. The community may be a sacrament of the kingdom but the kingdom is even larger. People outside church can share in its reality and foster its values. Jesus cared less about orthodoxy (I think) and more about whether religion enslaves people or sets them free. He cared about whether it fosters love and compassion.[1]

Again I thank the editors and authors for allowing me the privilege to interact with what they have had to say. May the discussion bear good fruit in the providence of God.

---

[1] Note: my book *A Wideness in God's Mercy: The Finality of Jesus Christ in a World of Religions*, though out of print, is still available. A book agent can place an order with Lightning Print Inc., a subsidiary of Spring Arbor/Ingram Distributors (Michigan), or it can also be obtained by e-mail from JonRStock@academicbooks.com in a cheaper edition.

12

Conclusion

Christopher Sinkinson

A volume such as this cannot really have a conclusion. Gray and myself have been discussing the ideas presented by Pinnock and his like-minded theologians for quite a few years now. Particularly, through our involvement in Christian ministry among students it was obvious how significant and appealing these ideas could be to many people. We have not reached a conclusion on all these issues, nor does this volume intend to reach closure on the debate. In many respects we have simply sought to raise awareness of the questions that need to be addressed. We have no doubt that the cluster of questions raised by Pinnock's openness theism will be vigorously debated for many years. However, for now, we may be able to identify whether we have succeeded in our more modest aims.

We stated at the outset our desire to avoid producing more heat than light in this crucial debate. It was our intention to generate a discussion devoid of name-calling and strong on substantive content. All contributors felt this to have been achieved. However, labels are to some extent helpful. They are a shorthand way of guiding the discussion. In particular, every contributor has been concerned with whether the new theology represented by Pinnock is properly described as 'evangelical'. There is no monopoly on the term, as we made clear in the introduction, but it is used as a shorthand way of asking whether a position is truly biblical. Pinnock commented that Gray's evaluation of his position as 'thoroughly non-evangelical' stung. However, this is simply the implication of most of the arguments in the book. Whether it stings or not is another question.

Use of the term 'non-evangelical' is far from name-calling. What we mean by our use of the term 'evangelical' is too significant to dispense with it, as Strange showed in his opening essay. Most of the contributors felt that Pinnock is seriously compromising the meaning of the term by describing his own work as evangelical. Nonetheless, we remain convinced that the labels we use are not the key issue but that they point to more substantive matters. So did the book produce more heat or more light? No apology is needed for the debate being, in Pinnock's words, 'hard-hitting'. The matters discussed are serious. The contributors care about the issues not as mere academic pursuit but as matters close to the heart. Given such seriousness, the dialogue was certainly courteous.

On to more substantive matters. What may we conclude? The majority of contributors were convinced that Pinnock's theology is much less than biblical. The idea that God neither determines nor knows the future raised great concern. MacDonald and Gathercole provided the exegetical difficulties this idea creates. In particular, they presented many examples of prophecy that suggest much more than simply a declaration of God's intentions. Indeed, many prophecies predict the future behaviour of human beings – of Pharaoh and Cyrus for example. God is not simply, as Pinnock suggests, 'announcing his purposes and intentions for the future'. God reveals what the purposes and intentions of his future creatures will be. This must surely remain a problem for Pinnock's treatment of the relationship between divine knowledge and human freedom.

Gray and Richmond develop more philosophical considerations on the theme of foreknowledge and this generates a particularly vigorous response in Part 2. A central issue here is the relationship of biblical Christianity to various forms of non-Christian thought. The contributors were convinced that much of Pinnock's worldview owes more to non-Christian philosophical assumptions than to the Bible. It is interesting to note how much Pinnock resented this suggestion and was adamant that his only crime was the exact opposite: to 'prefer the Bible to Plato'. He has a point in saying that two thousand years of Christian theology show plenty of room for disagreement among Christians and divergent models for understanding God. That diversity itself shows the importance of Christian tradition. Whatever their differences, Christian theologians have usually maintained that the truth matters and that, in principle, doctrinal disagreements may be settled. Richmond and Gray are both well aware of theological diversity in this tradition.

What Pinnock fails to show is that there is room among Christians committed to the authority of the Bible for the abandonment of divine foreknowledge altogether. The debates in church history concern *how* God can know the future free choices of his creatures; they do not concern *whether* he has such knowledge. Whether its inspiration is found in Wesley or Arminius, the impression remains that Pinnock is developing a novel theological position. That we find difficulty locating him in relation to Christian tradition does not in itself constitute a crime but most evangelicals would at least find this unsettling. In his response to Part 1 Pinnock points out that many people respond to his work by simply saying, 'That's nothing new – I've always thought that.' Pinnock finds it 'gratifying' but no one need find it surprising. The issue is whether this response indicates coherent scriptural exegesis on the part of most people or simply the prevailing worldview of our post-Christian western world.

Part 3 deals with one specific area in which openness theism has been applied. It is true that this could have been devoted to a different area, perhaps the doctrine of inspiration. However, the area chosen is one on which Pinnock has written a great deal and seems a natural one to pursue. The importance of the Part, and its reason for being somewhat longer, is that it helps us to clarify some implications of adopting openness theism. Pinnock claims in Part 2 that views on the nature of the future are not part of the criterion of being orthodox or unorthodox. This may be true in the sense that the Bible does not develop a philosophical description of freedom as compatibalist, determinist or any other.

However, it is in the implications for soteriology discussed in Part 3 that we can begin to see the impact of Pinnock's view on a whole range of foundational doctrines. Partridge, Strange and I were particularly interested in the issue of how we define faith and what knowledge is necessary for saving faith. While we came from different perspectives and would not share each others conclusions, we all recognized that important doctrinal claims were at stake. The implications for the doctrines of grace, judgement and general revelation were especially important and given wide-ranging treatment. Pinnock describes Part 3 as the most interactive given the breadth of viewpoints among the contributors. Sadly this is not reflected in Pinnock's response which interacts only a little with the relevant essays. Instead, Part 3 is primarily a restatement of Pinnock's thought on other religions.

There are at least two helpful points that we might establish from the interaction between Pinnock and the contributors.

Firstly, the most common charge against Pinnock was the imprecision of his work. What Partridge described as being a little 'nebulous' was something all the contributors felt in reading and hearing Pinnock explain elements of his theology. Ambiguous statements and vague passing remarks make it difficult to establish exactly what a theologian is proposing. This is one reason for the present book: it aims to help clarify, in a detailed way, the position Pinnock espouses and the implications of adopting that position as one's own. Pinnock's plea that we should not want to 'shut these discussions down' hardly falls on deaf ears in a collection devoted to that very discussion!

Whether the discussion is shut down or not is certainly not in the hands of any of these present contributors. The only question open to us is whether the discussion is one we can take part in and interact with. For the sake of evangelical self-understanding and our witness in the world we all felt the pressing need to engage seriously with these issues. Pinnock's opportunity to respond to the questions, concerns and objections raised here was obviously limited by space. We are grateful for the interaction he was able to give but it is our hope that at some stage he will answer the wider range of issues raised. To do so will not only help clarify his relationship to evangelicalism but also to clarify the internal coherence of openness theism.

Secondly, a great deal of attention has been drawn to the role of presuppositions in these discussions. Pinnock admits this role in his responses as do the contributors. No one can honestly say that their entire worldview is shaped by the Bible. We bring with us a mixture of false prejudices and assumptions as we read the text of Scripture. What words like 'freedom' and 'sovereignty' mean to us will depend upon a range of presuppositions. This is shown up in various places throughout this present work. It means that we cannot simply proof-text for or against any particular position. We have all striven to avoid that approach in our discussion and yet to remain faithful to the teaching of Scripture. However, while we all admit that various philosophical assumptions influence our reading of the

Bible none of the contributors think that this creates an insurmountable obstacle to establishing the truth. Meaningful dialogue and argument is possible because we are convinced that theological mistakes are being made somewhere and that God has provided the church with the resources to be able to identify those errors. It is left for readers to judge, with their own assumptions and prejudices, which positions make the most natural reading of Scripture. We submit this volume in the hope of continuing clarification among evangelicals today.

Bibliography

Abbot, W.M. (ed.), *The Documents of Vatican II* (New Jersey: New Century Publishers, 1966)

Albrektson, B., *History and the Gods* (Lund: CWK Gleerup, 1967)

Anderson, N., *Christianity and World Religions* (Leicester: IVP, 1984)

Armstrong, J.H., *The Coming Evangelical Crisis* (Chicago: Moody Press, 1996)

Badcock, G., 'Karl Rahner, the Trinity, and Religious Pluralism' in K.J. Vanhoozer (ed.), *The Trinity in a Pluralistic Age: Theological Essays on Culture and Religion* (Grand Rapids: Eerdmans, 1997) 143–54

Bangs, C., *Arminius: A Study in the Dutch Reformation* (Grand Rapids: Zondervan, 1985)

Barclay, J.M.G., *Obeying the Truth* (Edinburgh: T. & T. Clark, 1988)

Basinger, D., and R. Basinger (eds.), *Predestination and Free Will: Four Views of Divine Sovereignty and Human Freedom* (Downers Grove: IVP, 1986)

Bavinck, J.H., 'Human Religion in God's Eyes: A Study of Romans 1:18–32', *The Scottish Bulletin of Evangelical Theology* 12 (1994) 44–52

Bebbington, D.W., *Evangelicalism in Modern Britain: A History from the 1730s to the 1980s* (London: Unwin Hyman, 1989)

Berkhof, L., *Systematic Theology* (Grand Rapids: Eerdmans, 1932)

Berkouwer, G.C., *General Revelation* (Grand Rapids: Eerdmans, 1995)

Best, E., *Essays on Ephesians* (Edinburgh: T. & T. Clark, 1997)

—, *Ephesians* (International Critical Commentary; Edinburgh: T. & T. Clark, 1998)

Blocher, H., 'Immanence and Transcendence in Trinitarian Theology' in Vanhoozer, *Trinity*, 104–23

Bloesch, D.G., *A Theology of Word and Spirit: Authority and Method in Theology* (Carlisle: Paternoster Press, 1992)

—, *God the Almighty* (Carlisle: Paternoster Press, 1995)

Boettner, L., *The Reformed Doctrine of Predestination* (Philadelphia: Presbyterian and Reformed, 1965)

Bornkamm, G., *Der Lohngedanke im Neuen Testament* (Munich: Kaiser, 1959)

Brettler, M.Z., *God Is King: Understanding an Israelite Metaphor* (Sheffield: Sheffield Academic Press, 1989)

Brooks, V.B., *The Neural Basis of Motor Control* (Oxford: Oxford University Press, 1976)

Bruce, F.F., *The Acts of the Apostles* (Aberdeen: Aberdeen University Press, 1952)

Brueggemann, W., *Theology of the Old Testament: Testimony, Dispute and Advocacy* (Minneapolis: Fortress Press, 1997)

Brümmer, V., *The Model of Love* (Cambridge: Cambridge University Press, 1993)

De Bruyn, T., *Pelagius's Commentary on St Paul's Epistle to the Romans* (Oxford: Clarendon Press, 1993)

Calvin, J., *Institutes of the Christian Religion*, ed. J.T. McNeill, tr. F.L. Battles (Philadelphia: Westminster Press, 1960)

Cameron, C., 'Arminius – Hero or Heretic?', *Evangelical Quarterly* 64 (1992) 213–27

Carson, D.A., review of C.H. Pinnock (ed.) *Grace Unlimited*, *Journal of the Evangelical Theological Society* 20 (1977) 177–8

—, *Divine Sovereignty* (London: Marshall, Morgan, and Scott, 1981

—, *How Long, O Lord? Reflections on Suffering and Evil* (Grand Rapids: Baker Book House, 1990)

—, *The Gagging of God* (Leicester: IVP, 1996)

Childs, B.S., *Exodus* (London: SCM Press, 1974)

Chisholm, R.B., 'Does God "Change His Mind"?', *Bibliotheca Sacra* 152 (1995) 378–99

Cook, R., 'God, Middle Knowledge and Alternative Worlds', *Evangelical Quarterly* 62 (1990) 293–310

Cracknell, K., *Justice, Courtesy and Love: Theologians and Missionaries Encountering World Religions, 1846–1914* (London: Epworth Press, 1995)

Craig, W.L., 'Middle Knowledge, a Calvinist-Arminian Rapprochement?' in Pinnock, *Grace of God*, 141–64

Cranfield, C.E.B., *A Critical and Exegetical Commentary on the Epistle to the Romans*, vol. 1 (Edinburgh: T. & T. Clark, 1975)

—, *On Romans* (Edinburgh: T. & T. Clark, 1998)

Cox, J.L., *Expressing the Sacred* (Harare: University of Zimbabwe, 1992)

Davidson, A.B., *The Theology of the Old Testament* (Edinburgh: T. & T. Clark, 1904)

Davies, B., *The Thought of Thomas Aquinas* (Oxford: Clarendon Press, 1992)

Davies, W.D., and D.C. Allison, *Matthew* (International Critical Commentary; Edinburgh: T. & T. Clark, 1991)

D'Costa, G., *Theology and Religious Pluralism* (Oxford: Basil Blackwell, 1986)

—, 'John Hick and Religious Pluralism: Yet Another Revolution' in H. Hewitt (ed.), *Problems in the Philosophy of Religion* (London: Macmillan, 1991) 324–34

—, 'The End of Systematic Theology', *Theology* 95 (1992)

—, 'The Impossibility of a Pluralist View of Religions', *Religious Studies* 32 (1996) 223–32

Dekker, E., 'Was Arminius a Molinist?', *SCJ* 27 (1996) 337–52

Demarest, B., *General Revelation: Historical Views and Contemporary Issues* (Grand Rapids: Zondervan, 1982)

—, 'General and Special Revelation: Epistemological Foundations of Religious Pluralism' in A.D. Clarke and B.W. Winter (eds.), *One God One Lord in a World of Religious Pluralism* (Cambridge: Tyndale House, 1991) 135–52

Duffy, S.J., *The Graced Horizon: Nature and Grace in Modern Catholic Thought* (Minnesota: Michael Glazier Books, 1992)

Dunn, J.D.G., *Romans* (Word Biblical Commentary; Waco: Word Books, 1988)

—, *Colossians* (The New International Greek Testament Commentary; Carlisle: Paternoster Press, 1996)

—, *Theology of Paul the Apostle* (Edinburgh: T. &. T. Clark, 1998)

Dunning, H.R., *Grace, Faith and Holiness: A Wesleyan Systematic Theology* (Kansas City: Beacon Hill Press, 1988)

Edwards, D.L., *Essentials: A Liberal-Evangelical Dialogue* (London: Hodder & Stoughton, 1992)

Erickson, M., *Christian Theology* (Grand Rapids: Baker Book House, 1985)

—, *The Evangelical Left: Encountering Postconservative Evangelical Theology* (Grand Rapids: Baker Book House, 1997)

Evans, C.F., *Saint Luke* (London: SCM Press, 1990)

Fackre, G., *The Doctrine of Revelation: A Narrative Interpretation* (Edinburgh: Edinburgh University Press, 1997)

Farmer, H.H., *Things Not Seen: Studies in the Christian Interpretation of Life* (London: Nisbet, 1929)

—, *The World and God: A Study of Prayer, Providence and Miracle in Christian Experience* (London: Nisbet, 1936)

—, 'The One Foundation', *Christian World Pulpit* 135 (1939) 205–7

—, *God and Men* (London: Nisbet, 1948)

Feinberg, J., 'God Ordains All Things' in Basinger and Basinger, *Predestination*, 29–32

Ferguson, S., *The Holy Spirit* (Leicester: IVP, 1996)

Forster, R., and P. Marston, *God's Strategy in Human History* (Crowborough: Highland, 1973)

Fretheim, T.E., *The Suffering of God: An Old Testament Perspective* (Philadelphia: Fortress Press, 1984)

—, 'Suffering God and Sovereign God in Exodus: A Collision of Images', *Horizons in Biblical Theology* 11 (1989) 31–56

—, *Exodus* (Louisville: John Knox Press, 1991)

Gammie, J.G., *Holiness in Israel* (Minneapolis: Fortress Press, 1989)

Geisler, N., *Creating God in the Image of Man? The New Open View of God – Neotheism's Dangerous Drift* (Minneapolis: Bethany House, 1997)

George, T., *Theology of the Reformers* (Leicester: Apollos, 1988)

Gibson, J.C.L., *Language and Imagery in the Old Testament* (London: SPCK, 1998)

Goldhill, S.D., *Reading Greek Tragedy* (Cambridge University Press, 1986)

Gordon, J.M., *Evangelical Spirituality: From the Wesleys to John Stott* (London: SPCK, 1991)

Graham, W., *Just as I Am: The Autobiography of Billy Graham* (London: Harper Collins, 1997)

Gray, T., 'Hell: An Analysis of the Doctrine of Hell in Modern Theology' (DPhil thesis, Oxford University, 1995)

—, 'God does not Play Dice', *Themelios* 24.2 (1999) 21–34

Green, J.B., *Luke* (New International Commentary on the New Testament; Grand Rapids: Eerdmans, 1997)

Green, M., *I Believe in the Holy Spirit* (London: Hodder & Stoughton, 1979)

Griffin, D.R., *God, Power and Evil* (New York: University Press of America, 1991)

Grudem, W., *Systematic Theology: An Introduction to Biblical Doctrine* (Grand Rapids: Zondervan/Leicester: IVP, 1994)

Gunton, C., 'The Trinity, Natural Theology and a Theology of Nature' in Vanhoozer, *Trinity*, 88–103

Hackett, S., *The Reconstruction of the Christian Revelation Claim* (Grand Rapids: Baker Book House, 1984)

Halbertal, K.D.M., and A. Margalit (eds.), *Idolatry*, tr. N. Goldblum (Cambridge, MA: Harvard University Press, 1992)

Hamilton, V.P., *Genesis 18–50* (Grand Rapids: Eerdmans, 1995)

Harrington, D.J., *The Gospel of Matthew* (Collegeville, MA: Liturgical Press, 1991)

Hasker, W., 'A Philosophical Perspective' in Pinnock et al., *The Openness of God: A Biblical Challenge to the Traditional Understanding of God* (Downers Grove: IVP/Carlisle: Paternoster Press, 1994) 126–54

Hawthorne, G., *Philippians* (Waco: Word Books, 1983)

Hays, R., *The Moral Vision of the New Testament* (Edinburgh: T. & T. Clark, 1996)

Heil, J.P., *The Gospel of Mark as Model for Action* (Mahwah, NJ: Paulist Press, 1992)

Helm, P., 'Are They Few That Be Saved?' in N.M. de S. Cameron, *Universalism and the Doctrine of Hell* (Carlisle: Paternoster Press, 1992), 257–81

—, *The Providence of God* (Leicester: IVP, 1993)

Hengel, M., *Judaism and Hellenism,* 2 vols. (Philadelphia: Fortress Press, 1974)

—, *The 'Hellenisation' of Judea in the First Century after Christ* (Philadelphia: Trinity Press International, 1989)

Henry, C.F., *God, Revelation and Authority*, 6 vols. (Carlisle: Paternoster Press, 1999)

Heschel, A.J., *The Prophets* (New York: Harper & Row, 1962)

Hick, J., *Faith and Knowledge* (London: Macmillan, 19882)

—, *God Has Many Names* (London: Macmillan, 1980)

—, *God and the Universe of Faiths* (London: Macmillan, 1988)

—, *An Interpretation of Religion* (London: Macmillan, 1989)

Hoolenweger, W., *The Pentecostals* (London: SCM Press, 1972)

Hughes, D.A., *Has God Many Names?* (Leicester: IVP, 1996)

Hughes, E.J., *Wilfred Cantwell Smith: A Theology for the World* (London: SCM Press, 1986)

Jenni, E., and C. Westermann (eds.), *Theological Lexicon of the Old Testament*, tr. M.E. Biddle (Peabody: Hendrikson, 1997)

Jensen, J., 'Yahweh's Plan in Isaiah and in the Rest of the Old Testament', *Catholic Biblical Quarterly* 48 (1986) 443–55

Kelly, J.N.D., *The Epistles of Peter and of Jude* (London: A. & C. Black, 1969)

Klostermaier, K., *Hindu and Christian in Vrindaban* (London: SCM Press, 1969)

Küng, H., *Does God Exist?* (London: SCM Press, 1991)

—, and K.-J. Kuschel (eds.), *A Global Ethic: The Declaration of the World's Parliament of Religions* (London: SCM Press, 1993)

Lampe, G.W.H., 'Christian Theology in the Patristic Period' in H. Cunliffe-Jones (ed.), *A History of Christian Doctrine* (Edinburgh: T. & T. Clark, 1978)

Langford, T., 'John Wesley's Doctrine of Justification by Faith', *Bulletin of the United Church of Canada Committee on Archives and History* 29 (1980) 55–8

Lee, U., *John Wesley and Modern Religion* (Nashville: Kingswood, 1936)

Leftow, B., 'Eternity' in P. Quinn and C. Taliaferro (eds.), *A Companion to Philosophy of Religion* (Oxford: Blackwell, 1997) 257–63

Letham, R., *The Work of Christ* (Leicester: IVP, 1993)

Lewis, C.S., *The Screwtape Letters* (London: Fontana, 1942)

Lewis, G.R., and B. Demarest, *Integrative Theology*, vol. 2 (Grand Rapids: Zondervan, 1990)

Lindbeck, G.A., *The Nature of Doctrine* (London: SPCK, 1984)

H. Lindstrom, *Wesley and Sanctification: A Study in the Doctrine of Salvation* (London: Epworth Press, 1946)

Lochhead, D., *The Dialogical Imperative* (London: SCM Press, 1988)

Lodge, D., *The British Museum is Falling Down* (London: Penguin Books, 1965)

MacMullen, R., *Roman Social Relations, 50 B.C. to A.D. 284* (New Haven: Yale University Press, 1974)

MacNicol, N., 'Is There a General Revelation? A Study in Indian Religion', *The International Review of Missions* 32 (1943) 241–57

Maddox, R.L., *Responsible Grace: John Wesley's Practical Theology* (Nashville: Kingswood, 1994)

Markham, I., 'Creating Options: Shattering the "Exclusivist, Inclusivist and Pluralist" Paradigm', *Religious Studies* 27 (1991) 259–67

Marshall, I.H., *Kept by the Power of God: A Study in Perseverance and Falling Away* (London: Epworth Press, 1969)

Martin, R.P., *Philippians* (New Century Bible; Grand Rapids: Eerdmans, 1989)

Martin, W., *The Billy Graham Story: A Prophet With Honour* (London: Hutchinson, 1991)

McGonigle, H., *John Wesley's Doctrine of Prevenient Grace* (Manchester: Wesley Fellowship, 1995)

McGrath, A.E., *The Genesis of Doctrine* (Oxford: Basil Blackwell, 1990)

—, *A Life of John Calvin* (Oxford: Basil Blackwell, 1990)

—, 'An Exclusivist View' in Okholm and Phillips, *Four Views*, 129–32

McGregor Wright, R.K., *No Place for Sovereignty: What's Wrong with Freewill Theism* (Downers Grove: IVP, 1996)

Meijer, F., and O. van Nijf, *Trade, Transport and Society in the Ancient World: A Sourcebook* (London: Routledge, 1992)

Miller, P.D., 'The Sovereignty of God' in D.G. Miller (ed.), *The Hermeneutical Quest: Essays in Honor of James Luther Mays on His Sixty-Fifth Birthday* (Alison Park: Pickwick Publications, 1986) 129–44

Moberly, R.W.L., *At the Mountain of God: Story and Theology in Exodus 32–34* (Sheffield: JSOT Press, 1983)

—, *The Old Testament of the Old Testament: Patriarchal Narratives and Mosaic Yahwism* (Minneapolis: Fortress Press, 1992)

—, ' "God is Not a Human That He Should Repent" (Numbers 23:19 and 1 Samuel 15:29)' in T. Linafelt and T.K. Beal (eds.), *God in the Fray: A Tribute to Walter Brueggemann* (Minneapolis: Fortress Press, 1998) 112–23

de Molina, L., *On Divine Foreknowledge* (Part 4 of the *Concordia*) tr., with an Introduction and Notes, A.J. Freddoso (Ithaca: Cornell University Press, 1988)

Muller, R.A., *God, Creation and Providence in the Thought of Jacob Arminius* (Grand Rapids: Baker Book House, 1991)

Murray, I.H., *Revival and Revivalism: The Making and Marring of American Evangelicalism 1750–1858* (Edinburgh: Banner of Truth, 1994)

Murray, J., *The Imputation of Adam's Sin* (Grand Rapids: Eerdmans, 1959)

Nazir-Ali, M., *Citizens and Exiles: Christian Faith in a Plural World* (London: SPCK, 1998)

Nisbet R., and T. Wilson, 'Telling More Than we Can Know: Verbal Reports on Mental Processes', *Psychological Review* 84 (1977) 231–59

Noble, P.R., 'The Sensus Literalis: Jowett, Childs, and Barr', *Journal of Theological Studies* 44.1 (1993) 1–23

Okholm, D.L., and T.R. Phillips (eds.), *More Than One Way? Four Views on Salvation in a Pluralistic World* (Grand Rapids: Zondervan, 1995)

Olson, G., *The Story of Christian Theology* (Leicester: Apollos, 1999)

Packer, J.I, 'Arminianisms' in R. Godfrey and T. Boyd (eds.), *Through Christ's Word: A Festschrift for P E Hughes* (Phillipsburg: P. & R., 1985) 121–48

Palmer, E., *The Person and Ministry of the Holy Spirit* (Grand Rapids: Baker Book House, 1958)

Partridge, C.H., *H.H. Farmer's Theological Interpretation of Religion: Towards a Personalist Theology of Religions* (Toronto Studies in Theology, 76; Lewiston: Edwin Mellen Press, 1998)

—, 'The Academic Study of Religions: Contemporary Issues and Approaches', *Evangel* (forthcoming)

Phillips, T.R., and D.L. Okholm (eds.), *The Nature of Confession* (Downers Grove: IVP, 1996)

Pinnock, C.H., *A New Reformation: A Challenge to Southern Baptists* (Tigerville: Jewel Books, 1968)

—, *Evangelism and Truth* (Tigerville: Jewel Books, 1969)

—, 'Appendix: On Method in Christian Apologetics' in idem, *Set Forth Your Case: Studies in Christian Apologetics* (Chicago: Moody Press, 1971)

—, *Biblical Revelation: The Foundation of Christian Theology* (Chicago: Moody Press, 1971)

—, 'The Problem of God', *Journal of the Evangelical Theological Society* 16 (1973) 11–16

—, 'Responsible Freedom and the Flow of Biblical History' in idem (ed.), *Grace Unlimited* (Minneapolis: Bethany House, 1975) 95–109

—, 'The Need for a Scriptural, and Therefore a Neo-Classical Theism' in K.S. Kantzer and S.N. Gundry (eds.), *Perspectives in Evangelical Theology: Papers from the Thirtieth Meeting of the Evangelical Theological Society* (Grand Rapids: Baker Book House, 1979) 37–42

—, *A Case For Faith* (Minneapolis: Bethany House, 1980)

—, 'I Was a Teenage Fundamentalist', *The Wittenburg Door* 70 (December 1982/January 1983)

—, 'How I Use the Bible in Doing Theology' in R. Johnston (ed.), *The Use of the Bible in Theology* (Atlanta: John Knox, 1985) 18–34

—, *The Scripture Principle* (London: Hodder & Stoughton, 1985)

—, 'God Limits His Knowledge' in Basinger, D., and R. Basinger (eds.), *Predestination and Free Will: Four Views of Divine Sovereignty and Human Freedom* (Downers Grove: IVP, 1986)

—, 'Between Classical and Process Theism' in R. Nash (ed.), *Process Theology* (Grand Rapids: Baker Book House, 1987) 309–29

—, 'The Finality of Jesus Christ in the World Religions' in M.A. Noll and D.F. Wells (eds.), *Christian Faith and Practice in the Modern World* (Grand Rapids: Eerdmans, 1988) 152–68

—, 'From Augustine to Arminius: A Pilgrimage in Theology' in idem, *The Grace of God*, 15–30

— (ed.), *The Grace of God and the Will of Man: A Case For Arminianism* (Grand Rapids: Zondervan, 1989)

—, and D. Brown, *Theological Crossfire: An Evangelical/Liberal Dialogue* (Grand Rapids: Zondervan, 1990)

—, 'Toward an Evangelical Theology of Religions', *Journal of the Evangelical Theological Society* 33 (1990) 359–68

—, *A Wideness in God's Mercy: The Finality of Jesus Christ in a World of Religions* (Grand Rapids: Zondervan, 1992)

—, 'Foreword' in R.C. Roennfeldt, *Clark H. Pinnock on Biblical Theology: An Evolving Position* (Grand Rapids: Andrews University Press, 1993) xv–xxiii

—, R. Rice, J. Sanders, W. Hasker and D. Basinger (eds.), *The Openness of God: A Biblical Challenge to the Traditional Understanding of God* (Downers Grove: IVP/Carlisle: Paternoster Press, 1994)

—, 'Systematic Theology' in idem et al., *Openness*, 101–25

—, 'The Holy Spirit as a Distinct Person in the Godhead' in M. Wilson (ed.), *Spirit and Renewal* (*Journal of Pentecostal Theology*, Supplement Series, 5; Sheffield: Sheffield Academic Press, 1994) 34–41

—, and R.C. Brow, *Unbounded Love: A Good News Theology for the 21st Century* (Downers Grove: IVP/Carlisle: Paternoster Press, 1994)

—, 'An Inclusivist View' in D.L. Okholm and T.R. Phillips (eds.), *Four Views on Salvation in a Pluralistic World* (Grand Rapids: Zondervan, 1995) 93–123

—, *Flame of Love: A Theology of the Holy Spirit* (Downers Grove: IVP, 1996)

—, 'Evangelical Theologians Facing the Future: An Ancient and a Future Paradigm', Keynote address for the 33rd Annual Meeting of the Wesleyan Theological Society, 7–8 November 1997

—, *Theology for Revival*, 21 November 1997 (London: Emmanuel Evangelical Church, 1997) (audio cassettes)

—, 'The Role of the Spirit in Redemption', *Ashbury Theological Journal* 52 (1997) 47–54

Plantinga, E. (ed.) *Christianity and Plurality: Classic and Contemporary Readings* (Oxford: Blackwell, 1999)

Platt, J.E., 'The Denial of the Innate Idea of God in Dutch Remonstrant Theology: From Episcopius to Van Limborch' in C.R. Trueman and R.S. Clark (eds.), *Protestant Scholasticism: Essays in Reassessment* (Carlisle: Paternoster Press, 1999) 213–26

du Preez, J., 'Johan Herman Bavinck on the Relation Between Divine Revelation and the Religions', *Missionalia* 13 (1985) 111–20

Price, R.M., 'Clark H. Pinnock: Conservative and Contemporary', *Evangelical Quarterly* 88.2 (1988) 157–83

Race, A., *Christians and Religious Pluralism* (London: SCM Press, 1993)

von Rad, G., *Genesis*, tr. J.H. Marks and J. Bowden (London: SCM Press, 1972)

Rahner, K., 'Christianity and the Non-Christian Religions' in idem (ed.), *Theological Investigations* (London: DLT, 1966) 5:115–34

—, 'Nature and Grace' in idem (ed.), *Theological Investigations*, vol. 4 (London: DLT, 1966) ch. 7

—, 'Baptism of Desire' in idem (ed.), *Sacramentum Mundi: An Encyclopedia of Theology* (New York: Burns & Oats, 1968) 144–46

—, 'Church, Churches and Religions' in idem (ed.), *Theological Investigations*, vol. 10 (London: DLT, 1974) 30–49

—, *Foundations of the Christian Faith* (New York: Seabury, 1978)

—, 'The Supernatural Existential' in G.B. Kelly (ed.), *Karl Rahner: Theologian of the Graced Search for Meaning* (Edinburgh: T. & T. Clark, 1993) 110–17

Rakestraw, R.V., 'Clark H. Pinnock: A Theological Odyssey', *Christian Scholars Review* 3 (1990) 252–70

Rice, R., 'Divine Foreknowledge and Free-Will Theism' in Pinnock, *Grace of God*, 121–39

—, 'Biblical Support for a New Perspective' in Pinnock et al., *Openness*, 11–58

Richard, R.P., *The Population of Heaven: A Biblical Response to the Inclusivist Position on who will be Saved* (Chicago: Moody Press, 1994)

Richardson, D., *Eternity in Their Hearts* (California: Regal, 1984)

Roennfeldt, R.C., *Clark H. Pinnock On Biblical Theology: An Evolving Position* (Grand Rapids: Andrews University Press, 1993)

Rowley, H.H., *The Biblical Doctrine of Election* (London: Lutterworth, 1950)

Ruokanen, M., *The Catholic Doctrine of Non-Christian Religions According to the Second Vatican Council* (Leiden: E.J. Brill, 1992)

Sanders, E.P., *Paul and Palestinian Judaism* (Minneapolis: Fortress Press, 1977)

—, *Jesus and Judaism* (London: SCM Press, 1985)

Sanders, J., *No Other Name* (Grand Rapids: Eerdmans, 1991)

—, 'God as Personal' in Pinnock et al., *Openness*, 59–100

—, *The God who Risks: A Theology of Providence* (Downers Grove: IVP, 1998)

Schaeffer, F.A., *Collected Writings*, 5 vols. (Carlisle: Paternoster Press, 1996)

Schreiner, T.R., 'Does Scripture Teach Prevenient Grace in the Wesleyan Sense?' in T.R. Schreiner and B.A. Ware (eds.), *The Grace of God, The Bondage of the Will: Historical and Theological Perspectives on Calvinism* (Grand Rapids: Baker Book House, 1995) 365–83

Sinkinson, C., *John Hick: An Introduction to his Theology* (Leicester: RTSF, 1995)

Smail, T., *The Giving Gift: The Holy Spirit in Person* (London: Hodder & Stoughton, 1988)

Smalley, S.S., *1,2,3 John* (Waco: Word Books, 1984)

Smart, N., *Dimensions of the Sacred: An Anatomy of the World's Beliefs* (Berkeley: University of California Press, 1996)

Smith, W.C., *The Meaning and End of Religion: A Revolutionary Approach to the Great Religious Traditions* (London: SPCK, 1978)

—, *Towards a World Theology* (London: Macmillan, 1981)

—, *Patterns of Faith around the World* (Oxford: Oneworld, 1998)

Soggin, J.A., *Judges* (London: SCM Press, 1987)

Strange, D., 'The Possibility of Salvation Among the Unevangelised: An Analysis of Inclusivism in Recent Evangelical Theology' (PhD thesis, Bristol University, 1999)

Swidler, L. (ed.), *Death or Dialogue?* (London: SCM Press, 1990)

Taylor, J.V., *The Go-Between God: The Holy Spirit and the Christian Mission* (London: SCM Press, 1972)

Tomberlin, J., and P. van Inwagen (eds.), *Alvin Plantinga* (Profiles, 5; Dordrecht: Reidel, 1985)

Torrance, T.F., 'The Atonement. The Singularity of Christ and the Finality of the Cross: The Atonement and the Moral Order' in N.M. de S. Cameron, (ed.), *Universalism and the Doctrine of Hell* (Carlisle: Paternoster Press, 1992), 223–56

—, *Divine Meaning: Studies in Patristic Hermeneutics* (Edinburgh: T. & T. Clark, 1995)

Treggiari, S., *Roman Marriage: Iusti Coniuges from the Time of Cicero to the Time of Ulpian* (Oxford: Clarendon Press, 1991)

Trueman, C.R., *The Claims of Truth: John Owen's Trinitarian Theology* (Carlisle: Paternoster Press, 1998)

Turretin, F., *Institutes of Elenctic Theology*, vol. 1, tr. G.M. Giger, ed. J.T. Dennison, Jr. (Phillipsburg: P. & R., 1992)

Vanhoozer, K.J., 'Does the Trinity Belong in a Theology of Religions: On Angling in the Rubicon and the "Identity" of God' in idem (ed.), *The Trinity in a Pluralistic Age: Theological Essays on Culture and Religion* (Grand Rapids: Eerdmans, 1997) 41–71

Visser't Hooft, W.A., *No Other Name* (London: SCM Press, 1963)

Vroom, H.M., *Religions and the Truth* (Michigan: Eerdmans, 1989)

Ward, K., *Holding Fast to God: A Reply to Don Cupitt* (London: SPCK, 1982)

Warfield, B.B., 'The Development of the Doctrine of Infant Salvation' in idem, *Studies in Theology* (Edinburgh: Banner of Truth, 1988) 411–44

—, 'The Spirit of God in the Old Testament' in idem, *Biblical Doctrines* (Edinburgh: Banner of Truth, 1988) 101–29

Webb, R.A., *The Theology of Infant Salvation* (Harrisonburg: Sprinkle, 1981)

Weinfeld, M., *Social Justice in Ancient Israel and in the Ancient Near East* (Minneapolis: Fortress Press, 1995)

Wells, D.F., *God the Evangelist* (Exeter: Paternoster Press, 1987)

Wesley, J., *The Letters of John Wesley*, vol. 2, J. Telford (ed.) (London: Epworth Press, 1931)

—, *The Works of John Wesley*, T. Jackson, (ed.) 14 vols. (Grand Rapids: Zondervan, repr. 1979)

Westerholm, S., *Israel's Law and the Church's Faith: Paul and his Recent Interpreters* (Grand Rapids: Eerdmans, 1988)

Westermann, C., *Genesis 37–50: A Commentary*, tr. J.J. Scullion (London: SPCK, 1987)

White, V., *Atonement and Incarnation: An Essay in Universalism and Particularity* (Cambridge: Cambridge University Press, 1991)

Whitelam, K.W., *The Just King: Monarchical Judicial Authority in Ancient Israel* (Sheffield: JSOT Press, 1979)

Wiles, M., and M. Santer, *Documents in Early Christian Thought* (Cambridge: Cambridge University Press, 1975)

—, *Christian Theology and Inter-religious Dialogue* (London: SCM Press, 1992)

Williams, C.M., *John Wesley's Theology Today* (London: Epworth Press, 1960)

van Winkle, D.W., '1 Kings XIII: True and False Prophecy', *Vetus Testamentum* 29 (1989) 31–43

Wolf, S., *Freedom Within Reason* (Oxford: Clarendon Press, 1990)

Wright, C., *The Uniqueness of Jesus* (Crowborough, East Sussex: Monarch, 1997)

Wright, D.F, 'Pelagianism' in S. Fergusson and D.F. Wright (eds.), *New Dictionary of Theology* (Leicester: IVP, 1988) 499–501

—, 'The Watershed of Vatican II: Catholic Attitudes Towards Other Religions' in A.D. Clarke and B.W. Winter (eds.), *One God, One Lord in a World of Religious Pluralism* (Cambridge: Tyndale House, 1991) 153–71

Wright, N.T., *Climax of the Covenant* (Edinburgh: T. & T. Clark, 1991)

—, *The New Testament and the People of God* (London: SPCK, 1992)

Zimmerli, W., 'Knowledge of God according to the Book of Ezekiel' in W. Brueggemann (ed), *I Am Yahweh*, tr. D.W. Stott (Atlanta: John Knox Press, 1982) 29–98 (tr. from *Erkenntnis Gottes nach dem Buch Ezekiel: Eine theologische Studie* [Zürich: Zwingli, 1954])